D1126749

Jane Greenberg, PhD
Editor

Metadata and Organizing Educational Resources on the Internet

Metadata and Organizing Educational Resources on the Internet has been co-published simultaneously as *Journal of Internet Cataloging*, Volume 3, Numbers 1 and 2/3 2000.

Pre-publication
REVIEWS,
COMMENTARIES,
EVALUATIONS . . .

"**T**his book is timely and an essential reference for those working in the area of developing meaningful metadata in support pathways to, and through, the 'knowledge-age'. As a compilation of important issues and views it provides the reader with a balanced and practical presentation of empirical case-studies and theoretical elaboration. All communities depend upon standards for their well being and one transformation of the 'educational terrain' unleashed by the technologies of the Internet, as Jane Greenberg describes it, will depend upon coherency enabled by metadata standards and interoperable classification systems.

The challenge of developing the potential of the Internet as a platform for a truly global educational information infrastructure is one that has been met by some of the pioneer projects described in this book. Continuation of this effort is best informed through both collaboration and comparative exposure such as that presented in this volume. I commend the reader to explore deeper the issues uncovered through projects such as GEM, IMS, ARIADNE and others."

Jon Mason, BA, MA
Co-Chair, Dublin-Core Education
Working Group
and Technical Director
Education Au LTD
(Education Network Australia)

"**R**ecent developments in metadata applications have led to the reconceptualization of the design and construction of tools for resource discovery. From the experience of the many who have undertaken site-specific or function-specific models for metadat applications comes this volume dedicated to the organization of educational resources on the Internet. This compilation is extremely valuable and well-timed. As the need for metadata escalates, so too does the demand for teaching metadata concepts and applications. Sources such as this go a long way toward meeting those demands.

This volume's specific focus is on the organization of educational resources. The breadth of experience reported in the individual papers suggests that a wide variety of models exist and are applicable. Of particular pragmatic value is the crosswalk suggested for GEM, IMS and CDL. Discussions on metadata issues and document architecture, and the use of structured metadata spaces contribute greatly to potential theoretical developments."

Richard P. Smiraglia, PhD
Professor, Palmer School of LIS
Long Island University, New York

"One of the most glorious uses of the Internet is for education. But how to document the huge mass of online data so that it can be used effectively to educate? This timely book begins to answer this question.

The authors of the essays in this book are some of the pioneers in recognizing the importance of standardizing the cataloging of Internet resources. Their reports will be of use to all catalogers and educators, who will find in them not only the practical details of metadata creation, but also inspiration.

A sampling of the many leading projects described in this book includes James Briggs Murray's article, which makes the reader feel how exciting it is to be able to catalog Internet resources so that a large body of specialized information becomes coherent and available to the public for the first time; Amy C. Smith's article, which shows how metadata can be created in such a way that it reveals relationships between objects previously disassociated; and Richard Giordano's article, which discusses how metadata can be used to bring together information on the same subject but in completely disparate form.

These articles, as well as many others in this book, demonstrate how metadata can be used to gather together pieces of the Internet to make a synergistic whole for education."

Frances Adams, BA
Bibliographic Assistant
(Copy Cataloger for 14 Years)
Columbia University Libraries

More pre-publication
REVIEWS, COMMENTARIES, EVALUATIONS . . .

"**T**his volume contains a series of articles that collectively address a wide variety of metadata issues related to the complex task of disseminating electronic educational resources to specific target audiences.

Taken as a whole, the volume provides the reader with a lens with which to view the various approaches catalogers, indexers, library administrators, and educators are taking in order to cull together Internet resources in a user-friendly way. However, each article may be read individually, without the context of the entire volume.

The book is an important and truly work, which details the application of various metadata standards. The use of these standards as illustrated here will shape the practice of indexers and catalogers as they too embark on the road to organizing the content of the Internet for their patrons."

Kristin Freda, MLS
Technical Services Librarian
Bank Street College of Education
New York, New York

The Haworth Information Press
An Imprint of The Haworth Press, Inc.

Metadata and Organizing Educational Resources on the Internet

Metadata and Organizing Educational Resources on the Internet has been co-published simultaneously as *Journal of Internet Cataloging,* Volume 3, Numbers 1 and 2/3 2000.

The *Journal of Internet Cataloging* Monographic "Separates"

Below is a list of "separates," which in serials librarianship means a special issue simultaneously published as a special journal issue or double-issue *and* as a "separate" hardbound monograph. (This is a format which we also call a "DocuSerial.")

"Separates" are published because specialized libraries or professionals may wish to purchase a specific thematic issue by itself in a format which can be separately cataloged and shelved, as opposed to purchasing the journal on an on-going basis. Faculty members may also more easily consider a "separate" for classroom adoption.

"Separates" are carefully classified separately with the major book jobbers so that the journal tie-in can be noted on new book order slips to avoid duplicate purchasing.

You may wish to visit Haworth's website at . . .

http://www.HaworthPress.com

. . . to search our online catalog for complete tables of contents of these separates and related publications.

You may also call 1-800-HAWORTH (outside US/Canada: 607-722-5857), or Fax 1-800-895-0582 (outside US/Canada: 607-771-0012), or e-mail at:

getinfo@haworthpressinc.com

Metadata and Organizing Educational Resources on the Internet, edited by Jane Greenberg, PhD (Vol. 3, No. 1/2/3/, 2000). *"A timely and essential reference. . . . A compilation of important issues and views . . . provides the reader with a balanced and practical presentation of empirical case studies and theoretical elaboration." (John Mason, Co-Chair, Dublin Core-Education Working Group, and Technical Director, Education, Au LTD [Education Network Australia])*

Internet Searching and Indexing: The Subject Approach, edited by Alan R. Thomas, MA, and James R. Shearer, MA (Vol. 2, No. 3/4, 2000). *This handy guide examines the tools and procedures available now and for the future that will help librarians, students, and patrons search the Internet more systematically, and also discusses how Internet pages can be modified to facilitate easier and efficient searches.*

Metadata and Organizing Educational Resources on the Internet

Jane Greenberg, PhD
Editor

Metadata and Organizing Educational Resources on the Internet has been co-published simultaneously as *Journal of Internet Cataloging,* Volume 3, Numbers 1 and 2/3 2000.

The Haworth Information Press
An Imprint of
The Haworth Press, Inc.
New York • London • Oxford

Published by

The Haworth Information Press, 10 Alice Street, Binghamton, NY 13904-1580 USA

The Haworth Information Press is an imprint of The Haworth Press, Inc., 10 Alice Street, Binghamton, NY 13904-1580 USA.

Metadata and Organizing Educational Resources on the Internet has been co-published simultaneously as *Journal of Internet Cataloging,* Volume 3, Numbers 1 and 2/3 2000.

© 2000 by The Haworth Press, Inc. All rights reserved. No part of this work may be reproduced or utilized in any form or by any means, electronic or mechanical, including photocopying, microfilm and recording, or by any information storage and retrieval system, without permission in writing from the publisher. Printed in the United States of America.

The development, preparation, and publication of this work has been undertaken with great care. However, the publisher, employees, editors, and agents of The Haworth Press and all imprints of The Haworth Press, Inc., including The Haworth Medical Press® and Pharmaceutical Products Press®, are not responsible for any errors contained herein or for consequences that may ensue from use of materials or information contained in this work. Opinions expressed by the author(s) are not necessarily those of The Haworth Press, Inc.

Cover design by Thomas J. Mayshock Jr.

Library of Congress Cataloging-in-Publication Data

Metadata and organizing educational resources on the Internet / Jane Greenberg, editor.
     p. cm.
    Co-published simultaneously as Journal of Internet cataloging, v. 3, nos. 1 and 2/3 2000.
    Includes bibliographical references and index.
    ISBN 0-7890-1178-6 (alk. paper)–ISBN 0-7890-1179-4 (alk. paper)
    1. Web databases. 2. Metadata. 3. Internet in education. I. Greenberg, Jane. II. Journal of Internet cataloging.
QA76.9.W43 M48 2000
025.3'44–dc21
                                                       00-044871

INDEXING & ABSTRACTING

Contributions to this publication are selectively indexed or abstracted in print, electronic, online, or CD-ROM version(s) of the reference tools and information services listed below. This list is current as of the copyright date of this publication. See the end of this section for additional notes.

- *AGRICOLA Database*
- *Applied Social Sciences Index & Abstracts (ASSIA) (Online: ASSI via Data-Star) (CDRom: ASSIA Plus)*
- *BUBL Information Service, an Internet-based Information Service for the UK higher education community <URL: http://bubl.ac.uk/>*
- *CNPIEC Reference Guide: Chinese National Directory of Foreign Periodicals*
- *Combined Health Information Database (CHID)*
- *Computer Literature Index*
- *Current Awareness Abstracts of Library & Information Management Literature, ASLIB (UK)*
- *Current Cites (Digital Libraries) (Electronic Publishing) (Multimedia & Hypermedia) (Networks & Networking) (General)*
- *Current Index to Journals in Education*
- *FINDEX, free Internet Directory of over 150,000 publications from around the world <www.publist.com>*
- *Index to Periodical Articles Related to Law*
- *Information Science Abstracts*
- *INSPEC*
- *Internet & Personal Computing Abstracts can be found Online at: DIALOG, File 233, HRIN & OCLC and on Internet at: Cambridge Scientific Abstracts, Dialog Web & OCLC <www.infotoday.com/mca/default.htm>*
- *Konyvtari Figyelo–Library Review*
- *Library & Information Science Abstracts (LISA)*
- *Library and Information Science Annual (LISCA) <www.lu.com/arba>*

(continued)

- *MLA International Bibliography*

- *PASCAL, c/o Institute de L'Information Scientifique et Technique. Cross-disciplinary electronic database covering the fields of science, technology & medicine. Also available on CD-ROM, and can generate customized retrospective searches <www.inist.fr>*

- *Referativnyi Zhurnal (Abstracts Journal of the All-Russian Institute of Scientific and Technical Information)*

- *Social Work Abstracts*

- *World Publishing Monitor*

Special Bibliographic Notes related to special journal issues (separates) and indexing/abstracting:

- indexing/abstracting services in this list will also cover material in any "separate" that is co-published simultaneously with Haworth's special thematic journal issue or DocuSerial. Indexing/abstracting usually covers material at the article/chapter level.
- monographic co-editions are intended for either non-subscribers or libraries which intend to purchase a second copy for their circulating collections.
- monographic co-editions are reported to all jobbers/wholesalers/approval plans. The source journal is listed as the "series" to assist the prevention of duplicate purchasing in the same manner utilized for books-in-series.
- to facilitate user/access services all indexing/abstracting services are encouraged to utilize the co-indexing entry note indicated at the bottom of the first page of each article/chapter/contribution.
- this is intended to assist a library user of any reference tool (whether print, electronic, online, or CD-ROM) to locate the monographic version if the library has purchased this version but not a subscription to the source journal.
- individual articles/chapters in any Haworth publication are also available through the Haworth Document Delivery Service (HDDS).

To David S. Hill, ex-Wallstreeter, Zen Buddhist, and supporter of metadata.

ABOUT THE EDITOR

Jane Greenberg, PhD, is Assistant Professor at the University of North Carolina (UNC), School of Information and Library Science. She holds an MS in Library Science from Columbia University and a PhD from the School of Information Sciences, University of Pittsburgh. Her current metadata research involves serving as the Metadata Coordinator for the North Carolina Plant Information Center, a project that supports botanical science education by linking students at all levels to a virtual herbarium and scientific resources. Greenberg is a member of UNC's Open Source Research Team, where she has examined the production of Linux Software Maps (LSMs) and participated in metadata-based analyses that examine the evolution of the open source community. Greenberg's metadata work has also involved working on the Pennsylvania Educational Network Digital Object Repository (PEN-DOR) project, which is part of a Link-2-Learn initiative to connect Pennsylvania schools statewide through a shared digital library. Prior to earning her doctorate, Greenberg was the Coordinator of Special Collections Cataloging at the Schomburg Center for Research in Black Culture, a Research Division of the New York Public Library.

Metadata
and Organizing Educational Resources
on the Internet

CONTENTS

Acknowledgments   xiii

Metadata Questions in Evolving Internet-Based
    Educational Terrain   1
       Jane Greenberg

The School Library Media Center in the Digital Age:
    Issues in the Cataloging of Electronic Resources   13
       Karen Letarte

ALADIN: An Example of Integrating Traditional
    and Electronic Services in the Digital Environment   41
       Ursula Giere
       Eva Kupidura

Cataloging K-12 Math and Science Curriculum Resources
    on the Internet: A Non-Traditional Approach   53
       Karen A. Plummer

Dewey Applications for the Simple Arrangement of a Link
    Library: The Case of Science Net   67
       Cheryl Martin
       Wayne Daniels

Straining the Standards: How Cataloging Websites
    for Curriculum Support Poses Fresh Problems
    for the *Anglo-American Cataloging Rules*   79
       D. Grant Campbell

Democratizing Education at the Schomburg: Catalog
   Development and the Internet   93
    James Briggs Murray

GEM: Design and Implementation of a Metadata Project
   for Education   109
    Carrie Lowe

Metadata for a Digital Library of Educational Resources   127
    Jane Greenberg
    Karen Fullerton
    Edie Rasmussen

Managing Digital Educational Resources with the ARIADNE
   Metadata System   145
    E. Duval
    E. Vervaet
    B. Verhoeven
    K. Hendrikx
    K. Cardinaels
    H. Olivié
    E. Forte
    F. Haenni
    K. Warkentyne
    M. Wentland Forte
    F. Simillion

Disiecta Membra: Construction and Reconstruction
   in a Digital Catalog of Greek Sculpture   173
    Amy C. Smith

The National Engineering Education Delivery System (NEEDS)
   Project: Reinventing Undergraduate Engineering Education
   Through Remote Cataloging of Digital Resources   191
    Brad Eden

Providing Access to Course Material at Deakin University   203
    Cate Richmond
    Ebe Kartus

Using the Online Catalog as a Publishing Source
   in an Academic Institution   217
     Ana Torres
     Cynthia Wolff

Cataloging Economics Preprints: An Introduction
   to the RePEc Project   227
     José Manuel Barrueco Cruz
     Thomas Krichel

Metadata Issues, Document Architecture, and Best
   Educational Practices   243
     Richard Giordano

Structured Metadata Spaces   263
     Thomas D. Wason
     David Wiley

Discovering and Using Educational Resources on the Internet:
   Global Progress or Random Acts of Progress?   279
     William H. Graves

Index   289

ALL HAWORTH INFORMATION PRESS
BOOKS AND JOURNALS ARE PRINTED
ON CERTIFIED ACID-FREE PAPER

Acknowledgments

There are many people to thank in putting together this volume. First, I'd like to thank Ruth Carter, Editor of the *Journal of Internet Cataloging*, for her encouragement and faith as I pursued this topic. I'd like to extend a thank you to the authors for their hard work, without which this special volume would not be possible. A thank you also needs to be extended to the excellent help that Haworth Press editors gave in preparing this volume and to Miles Effron, doctoral student at the School of Information and Library Science at the University of North Carolina at Chapel Hill, for assistance in getting this product to Haworth Press. Finally, I'd like to thank my husband David S. Hill, whose understanding of information in the larger world in addition to his love and support has helped immeasurably as I pulled this work together.

Jane Greenberg

Metadata Questions in Evolving Internet-Based Educational Terrain

Jane Greenberg

SUMMARY. This article begins by defining the evolving Internet-based educational terrain. Questions about cataloging tools and the development of metadata standards are examined, followed by inquiry on metadata creation. The final section introduces the articles contained in this special volume. *[Article copies available for a fee from The Haworth Document Delivery Service: 1-800-342-9678. E-mail address: <getinfo@ haworthpressinc.com> Website: <http://www.HaworthPress.com>]*

KEYWORDS. Metadata, cataloging, educational resources on the Internet, Internet-based educational resources, online catalogs, OPACs, digital libraries

INTRODUCTION

The tremendous growth of the Internet, particularly the World Wide Web, has had a remarkable impact on availability of educational resources in K-12, secondary, adult, and other distinct educational communities. Digital objects in a variety of formats (e.g., text, image, audio, moving image, and multi-me-

Jane Greenberg is Assistant Professor, School of Information and Library Sciences, University of North Carolina at Chapel Hill. Dr. Greenberg teaches and conducts research in the area of metadata.

[Haworth co-indexing entry note]: "Metadata Questions in Evolving Internet-Based Educational Terrain." Greenberg, Jane. Co-published simultaneously in *Journal of Internet Cataloging* (The Haworth Information Press, an imprint of The Haworth Press, Inc.) Vol. 3, No. 1, 2000, pp. 1-11; and: *Metadata and Organizing Educational Resources on the Internet* (ed: Jane Greenberg) The Haworth Information Press, an imprint of The Haworth Press, Inc., 2000, pp. 1-11. Single or multiple copies of this article are available for a fee from The Haworth Document Delivery Service [1-800-342-9678, 9:00 a.m. - 5:00 p.m. (EST). E-mail address: getinfo@haworthpressinc.com].

© 2000 by The Haworth Press, Inc. All rights reserved.

dia creations), fully developed lesson plans, and curriculum standards documentation are examples of the types of resources that are increasingly being accessed through online public access catalogs (OPACs) and educationally focused digital libraries. The development of interactive lesson plans and distance education initiatives, both of which rely heavily on access to Internet resources, are also becoming more commonplace. Underlying the success of this evolving educational environment is the development and deployment of metadata standards that support the discovery, use, and integrity of Internet resources.

This special volume documents the experiences of metadata creators (both catalogers and indexers), library administrators, and educators who are actively engaged in projects that organize Internet resources for educational purposes. Education is broadly defined and includes K-12, higher education, adult education, public education, and education of distinct communities, such as art historians and economists, and life long learners. While there are many educational projects that involve metadata, this is the first time that a series of articles specifically addressing this topic have been brought together in a single work.

This introduction begins by defining the evolving Internet-based educational terrain. Questions about cataloging tools and the development of metadata standards are presented, followed by questions about the creation of metadata. The final section introduces the articles contained in this special volume.

THE INTERNET-BASED EDUCATIONAL TERRAIN

Traditionally, there has always been a population of educators who are avid adopters of new technologies. It should therefore come as no surprise that the growth of the Internet has had a definite impact on the development of educational resources and offerings. Today, networking technologies have essentially forced a redefinition of part of the educational terrain, which now crosses traditional physical boundaries and exists as a collection of virtual environs. Internet resources designed for and incorporated into education curricula are accessed through both online public library catalogs (OPACs) and digital libraries in a variety of ways, making it difficult to define a single Internet-based educational environment. Despite this complexity, some cohesiveness can be given to this terrain by looking at content, access, and modeling practices.

Content. Content is primarily understood as the subject or thematic matter of a particular project. Many of the educational projects dealing with Internet resources are discipline-specific and developed for a target audience. For example, the Eisenhower National Clearinghouse for Mathematics and Science Education (ENC) project discussed in this volume (Plummer, pp. 53-65)[*] focuses on K-12 math and science curriculum resources. Internet-based educational projects may also focus on a specific resource type, such as all photographs or video. The Greek Sculpture Catalog (Smith, pp. 173-189), which is comprised of images of sculpture fragments and used for art historical and anthropological study, is both discipline- and resource-specific.

Content foci are generally initiated for reasons of economy and practicality. Without focus, it can be difficult to initiate let alone complete a project. Metadata must support the desired subject focus by using appropriate content value standards (e.g., subject thesauri) and providing resource descriptions at a level useful to the project's audience. Nearly all of the projects documented in this special volume have subject, audience-related, and in several cases resource type foci that are supported by a range of metadata practices.

Access. Access identifies who has permission to use a collection of resources, and is often related to content. The evolving Internet-based educational terrain includes local, statewide, national, and international access. An example of local access, controlled by passwords, is viewed with the digital library that delivers course material through the online catalog at the Bern Dibner Library of Science and Technology, Polytechnic University in Brooklyn, New York (Torres and Wolff, pp. 217-225). An example of statewide access, also password controlled, is viewed with the Pennsylvania Educational Network-Digital Object Repository (PEN-DOR) project, which is part of the Link-2-Learn initiative to connect Pennsylvania schools statewide through a shared digital library of educational resources and lesson plans (Greenberg, 127-144). And an example of international access is viewed with UNESCO's ALADIN (Adult Learning Documentation and Information Network), which consists of a network of over 90 worldwide adult learning documentation and information services (Giere and Kupidura, pp. 41-52).

The degree of geographical access scale-wise (local to international) combined with the diversity of audiences that are permitted access impacts the metadata assigned for resource discovery. With international access, there are issues of multilingual metadata and metadata localization, and with various user audiences, there are different degrees of granularity in terms of description. Overall, metadata standards permit Internet-based educational resources to be accessed and used within their proper context.

Modeling. Modeling defines a project's architecture. Many of the Internet-based educational projects follow a centralized model in which a single OPAC system or digital library environment coordinates all of the metadata and related activities (e.g., metadata creation, maintenance, etc.). The central-

---

[*]All parenthetical references in this introduction are for articles appearing in this special volume. Homepages for individual projects are found in these articles.

ized model limits communication bottlenecks that can lead to problems such as duplicative cataloging.

At the other end of the spectrum is the distributed approach. Increasingly, Internet-based educational projects are adopting a distributed model, which can involve any number of host sites. This model is generally selected for reasons of economy, access, and collaboration. Through shared collection building and metadata creation, a project can grow at a more expedient pace, and richer collections can be developed. There is also a benefit of multiple means of access via project mirroring. The RePEc (Research Papers in Economics) project, which consists of over 80 archival sites that actively collect and catalog economics papers for educational and documentary purposes (Cruz and Krichel, pp. 227-241), is an example of a distributed approach. Another example is provided by the Alliance of Remote Instructional Authoring and Distribution Networks for Europe (ARIADNE) project (Duval et al., pp. 145-171). ARIADNE promotes that computer-based and telematics-supported educational activities should rely primarily on an international system of interconnected knowledge pools (KPS).

The content, access, and modeling practices presented above provide only a general picture of several aspects of the evolving Internet-based educational terrain. These varied practices have introduced a number of metadata-related questions, several of which are explored in the next section of this introduction.

METADATA QUESTIONS

The evolving Internet-based educational terrain is made up of a wide range of projects that rely on the organization, access, and use of Internet resources. These activities have introduced a series of questions about cataloging tools, new metadata standards, and metadata creation options.

What Tools Assist with Internet Cataloging?

While the Internet and its educational offerings appear to have grown overnight, these developments have actually emerged through an evolutionary process, albeit a fast-paced one. Many tools developed for non-print cataloging in the pre-Internet environment are also applicable to Internet cataloging. Also useful are a host of cataloging tools that have universal application, such as subject thesauri and classificatory systems–many of which have been identified as acceptable content value standards to be used with existing metadata schemes. A rule of thumb for any Internet-based educational initiative is to evaluate existing cataloging tools, and determine what will aid the cataloging function. In taking this step, questions should also be asked about the degree of revision required when working with a set of guidelines or an official standard, especially prior to creating a whole new approach that will most likely duplicate an existing tool to some degree.

This introduction is not the place to provide an inclusive list of useful cataloging tools; however; the *Anglo-American Cataloguing Rules* (AACR)[1] and Machine Readable Cataloging (MARC) standards documentation[2] can be highlighted as two pre-Internet cataloging tools that guide descriptive cataloging and encoding of Internet resources in the OPAC environment. *Cataloging Internet Resources: A Manual and Practical Guide*,[3] and *ISBD(ER): International Standard Bibliographic Description for Electronic Resources*[4] should be highlighted as important tools developed specifically for Internet cataloging. (*ISBD/ER* is based on the International Standard Bibliographic Description for Computer Files [*ISBD/CF*].) And there is the *Library of Congress Subject Headings* (LCSH)[5] and the *Dewey Decimal Classification* (DDC) system,[6] both of which appear to be frequently used for content cataloging in this new environment. There exists a collection of general and perhaps even a wider assortment of subject-specific verbal and classificatory tools that can also be employed for Internet-based learning initiatives (e.g., *Medical Subject Headings* [MeSH][7] for Internet-based educational tools in medicine). What's important to recognize is that many cataloging tools supporting more traditional practices can be used for cataloging Internet resources in the OPAC environment, and that many of the content-oriented tools are also used in educationally focused digital library projects.

Are New Metadata Standards Needed?

Cataloging practices have primarily been concerned with resource discovery via metadata elements such as author, subject, and title. *AACR*, MARC standards documentation, and subject tools such as those noted above have proved fairly adequate for dealing with content and structural cataloging processes. Over the years, MARC has expanded its metadata encoding options with the introduction of fields for rights management (MARC field 506, Restrictions on Access Note); systems requirements (MARC field 538, System Details Note); and processing, reference, and preservation documentation (MARC field 583, Action Note). The MARC community has also endorsed the Curriculum Enhanced (CE) MARC fields (520 "Summary Note"; 521, "Target Audience Note"; 526, "Study Program Note"; and 658, "Curriculum Objective"). And most recently MARC has introduced the 856 field, "Electronic Location and Access," for encoding location and access protocol data.

While these and other existing MARC enhancements have supported growing metadata needs, there are a number of shortcomings with this approach. The most notable limitation with the above examples is that all but two of them have been relegated (*jammed in*) to MARC note fields. Although OPAC note fields are generally accessible via free text searching, they are not searchable in the controlled way that subject heading and name heading fields data are, which lends to a greater recall result. This limitation, the general crowding of metadata elements into the existing MARC format, and the desire to explore new modeling and access options has encouraged those involved with Internet-based educational projects to experiment with metadata schemes, such as the Dublin Core.[8] Moreover, these existing limitations and new design needs have prompted the development of a number of educational-based metadata schemas. The following are among the most well known metadata schemes developed for organizing and providing access to educational resources on the Internet, and are a testimony of the need for new standards in this area:

- The GEM (Gateway to Educational Materials) Element Set,[9]
- IMS (Instructional Management Systems) Meta-data Specification,[10]
- IEEE Learning Technology Standards Committee (LTSC) Learning Object Metadata (LOM),[11]
- EUN European School Net metadata scheme,[12] and
- EdNA (Education Network Australia) metadata scheme.[13]

The list given above is far from inclusive, as there are a host of project-specific schemes, many of which incorporate elements of these schemes (e.g., the PEN-DOR scheme builds on the GEM scheme, and the ARIADNE scheme builds on the IEEE/LOM). Related to this is that fact that all of the schemes listed above and many project specific schemes incorporate the Dublin Core at a base level. Also significant is the Dublin Core community's establishment of the Education Work Group, which plans make the Dublin Core scheme more suited for national and cross-sectoral communities (e.g., K-12, higher education, and lifelong learning).[14] The Education Working Group includes representatives from a number of Internet-based educational initiatives, including representatives from projects endorsing the above-noted schemes.

Who Should Create Metadata?

Historically, catalogers and indexers have been recognized as expert metadata creators. This is because they have generally received formal training and are known to have acquired both the skills and principled knowledge to create document representations. There is also a body of metadata creators (e.g., para-professionals) who lack formal education, but have learned this activity through on-the-job training. And there are authors who compose a third category of metadata creators. Abstracting and indexing services frequently use author abstracts and keywords with trained staff creating other metadata, such as journal title and subject code. This practice initiated in the pre-Internet environment.

There is no single answer to *who should create metadata* in the evolving Internet-based educational environment. In determining what works, a project team must consider the human, financial, and technical support costs together with the goal to provide resource access. Professionally trained metadata creators, while the most skilled in this activity, are costly and limited in availability–especially for short-term projects. Most Internet-based educational resource projects include an array of team members beyond cataloging librarians who may be able to assist with metadata creation given training and guidelines (e.g., educators, instructional-technology experts, graduate students, etc.). Overall, the question of who should create metadata now extends to how can the professionally trained metadata creator help other individuals produce quality metadata records in an efficient fashion.

How Should Metadata Be Created?

Related to the "who" of metadata creation is the "how" in terms of technological production. Metadata creation methods can be human, machine, or a combination of the two. The historical debate of controlled vocabulary versus natural language processing lends itself to this question in some respect in that the emphasis is reflected in the human versus the machine.[15]

The Internet is growing at a phenomenal pace, and it seems reasonable that those involved in educational related projects, or any sort of Internet organization project, investigate the potential for automatic metadata generation. An excellent list of metadata related tools is found via the homepage of the Dublin Core Metadata Initiative.[16] Likewise, many projects have or are in the process of developing their own toolkits to assist with metadata creation. While the automatic generation of metadata records has a way to go, we should be mindful of the controlled vocabulary versus the natural language processing debate, which has reasonably concluded that both techniques have their strengths and weaknesses. In time, we may have similar conclusion for the creation of metadata for educational resources on the Internet as well as for Internet resources beyond this domain.

ABOUT THE ARTICLES IN THIS VOLUME

The articles in this volume document the experiences of metadata creators (catalogers and indexers), library administrators, and educators who are actively engaged in projects that organize Internet resources for educational purposes. The volume is divided into two sections: the first part examines the status quo of cataloging Internet resources and explores the relationship between traditional cataloging practices and Internet cataloging; the second part introduces three metadata schemes, presents a sample of Internet-based educational projects in which metadata plays a central role, and examines best practices and theoretical aspects of metadata in relation to the evolving Internet-based educational terrain. A synopsis is presented below to provide readers with an overview of this entire volume.

Part I

This volume opens with Karen Letarte's report on a survey study that examines how school library media centers are providing access to range of electronic resources (educational software, interactive multimedia, and Internet resources). Letarte's article is followed by Ursula Giere and Eva Kupidura's report on a world-wide survey that examined networking issues and traditional and electronic resources cataloging for the ALADIN (Adult Learning Documentation and Information Network) project. Next are three articles that examine the integration of traditional and Internet cataloging practices. Karen A. Plummer presents a non-traditional approach to cataloging K-12 math and science curriculum resources via the Eisenhower National Clearinghouse for Mathematics and Science Education (ENC) project. Cheryl Martin and Wayne Daniels illustrate the use of Dewey Decimal Classification (DDC) for ordering K-12 science curriculum resources in Science Net, which is for Canadian schools. Their article also explores the use of the Dublin Core for both Science Net and the Virtual Reference Library project. And D. Grant Campbell presents a theoretical analysis the concept *document extent* via a series of genres and the evolving notion of *edition statement*. The first part concludes with an article by James Briggs Murray on the democratization of education and the role of the Schomburg Center's library catalog. The article documents the Center's catalog from its beginnings up to present day and highlights current metadata within the context of the Digital Schomburg project.

Part II

The second part begins by highlighting three metadata schemes for educational resources. Carrie Lowe's article introduces the Gateway to Educational Materials (GEM) project and development of the GEM metadata profile, which is among one of the most popular educationally focused metadata schemes. Lowe's article covers two case studies that apply the GEM metadata profile. An article documenting the development and implementation of the PEN-DOR metadata scheme follows next. The PEN-DOR scheme is based on input from project team members as well as an advisory board composed of educators and school media specialists. The ARIADNE metadata system, which is based on the Learning Object Model (LOM) scheme developed by IEEE, is the third scheme highlighted in this group of articles. The use of this scheme is meant to support the sharing and reuse of digital pedagogical materials on a European-wide basis.

The increased use of Internet-based technology for educational purposes has given rise to a wide variety of projects in which metadata creation and development has played a central role. The following group of articles is a sample of some of these projects. Amy C. Smith's article documents the evolution of a Greek sculpture catalog that is part of the Perseus Project. Categorization of artworks and multi-relational database issues are discussed along with the potential to eventually reconstruct lost original artworks during the next phase of catalog development. Next, Brad Eden shares his cataloging and telecommuting experiences with the Synthesis Coalition's National Engineering Education Delivery System (NEEDS) project. Eden discusses the use of library standards for cataloging engineering computer courseware modules, and comments on the future of telecommuting and remote cataloging of digital resources. Cate Richmond and Ebe Kartus examine how metadata can be retrospectively incorporated into new print and electronic course material, and outlines a series of issues that any Library needs to consider when providing access to a university's general course material. And Ana Torres and Cynthia Wolff share their experience in providing access to Internet-based and other electronic course material via the OPAC at the Bern Dibner Library of Science and Technology at Polytechnic University. The final article in this section is on the RePEc project, which is a distributed catalog of economics papers primarily for academic community education and research. Cruz and Krichel evaluate the success in providing metadata of reasonable quality through a decentralized approach.

The last section, and the volume in total examines best practices and theoretical aspects of metadata in relation to the evolving Internet-based educational terrain. Richard Giordano emphasizes contextual aspects of metadata for describing documents and their relationship to educational practice. Giordano also discusses document architecture and the Dublin Core and GEM metadata schemes. Thomas D. Wason and David Wiley present concepts of a metadata space in relation to cataloging and discovery. The scope of the concepts encompasses both educational related and general metadata systems. The last article in this special volume is by William H. Graves, who among many outstanding achievements in the area of educational technology is Chairman and Founder of eduprise.com, on EDUCAUSE's Board of Directors, and on the steering committees for the Instructional Management Systems (IMS) Cooperative and the ARL/EDUCAUSE Coalition for Networked Information. Graves shares his vision of the strategic impact of the Internet on education. In doing so he highlights the importance of metadata for resource discovery as the central topic of this volume.

CONCLUSION

The Internet, no doubt, is reshaping the educational terrain. Catalogers, educators, and other parties have experimented with and been successful in providing electronic access to curricula materials through the OPAC and digital library environment. Project success has relied on revised cataloging practices and the development and implementation of metadata schemes. Through further exploring the metadata-related question introduced above, these and other related projects will have a better chance of reaching their full potential in the Internet-based educational environment.

NOTES

1. *Anglo-American Cataloguing Rules*, 2nd edition, 1988 revision, Amendments 1993. (1993). Chicago: American Library Association.
2. MARC Standards: Library of Congress Network Development and MARC Standards Office. Documentation and references to resources available [on-line] at: *http://lcweb.loc.gov/marc/* This Website also provides information on printed resources for MARC.
3. *Cataloging Internet Resources: A Manual and Practical Guide*, 2nd edition. (1997). Ed., Olson, N. B. Available [on-line] at: *http://www.purl.org/oclc/cataloging-internet*
4. *ISBD(ER): International Standard Bibliographic Description for Electronic Resources.* (1997). Revised from the ISBD(CF): International Standard Bibliographic Description for Computer Files Recommended by the ISBD(CF) Review Group (Originally issued by K. G. Saur, Muenchen, 1997 as Vol. 17 in the UBCIM Publications, New Series). Available [on-line] at: *http://www.ifla.org/VII/s13/pubs/isbd.htm*
5. *Library of Congress Subject Headings*, 22nd edition (1999). Washington, D.C.: Library of Congress, Office for Subject Cataloging Policy. Annual.
6. *Dewey Decimal Classification and Relative Index*, 21st edition. Albany, N.Y.: Forest Press Dewey for Windows. Version 1.1. (Compact disc with documentation.) Albany, N.Y.: Forest Press, 1996. DDC 21 editions available in CD-ROM from Forest Press. See: *http://www.oclc.org/oclc/fp/deweywin/7037.htm*
7. Medical Subject Headings (MeSH). (1999). National Library of Medicine. (Contains Supplementary Concept Records Through October 20, 1999). Available [on-line] at: *http://www.nlm.nih.gov/mesh/99MBrowser.html*
8. Dublin Core Metadata Initiative (DCMI) homepage. (1999). Available [on-line] at: *http://purl.org/dc*
9. The GEM Element Set. (1999). Available [on-line] at: *http://www.geminfo. org/Workbench/Metadata/GEM_Element_List.html*

10. IMS Meta-data Specification. (1999). Available [on-line] at: *http://www. imsproject.org/metadata/index.html*

11. IEEE Learning Technology Standards Committee (LTSC) Learning Object Metadata (LOM) (September 5, 1999, Draft Document v3.6). Available [on-line] at: *http://ltsc.ieee.org/doc/wg12/LOM3.6.html*

12. European School Net. Available [on-line] at: *http://www.ub.lu.se/EUN/metadata/*

13. Education Network Australia (EdNA) metadata scheme. Available [on-line] at: *http://www.edna.edu.au/metadata*

14. Dublin Core. Education Working Group. Available [on-line] at: *http:// purl.org/DC/groups/education.htm*

15. Rowley, J. (1994). The controlled versus natural indexing languages debate revisited: a perspective on information retrieval practice and research. Journal of Information Science 20: 108-119. Svenonius, E. (1986). Unanswered questions in the design of controlled vocabularies. Journal of the American Society for Information Science 37: 331-340.

16. Metadata Related Tools. Available [on-line] at: *http://purl.org/DC/tools/index. htm*

The School Library Media Center in the Digital Age: Issues in the Cataloging of Electronic Resources

Karen Letarte

SUMMARY. In May 1999 a survey was distributed to 214 school library media specialists to explore the ways in which school library media centers provide access to electronic resources such as educational software, interactive multimedia, and Internet resources. The survey also addressed the use of curriculum enhancements to the MARC format, including fields 856, 658, 526, and 521 in school library catalogs. Results show that while direct-access electronic resources are being fully integrated into collections and services in the library media center, Internet resources are not yet at that point and most library media center catalogs do not reflect the use of curriculum-enhanced MARC for electronic or other materials. The need to develop cooperative cataloging ventures to create curriculum linkages for electronic educational resources is identified. *[Article copies available for a fee from The Haworth Document Delivery Service: 1-800-342-9678. E-mail address: <getinfo@haworthpressinc.com> Website: <http://www.HaworthPress.com>]*

Karen Letarte is Assistant Professor of Library Science and Cataloger at Southwest Missouri State University (e-mail: KML879f@mail.smsu.edu). As part of her responsibilities Ms. Letarte catalogs electronic resources and the collection of the Greenwood K-12 Laboratory School, and teaches cataloging and classification.

The author gratefully acknowledges the support of the administration and colleagues of the Libraries of Southwest Missouri State University, including Karen Horny, Neosha Mackey, J. B. Petty, Marilyn McCroskey, Mark Arnold, Dea Borneman, Michelle Turvey and the ILL staff.

[Haworth co-indexing entry note]: "The School Library Media Center in the Digital Age: Issues in the Cataloging of Electronic Resources." Letarte, Karen. Co-published simultaneously in *Journal of Internet Cataloging* (The Haworth Information Press, an imprint of The Haworth Press, Inc.) Vol. 3, No. 1, 2000, pp. 13-40; and: *Metadata and Organizing Educational Resources on the Internet* (ed: Jane Greenberg) The Haworth Information Press, an imprint of The Haworth Press, Inc., 2000, pp. 13-40. Single or multiple copies of this article are available for a fee from The Haworth Document Delivery Service [1-800-342-9678, 9:00 a.m. - 5:00 p.m. (EST). E-mail address: getinfo@haworthpressinc.com].

© 2000 by The Haworth Press, Inc. All rights reserved.

KEYWORDS. School libraries, cataloging of Internet resources, cataloging of computer files, MARC Field 856, MARC Field 658, MARC Field 526, MARC Field 521, curriculum-enhanced MARC, electronic educational resources

INTRODUCTION

School library media specialists of today have increasingly complex roles. Not only must they provide support for rapidly shifting curricula and instructional techniques, they also must cope with the explosion of information resources and new formats, particularly electronic ones. The number of electronic educational resources, including Internet resources, has expanded dramatically in recent years. The proliferation and availability of information raise several significant questions. How do school library media centers (LMCs) provide access to electronic resources such as educational software, interactive multimedia, and Internet resources? Are these educational resources available in the LMC for students? To what degree are these materials integrated into the library's services? Do LMCs typically provide access to electronic resources through the catalog or by some alternate means?

A paucity of literature on the subject of cataloging electronic resources in LMCs suggests that these resources are not cataloged, but rather, made available through alternate means, such as computer labs, print guides, or special storage and browsing shelves. An exploratory survey was conducted to gain an understanding of how these important resources are currently handled in the LMC.

METHODOLOGY

In May 1999, the survey was distributed to 214 school library media specialists (LMSs), most of whom were members of the American Association of School Librarians (AASL). Participants were chosen from all fifty states, representing both rural and urban areas, with most participants from public schools (Table 1). The total number of responses was 92, a response rate of 43%. As shown in Table 2, the schools represented included elementary, middle and high schools. Some respondents were district catalogers, who perform cataloging for an entire school district rather than a single library.

THE SURVEY

The survey addressed three major areas: (1) access to educational software in LMCs; (2) access to Internet resources; and, (3) use of enhancements to the

TABLE 1. Pool and Respondents by Region

Region	No. in pool (n = 214)	% of total	No. of respondents (n = 92)	% of total
Northeast	47	22.0%	22	23.9%
South	49	22.9%	14	15.2%
Midwest	60	28.0%	28	30.4%
West	58	27.1%	28	30.4%

TABLE 2. By School

Type of School	No. of respondents (n = 92)	% of respondents
K-12	1	1.1%
Elementary Schools	28	30.4%
Middle Schools	10	10.9%
High Schools	36	39.1%
District Catalogers	17	18.5%

MARC (Machine Readable Cataloging) record for electronically based curriculum materials. Instrument design was based on two surveys distributed in the spring of 1999 on the AUTOCAT electronic discussion list (Ward and VanderPol 1999, and Meyers and Deyoe 1999).

The first part of the survey dealt with issues of automation and connectivity. Participants reported that 96.7% of LMCs had Internet or Web access, a substantial increase over recent studies (Table 3) (Miller and Shontz 1998, NCES 1998).

In comparison with the 58% of libraries with online catalogs and circulation systems identified by Miller and Shontz (1998, 27), respondents demonstrated a much greater degree of automation, with 79% reporting use of an online catalog. Results also demonstrate an awareness of the potential for Web-based delivery of catalog information in LMCs: 19 respondents indicated that their catalog is Web-based, and 17 reported that their catalogs are accessible through the Internet (Table 4). This is particularly important in considering the cataloging of Internet resources in LMCs, since it affects the functionality of the Field 856 "hotlink" directly to the resource.

ACCESS TO ELECTRONIC RESOURCES IN LMCs:
REMOTE VS. DIRECT ACCESS

The distinction between *remote* and *direct access* resources is important to understand. *Anglo-American Cataloguing Rules* (AACR2) (1988, rev. 1998)

TABLE 3. Internet Access in LMCs, 1994-1999

Year	% of Library Media Centers with Internet Access
1994 (Miller and Shontz)	57%
1995-1996 (Miller and Shontz)	73% (high-tech LMCs, n = 365)
1998 (NCES)	51-89%[1]
May 1999 (Letarte)	96.7% (n = 92)

[1]Study found that 89% of public schools had Internet connections, with connections in 51% of the instructional rooms (including school libraries) in those schools (NCES 1992, 2).

TABLE 4. Automation and Connectivity Overview

May 1999	No. of respondents (n = 92)	% of respondents
Libraries with WWW/Internet Access	89	96.7%
Libraries with online catalogs	73	79.3%
Libraries with Internet access to catalog	17	18.5%
Libraries with Web-based catalogs	19	20.7%

defines direct access as "The use of computer files via carriers (e.g., disks, cassettes, cartridges) designed to be inserted into a computer or its auxiliary equipment by the user." Remote access is "the use of computer files via input/output devices connected electronically to a computer." For the sake of clarity, the survey addressed direct-access educational software (stored on disk or CD-ROM and housed in the library) separately from Internet (remote access) resources. "Electronic resources" were defined as software or interactive multimedia. The survey explored the ways in which LMCs provide access to electronic educational resources and the degree to which these materials are integrated into library services.

DIRECT-ACCESS RESOURCES: SOFTWARE AND INTERACTIVE MULTIMEDIA

Survey results show that direct-access electronic resources are indeed being fully integrated into collections and services in the LMC. Miller and Shontz's (1998, 27) study found that 91% of LMCs use CD-ROMS. Current survey data support this, with 91.3% of respondents providing access to direct-access resources either through the catalog or through an alternate means (Table 7). These results suggest that a majority of LMCs now treat software no differently than other types of resources. Access to electronic resources (software, interactive multimedia or both) is provided through the catalog by 63% of respondents (Table 5). Results, shown in Table 6, also demonstrate that a majority of LMCs (72.8%), provide access to software through means other than the catalog.

Clearly, LMSs recognize electronic resources as important and legitimate sources of information for their patrons. Although not all respondents catalog these resources, nearly all (91%) provide access of some kind (Table 7). For the 8.8% who do not, the lack of resources, funding and time may be a factor. Some simply do not collect in this area. Of the 8 respondents whose LMCs

TABLE 5

Cataloging of Direct-Access Resources	No. of respondents (n = 92)	% of respondents
Catalog electronic resources	58	63.0%
Do not catalog electronic resources	34	37.0%
Catalog software	58	63.0%
Catalog interactive multimedia	41	44.6%

TABLE 6

Other Access to Software	No. of respondents (n = 92)	% of respondents
Through Library homepage	30	32.6%
Print guides	34	37.0%
On select workstations or separate lab	57	62.0%
Through bibliographic instruction	47	51.1%
Provide access to software through means other than the catalog (Total)	67	72.8%

TABLE 7

Catalog vs. Other Means of Access	No. of respondents (n = 92)	% of respondents
Catalog electronic resources	58	63.0%
Do not catalog software but provide alternate access	26	28.3%
Provide access either through catalog or through alternate means	84	91.3%
Do not catalog software and do not provide alternate access	8	8.7%

provide no access, one does not own any software, three did not provide data on the amount of software in the collection, and three others report that software comprises 5% or less of the collection.

REMOTE ACCESS RESOURCES: INTERNET RESOURCES

Access to Internet resources in the LMC is a topic that has received much recent publicity, particularly in issues of censorship, filtering, and intellectual freedom. The issue of cataloging Internet resources remains complex, and presents many challenges. The debate continues over whether these resources should be included in the library catalog, given the fact that they do not represent physical items housed in a collection and can be ephemeral in nature. The problem of how best to keep Field 856 links current persists. The question of whether the *Anglo-American Cataloguing Rules* and the MARC format are the appropriate standards for describing these resources also remains, with new metadata standards such as Dublin Core yet to be explored fully.

Results show that although LMSs clearly provide access to these resources, with 96% reporting Internet or Web connections, only 4.3% catalog Internet resources (Table 9). Most (72.8%) provide access through alternate means (Table 8). The preferred method seems to be to bookmark files on workstations for student use, with 60.87% of respondents reporting this practice. In comparison, a recent survey of academic libraries conducted by David Ward and Diane VanderPol (1999) determined that 57.8% of respondents cataloged Web resources.

A majority of LMSs, 73.9%, provide access to Internet resources, whether through the catalog or through alternate means (Table 9). Conversely, 25% responded that access is not provided through either means. This figure seems at odds with the 96.7% of respondents who reported Internet access in

TABLE 8

Non-Catalog Access to Internet Resources in LMCs	No. of respondents (n = 92)	% of respondents
Through Library homepage	32	34.8%
Print guides	37	40.2%
Bookmark files on workstations	56	60.9%
Through bibliographic instruction	51	55.4%
Provide access to Internet resources through means other than the catalog (Total)	67	72.8%

TABLE 9

Catalog vs. Other Access to Internet Resources in LMCs	No. of respondents (n = 92)	% of respondents
Catalog Internet Resources	4	4.3%
Provide access to Internet resources only through means other than the catalog	64	69.6%
Provide access to Internet either through catalog or alternate means	68	73.9%
Provide WWW access neither through alternate means nor through catalog	23	25.0%

the library. However, of the 23 LMSs that do not provide access through either means, only two reported that they did not have Internet access in the library. Since respondents were not queried separately about Web access versus Internet access, it seems likely that this figure reflects Web access rather than Internet access.

MARC FIELD 856

The use of MARC Field 856 is of particular importance with respect to catalog access to Internet resources in LMCs. Field 856 is used to record the URL (Uniform Resource Locator), or address, for an Internet resource. In Web-based catalogs, this field provides a hot-link directly to the resource whose location is identified by the URL. Field 856 can be used in three cases: (1) when the item being cataloged is itself an Internet resource, (2) when it is a component or version of an Internet resource, and (3) when it is related to an Internet resource.

Only 8.7% of participants use Field 856. Some use of all three of the above functions of the field was reported (Table 10). Another question of interest is whether or how LMSs handle the maintenance of this field. None reported any formal procedures for maintaining the links. One librarian's creative maintenance strategy includes a plan to check the links once a year by doing a keyword search for the string "http" in the OPAC.

The low use of Field 856 by participants has powerful implications for the functionality of Web-based catalogs in school settings. Of the 19 respondents whose catalogs are Web-based, only 3 use Field 856. Thus, 84.2% of those with Web-based catalogs do not use this field. Although students in these schools could have "click and go" functionality within the catalog, the lack of Field 856 in records eliminates this capability. As more schools migrate to third-generation systems capable of access via the Web, this issue becomes increasingly important. The ways in which this field is used will also become more significant as LMC catalogs are accessible not just to local users, but to remote users as well. As this occurs, standardization in cataloging for all formats will assume greater importance.

Participants also described the evaluation of Internet resources for library use. Responses reveal that while most do not evaluate Websites for inclusion in the catalog, over half of the respondents (62%) do evaluate them for access through alternate means (Table 11). These results suggest that although the importance of Internet resources to users is recognized, they are only beginning to be integrated into LMC services and collections.

The final part of the survey focused on participants' use of enhancements to the MARC format for curricular materials. These enhancements encompass the inclusion of such elements as target audience, summary information, and contents in the record. These elements are especially desirable when describing non-print materials, since the browsing potential of such resources is often limited. The need for record enhancement for electronic materials is even greater, particularly for remote resources. An enhanced catalog record enables users to judge, solely from the record, whether the item described meets their need.

TABLE 10

Use of Field 856	No. of respondents (n = 92)	% of respondents
Libraries that use field 856	8	8.7%
For Internet resources	5	5.4%
For items that are versions or components of Internet resources	3	3.3%
For Internet resources that are related to the item being cataloged	3	3.3%

TABLE 11

Evaluation of Internet Resources in LMCs	No. of respondents (n = 92)	% of respondents
Actively seek and evaluate educational Websites for inclusion in the catalog	9	9.8%
Actively seek and evaluate educational Websites for inclusion through an alternate means	57	62.0%

Since 1993, several fields have been created or enhanced to provide better access to curriculum materials. The survey examined the use of Fields 658 (Curriculum Objectives), 526 (Study Program Information), 520 (Summary Note) to record reviews, and 521 (Target Audience Note). These fields allow powerful connections to be made between the curriculum and information resources.

The survey explored the degree to which LMSs currently exploit the power of the curriculum enhanced MARC format (CEMARC) to make such connections. Results, shown in Table 12, suggest that these enhancements are not used in LMCs. In particular, Field 658, which links the curriculum objective fulfilled to the resource, is not used, with only one respondent indicating its use.

Field 526, for Study Program Information (formerly, Reading Program Information), was approved by the Machine Readable Bibliographic Information Committee of the American Library Association (MARBI) in June 1998 (MARBI 1997, 1998). To date, it has not yet been implemented in the OCLC system. Only 2 respondents indicated plans to use the field. Use of Fields 520 and 521 was much higher. Participants were asked whether they used Field 520 (with a first indicator of 1) to record reviews of items being cataloged. Although 15.2% use the field for this purpose, it is used mostly for print items, with much lower usage reported for software and other audiovisual materials. Three respondents use Field 510 to record reviews, mostly in records purchased from vendors.

Results also reveal that Field 521 is used mainly to describe reading level, with indicators for reading grade level, reading age level and interest age level used most frequently (see Table 13). Thirty-one percent of respondents record the reading grade level. Most respondents did not indicate use of this field for any particular format. Only 8.7% of respondents use first indicators of 3 (special audience characteristics) and/or 4 (motivation level). Factors

TABLE 12

Use of Curriculum Enhancements to the MARC Format	No. of respondents (n = 92)	% of respondents	For type of material
Use Field 658	1	1.1%	Print and AV
Use/Plan to Use Field 526	2	2.2%	N/A
Use Field 520 for Reviews	14	15.2%	
	12	13.0%	Print materials
	7	7.6%	Software
	2	2.2%	Internet
	8	8.7%	Other A/V

TABLE 13

Use 1st indicator in field 521	No. of respondents (n = 92)	% respondents	For type of material
0 (Reading grade level)	29	31.5%	N/A
	8	27.6% (n = 29)	Print
	1	3.4% (n = 29)	Software
	1	3.4% (n = 29)	AV
	19	65.5% (n = 29)	NR
1 (Interest age level)	20	21.7%	N/A
	2	10.0% (n = 20)	Print
	18	90.0% (n = 20)	NR
2 (Interest grade level)	24	26.1%	N/A
	4	16.7% (n = 24)	Print
	20	83.3% (n = 24)	NR
3 (Special audience characteristics)	8	8.7%	N/A
	2	25.0% (n = 8)	Special Ed.
	1	12.5% (n = 8)	Gifted
	5	62.5% (n = 8)	NR
4 (Motivation/interest level)	8	8.7%	NR

contributing to the low use of the field may be inconsistent terminology, lack of time, or inadequate staffing. One respondent observed:

> [Use of this field] is another area that I have proposed to study, in order to make our new catalog really useful for teachers. Currently this field has been used with little consistency. We would have to standardize it in a way that grade & age levels could be selected in a drop-down menu. Big project to go back retrospectively and fix.

CURRICULUM ENHANCEMENTS TO THE MARC FORMAT

The 1998 *Information Power* guidelines for LMC programs focus on the promotion of information literacy, particularly for electronic information, and the creation of linkages between the curriculum and the LMC. The following discussion encompasses both formal curriculum materials, such as textbooks and other instructional materials, and purely juvenile materials, such as fiction and computer games. LMC collections, and curriculum materials in particular, have been widely recognized as unique and deserving of special bibliographic treatment (EBSS 1990, Kranz 1987, Minier 1994, Murphy 1998, Rottenbucher and Lamb 1994, Wehmeyer, 1976).

Teachers and students have information needs that are both individual and quite specific (Wehmeyer 1976). In Lewis's (1989, 153-55) informal study of elementary school children's use of catalogs, children expressed interest in fiction elements such as character, theme and setting; other features of interest were reading level, detail of illustration, organization (e.g., in chapters), and award status. Teachers, on the other hand, may seek materials to support specific instructional goals, such as those "in a discovery approach with visual aids to teach division of fractions to a bright second-grader" (Wehmeyer 1976, 316). Obviously, the ability of LMC catalogs to meet these needs can directly affect the quality of teaching and learning (Murphy 1991, 92) in the schools served.

Awareness of the unique nature of LMC collections and their users has grown over the past twenty years. In 1976, Wehmeyer observed that traditional subject cataloging practices were inadequate for curriculum materials. She envisioned the development of computer-based information storage and retrieval systems that could match the specific information needs of teachers and students with curriculum resources (Wehmeyer 1976; Murphy 1998, 93). She also identified the following elements for inclusion in the cataloging record: difficulty, audience, use, and organization (1976, 324).

Recognition of the unique nature of these resources led to the development of the curriculum enhancements to the MARC format in 1993 (Murphy 1998). Although sometimes referred to as the Curriculum-Enhanced MARC Format or CEMARC, it is not actually a new format, but simply an enhancement of the existing USMARC. Enhancements include additions to fields 520 and 521 and the development of Field 658. In 1998, MARBI approved the addition of a new field, 526, study program information (MARBI 1997 and 1998).

The following elements are particularly helpful to users of LMC collections: level of difficulty, age appropriateness, audience characteristics, summary and/or contents, awards status, review information, format, form, relationship to curricula and curriculum resources, and analysis of items in collections. Rottenbucher and Lamb (1994) found vendor-supplied MARC records for the retrospective conversion of one LMC catalog to be inadequate for teacher and student needs. Enhancing the records with additional subject headings and analytics was effective for increasing the usefulness of the catalog (Rottenbucher and Lamb 1994). The creation of analytics for short stories and collections was particularly helpful.

Despite Murphy's (1991) prediction that catalogs of the 1990s would more effectively correlate the needs of young users and the information resources represented in the catalog, there is still significant work to be done. Although the *USMARC Format for Bibliographic Data* is fully capable of representing all elements named above, survey responses indicate that currently, these enhancements are not exploited in LMC catalogs.

CURRICULUM LINKAGES THROUGH FIELDS 658, 526, AND 521

Field 658, for curriculum objectives, holds the greatest potential for creating powerful curriculum linkages. For the LMC, the potential benefits of this connection are obvious: improved instruction and increased learning. This field records the curriculum objective (e.g., national, state, local, etc.) fulfilled by the item being described, the degree of correlation to the objective (e.g., highly correlated, lightly correlated, etc.), and the objective's source. Use of this coding would enable teachers to search the catalog by a specific curriculum objective to find resources that meet that objective and to determine the degree to which they meet it (Minier 1994). The examples throughout this section are based on those used by Murphy in her excellent discussion of curriculum-enhanced MARC (1998).

The *USMARC Format for Bibliographic Data* specifies that curriculum objectives, codes, and correlation factors be taken from standard published lists. The source is given in code form in subfield 2. A list of available codes appears in the *USMARC Code List for Relators, Sources, Description Conventions* (1997 ed.) in the section "Subject/Index Term Sources." The *Code List* permits the use of the code "local" (i.e., locally assigned) for terms taken from a local standard. Lists of local standards can also be submitted to the Library of Congress for coding and inclusion in the *Code List* (Murphy 1998).

The basic structure of the field is straightforward. The main objective appears in subfield a (‡a), the secondary objective in subfield b. Subfield c contains a code that represents the objectives, and subfield d shows the degree of correlation, with the source appearing in subfield 2. The following example is adapted from the *USMARC Format for Bibliographic Data*:

> 658)) ‡a Math objective 6 ‡b fractions, decimals, percents, whole numbers, integers ‡c NRPO6-1991 ‡d highly correlated. ‡2ohco

In this example, the main objective is Math objective 6 and the secondary objective is fractions, decimals, percents, etc. The material described is highly correlated to the objective, and the source of the objective, "ohco," is the *Ohio Curriculum Objectives*. (The code given in subfield c is taken from the *Ohio Curriculum Objectives*.)

Use of this field opens many possibilities for users of LMC catalogs. However, more than a few challenges of implementation must be met before the field can gain widespread use. First, who will evaluate the curriculum resources and determine the degree to which a resource is correlated to a particular objective? What criteria should be used to determine this? To what level of objectives or standards should resources be correlated: local, state, national? The answer to this question will have implications for possible cooperative ventures. Murphy (1998) suggests that correlation at the national level might be most useful, and also cites Ohio's NWOET project as an innovative model for cooperation at the state level (Murphy 1994). This would result in data that would be usable across a wider spectrum of users than if correlated to the local level. The need to use an authoritative list or thesaurus is clear, to ensure consistency of terminology. The process of choosing an appropriate authoritative list should involve library media specialists, curriculum specialists, and teachers. Possible sources include the ERIC thesaurus and the *Eisenhower National Clearinghouse for Mathematics and Science Vocabularies* (Murphy 1998) as well as local, state and national standards.

The greatest challenge for implementation will be to determine who will correlate resources with standards, and how. Printed guides may offer correlations for some resources (Murphy 1998), but they are not comprehensive. Though such correlation has obvious value to users of LMC collections, is it realistic to expect that LMSs could add this function to their duties? LMSs have many competing demands on their time, not the least of which is their direct instructional role. Research shows little time devoted to administrative activities such as cataloging in the LMC (Everhart 1994, Van Deusen 1996). In fact, Van Deusen's (1996, 86) time use study recorded no cataloging performed by elementary LMSs during the data collection period. Given these obstacles, the greatest potential for a solution to the challenges of implementation lies in cooperation, whether at a district, state, or national level.

Field 526, Study Program Information, was the newest field examined. Like Field 658, it links the curriculum to library resources. Field 526 records the name of an interactive multimedia study program that uses the print resource described in the record. *Accelerated Reader* is one popular example of such a program. This field was developed in response to a strong interest of the K-12 community for a formal catalog record linkage of study program information to the library resources represented in the programs (MARBI 1997). Follett Software Company was a major proponent of the proposal, which illustrates the nature of cooperation and interdependence between LMCs and vendors. The following example is taken from the *USMARC Format for Bibliographic Data* (available on the Library of Congress's Website).

```
100 1) ‡a Lowry, Lois.
245 10 ‡a Number the stars / ‡c Lois Lowry.
526 0) ‡a Accelerated Reader/Advantage Learning Systems ‡b 5.0 ‡c 4.0
‡d 75
526 0) ‡a That's A Fact, Jack! ‡b 5.5 ‡c 4.5 ‡d 100
```

Lois Lowry's book *Number the Stars* is used by two reading programs, *Accelerated Reader* and *That's A Fact, Jack!* The 100 and 245 fields describe the book. Each 526 field contains the name of the interactive multimedia program in subfield a. The first indicator, coded 0, shows the program is a reading program. Subfield b records the interest level; subfield c, the reading level; and subfield d, the point value assigned to the book. In the example above, in the Accelerated Reader/Advantage Learning Systems program, the interest level is fifth grade, the reading level is fourth grade, and the book is worth 75 points. In the *That's A Fact, Jack!* program, the interest level is the fifth month of the fifth grade, the reading level is the fifth month of the fourth grade, and the book's point value is 100. Use of this coding would enable reading program titles to be identified in the catalog, providing a desirable curriculum linkage. Despite the interest in the field's development expressed by the K-12 community, survey results show that few LMCs have begun to plan for its implementation. This demonstrates a strong need for vendor support of the field and also for continuing education in the MARC format for LMSs.

The last field examined was field 521, for target audience. Recent enhancements have defined new first indicator values for this field. Value 3 describes special audience characteristics, such as learning style. The characteristics are recorded in subfield a; the source of the information in subfield b. The following examples are taken from the *USMARC Format for Bibliographic Data*:

521 3) ‡a Vision impaired ‡a fine motor skills impaired ‡a audio learner ‡b LENOCA.

This coding shows that the item is appropriate for audio learners with vision and fine motor skills impairment, and was designated by the LENOCA agency.

Value 4 "identifies the motivation and/or interest level of the audience for which the item is best suited" (*USMARC Format for Bibliographic Data*) in subfield a; the source is specified in subfield b.

521 4) ‡a Highly motivated ‡a high interest ‡b LENOCA.

Coding shows that the item is most suitable for a highly motivated and highly interested audience and was designated by the LENOCA agency. Use of this coding would allow teachers to locate resources for a particular audience or those suitable for students with a particular learning style. Materials to supplement instructional resources could more effectively be chosen to meet the needs of the individual learner.

CATALOGING EXAMPLES

Several survey participants submitted MARC record examples for electronic resources. The examples below help to shed some light on current cataloging practices for electronic resources in LMCs. They will be examined in the light of the *Guidelines for Standardized Cataloging of Children's Materials* (RTSD 1982), as well as other national standard tools for cataloging.

Designed for use with all materials "deemed intellectually suitable for children" through junior-high age, the *Guidelines* (RTSD 1982) require the use of the second level of description as set forth in the *Anglo-American Cataloguing Rules* (AACR2). Use of the general material designation (GMD) is mandatory for most types of material. The *Guidelines* also require the use of either a summary note or a contents note describing the nature and scope of the work. The international standard book number (ISBN) is required when it is available. The preferred source of subject headings is the Annotated Card list, but Library of Congress (LC) subject headings should also be added if records are contributed to a shared cataloging database. Existing LC headings can be modified to modernize spelling or to anglicize foreign names. Both general and specific headings for the same concept may be used if needed. Either the Library of Congress or the Dewey Decimal classification systems should be used.

DIRECT-ACCESS FILES: EDUCATIONAL SOFTWARE

Examination of cataloging records for software revealed deviations from standard practice in several areas and showed that LMC catalogs describe these materials in very nonstandard ways. Variations occurred in several areas of the cataloging record.

LEVEL OF DESCRIPTION

In these examples, neither the first nor the second level of description (as required in the *Guidelines*) is followed consistently. All three records are quite brief. The record for *The Magic School Bus* (Figure 1), does not adhere to either level. A statement of responsibility is included, as for level 2, but the place of publication and other physical details and dimensions (subfields b and c of the 300 field) are not given. Examples in Figures 2 and 3 also omit the physical details and dimensions. Field 538, the system requirements note, does not appear in the record in Figure 3. None of the records include the

FIGURE 1. Magic School Bus

```
                                Cataloging
                                                    DYNIX #: 176409
LEADER 01201nmm 2200116    4500^
008    960529s1995                        eng
092    612 Col
100 1  Cole, Joanna
245 10 The magic school bus explores the human body /$cJoanna Cole.$h[in
       teractive multimedia].
260    $bMicrosoft Corp.,$c1995.
300    1 CD-ROM disc ;$eMicrosoft Windows Compatable. Macintosh.
520    An interactive science adventure.
521    For ages 6 to 10.
538    System requirements: Macintosh LC 550 or higher with color monito
       r, System 7.1 or later, 8 MB of memory (RAM), 8 MB of available h
       ard-disk space, double-speed CD-ROM drive, Optional:  printer. MS
       -DOS operating system version 5.0 or later, Microsoft Windows com
       patible.
650    Macintosh (Computer)
650    CD ROM(Compact disk read-only mem.).
650    Physiology$xComputer assisted instruction
650    Metabolism
650    Human body$xComputer assisted instruction
650  0 MS DOS (Computer operating system)
690    Human body$9HUM01$xComputer assisted instruction$8COM07
690    Metabolism$9MET00
690    Physiology$9PHY09$xComputer assisted instruction$8COM07
690    CD ROM(Compact disk read-only mem.).$9CD 00
690    Macintosh (Computer)$9MAC21
690    MS DOS (Computer operating system)$9MS 00
740 01 Scholastic's The magic school bus explores the human body.
                 - - - - End of Title Info - - - -
```

FIGURE 2. Holocaust Atlas

```
                    B R O W S E   R E C O R D S
ΓMMMMMMMMMMMMMMMMMMMMMMMMMMMMMMMMMMMMMMMMMMMMMMMMMMMMMMMMMMMMMMMMMMMMMMΓ
: Leader       LDR         nmm  22      u  4500^                       :
: Last Trans   005    19970530154936.0^                               :
: Fixed Data   008    970530s1996     nyu    |   ||      eng d^        :
: ISBN         020    _a0028974549^                                    :
: Location     049    _aWest^                                          :
: Title stmt   245  00_aHistorical atlas of the Holocaust_hCD-ROM^     :
: Edition stmt 250    _aWindows vers.^                                 :
: Imprint stmt 260    _aNew York :_bMacMillan,_c[1996].^               :
: Phys descrip 300    _a1 computer laser optical disc_e1 guide^        :
: Summary note 520    _aThe history of the Holocaust as it occurred geographic :
:                     ally, presented by the U.S. Holocaust Memorial Museum.^ :
: Tech det not 538    aMinimum system requirements: IBM or compatible 386 wit :
:                     h Windows 3.1; 256-color monitor: 4MB RAM; 2x speed CD-R :
:                     OM drive.^                                       :
: Local note   590    _a05-29-97/2^                                    :
: Subj:Topical 650   0_aHolocaust, Jewish (1939-1945)_xMaps.^          :
: Subj:Topical 650   4_aHolocaust, Jewish (1939-1945)_xComputer programs.^ :
: Subj:Topical 650   0_aHistorical geography_xMaps.^                   :
: Subj:Topical 650   7_2sears_aHistorical geography_xComputer programs.^ :
: AE:Corp name 710  2 _aU.S. Holocaust Memorial Museum.^               :
: Local call # 900    _aCDROM 940.53 HIS^                              :
{MMMMMMMMMMMMMMMMMMMMMMMMMMMMMMMMMMMMMMMMMMMMMMMMMMMMMMMMMMMMMMMMMMMMMM<
     Use^EscJExit    CURRENT INDEX:  900 _a Local Call        ^F1JHelp
```

mandatory "source of title" note in Field 500, so it is impossible to determine whether cataloging information was based on internal sources (title screens) or eye-readable data (disc labels and packaging). Since titles on software can vary greatly within a single item, depending on the source, this lack of information could create difficulties for the sharing of cataloging data.

FIGURE 3. Kinderventures

©1996-99 Brodart Co.

Bibliographic Record

Searching : Kinderventures: Amazing me: Understanding how the body works [computer file] 199

```
001      04327276
008      970806s19uu              000 0 eng dnam a
020      $a1564602818
069      $aAG$b60408261$cFL 1002
100 1    $aOptical Data Corporation.
245 10   $aKinderventures: Amazing me: Understanding how the body
         works$b[computer file].
260      $aWarren, NJ ;$bOptical Data Corp. ;$c1994.
300      $a1 laser disc ;$b1 CD-ROM ;$c1 teacher's guide + 1
         software guide.
440  0   $aKinderventures.
999      $4Region 5$3Dade$2$cLeewood ES$fNP 612 AMA
```

ORDER AND PUNCTUATION OF ELEMENTS

The prescribed punctuation is not used consistently in the examples, nor do elements follow the order prescribed in AACR2. In Figures 2 and 3, the punctuation preceding subfield e of Field 300 (for accompanying material) is nonstandard. In Figure 1, a semicolon appears rather than the prescribed space-plus sign-space. The example in Figure 2 shows no punctuation. In Figure 3, the prescribed punctuation is used, but the information on accompanying material is coded in subfield c rather than e. In Field 245, subfield tagging and punctuation vary from the standard. "Kinderventures" is clearly a series title and "Amazing me," the distinctive title of one volume in the series. Since "Kinderventures" is repeated in the 440 series field, it normally would be deleted from the title proper. If this information were retained in Field 245, standard coding and punctuation would place the distinctive title in subfield p:

245 10 ‡a Kinderventures. ‡p Amazing me ‡h [computer file] : ‡b understanding how the body works.

None of the examples follow the prescribed order of notes. Field 538, for system requirements, should always be the first note for computer files. Field 520, for summary information, should be last.

GMD (GENERAL MATERIAL DESIGNATION)
AND SMD (SPECIFIC MATERIAL DESIGNATION)

Use of both the GMD and the SMD deviated from the standard in place-ment, MARC tagging and usage. In Figure 1, the GMD follows the statement of responsibility rather than the title proper. In Figure 2, the GMD is tagged in subfield b, rather than subfield h. Figure 1 uses the GMD "CD-ROM," which does not appear on the list of approved GMDs. The prescribed GMD would be "computer file." Similarly, "maverick" SMDs were also used: "CD-ROM disc" (Figure 1) and "laser disc," "CD-ROM" (Figure 3). The authorized term would be "computer optical disc."

ACCESS POINTS AND SUBJECT CATALOGING

Other unusual practices were noted with respect to the choice of main entry headings for *The Magic School Bus* and *Kinderventures*. Under current rules, both would probably be considered works of diffuse authorship and entered under title. Instead, *The Magic School Bus* is entered under the heading appropriate for the books on which the software is based, probably for reasons of collocation. *Kinderventures* is entered under the heading for the publisher.

The *Guidelines* require the use of either a summary or contents note. Though the records in Figures 1 and 2 include summaries (Field 520), Figure 3 shows neither. Use of subject heading and classification are also inconsistent. Only the item in Figure 1 is classed. The example in Figure 3 gives neither class number nor subject headings. The other two examples include several subject headings, with use of local subject headings (690) evident in Figure 1. However, it is difficult to determine which subject heading system is used, since the second indicator of Field 650, describing the type of heading, is either absent or varies. The nonstandard application of form subdivisions is also evident in Figures 1 and 2. The example in Figure 2 uses "computer programs"; whereas the standard term from the *Library of Congress Subject Headings* would be "software." The topical subdivision "computer-assisted instruction," normally used only for works *about* computer-assisted instruction, is applied in Figure 2 as a form subdivision.

It can be hypothesized that the nonstandard practices seen above meet the needs of local users and LMCs while standard cataloging practices do not. Cataloging in all three examples is streamlined, perhaps including just the information that is absolutely needed. The nonstandard SMDs and GMDs may be more "kid-friendly" than standard terms. Main entry headings may be chosen to achieve a desired collocation not provided for in the rules, such as by publisher or with related print resources. For materials intended to be used only in the LMC, system requirements information may be of less use to patrons than to staff, so placing that information first in the record is not necessary. Clearly, there is a need for new form subdivisions for electronic curriculum materials, since juvenile form subdivisions are not used with Annotated Card headings. Further research in the nonstandard cataloging practices for electronic resources in LMCs is needed.

REMOTE ACCESS FILES: INTERNET RESOURCES

The catalog examples for Internet resources were taken from one school's Web-based catalog. The partial record examples below exhibit non-standard practices and reveal highly creative solutions to the challenges of providing catalog access to Internet resources in a school setting. In describing her experiences, the LMS commented:

> I try to catalog or link websites that are recommended for student projects. I feel very strongly that our library catalog should be like "one-stop" shopping. Students should be able to get the best resources from our library catalog. There really isn't a good way in [our] Library system to do this at present. You have to sort of pretend the site is a book.

Figure 4, "Mr. Klaus' favorite web sites," shows Internet resources that are treated like a book. The "book" icon, depicting the format, is visible on the record. The record for English 1 Shakespeare Websites (Figure 5), is similar, but here the Websites are treated like a direct-access file, hence the

FIGURE 4. Website Cataloged as Book

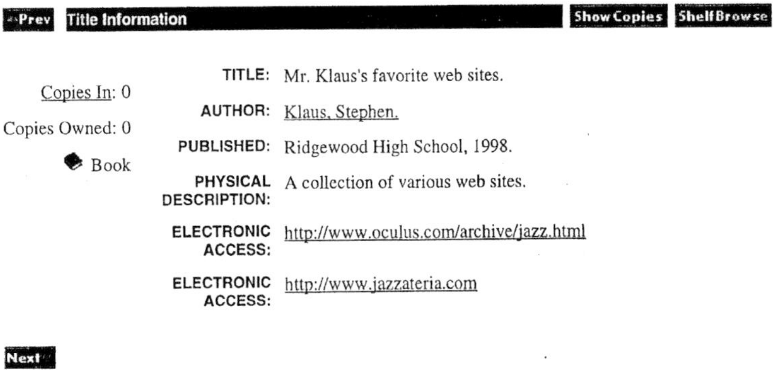

| **Prev** Title Information | | **Show Copies** **ShelfBrowse** |

Copies In: 0
Copies Owned: 0
◆ Book

TITLE:	Mr. Klaus's favorite web sites.
AUTHOR:	Klaus, Stephen.
PUBLISHED:	Ridgewood High School, 1998.
PHYSICAL DESCRIPTION:	A collection of various web sites.
ELECTRONIC ACCESS:	http://www.oculus.com/archive/jazz.html
ELECTRONIC ACCESS:	http://www.jazzateria.com

Next

FIGURE 5. Website Cataloged as Direct-Access File

◄Prev	Title Information		Show Copies	Shelf Browse

Online.	**TITLE:**	English I Shakespeare web sites [MRDF]	
Copies In: 1	**PHYSICAL DESCRIPTION:**	Internet sites.	
Copies Owned: 1 💻 Computer	**ELECTRONIC ACCESS:**	Virtual Renaissance. http://renaissance.district96.k12.il.us/	
	ELECTRONIC ACCESS:	Mr. William Shakespeare and the Internet. http://daphne.palomar.edu/shakespeare/	
	ELECTRONIC ACCESS:	Complete works of William Shakespeare (searchable full text, but slow to load) http://www-tech.mit.edu/Shakespeare/works.html	
	ELECTRONIC ACCESS:	Shakespeare Theme Page. http://www.cln.org/themes/shakespeare.html	
	ELECTRONIC ACCESS:	Carnegie Mellon University literature server. http://english.hss.cmu.edu/	
	ELECTRONIC ACCESS:	Shakespearean Insult http://www.emap.mtu.edu/mdh/Insult.html	

disk icon. Both Figures 4 and 5 function as collection-level records, describing, in minimal detail, more than one resource. Since neither record includes subject headings, the resources are retrievable only by a keyword search.

The example in Figure 6 is quite fascinating, because it displays an interesting use of Field 856. As discussed above, bibliographic records for print items can be enhanced to include the URLs of related Websites. For example, the URL for an educational Website on the U.S. Civil War could be added (in Field 856) to the bibliographic record for a novel about the Civil War, such as Irene Hunt's *Across Five Aprils*. In Figure 6, the record describes a book, *Bullfinch's Mythology* and the URLs below link the record to Websites devoted to mythology. This cataloging is an excellent example of the non-standard but creative ways that one school librarian uses to provide access to remote resources through the library catalog, despite the limitations of her local system.

These nonstandard cataloging practices very strongly reflect local needs and practices. Though non-standard, these records "work" for schools and serve the needs of local users. As one librarian commented: "We do a minimal cataloging, including just the areas we feel are necessary for patrons and for performing the searches and reports required and needed by our schools and ourselves."

This comment reveals two important points. First of all, LMSs perceive their software cataloging to be non-standard. Several indicated that they were unwilling to submit cataloging examples specifically because of nonstandard cataloging practices in their records. Second, many factors must be balanced

FIGURE 6. Print Resource with Links to Related Internet Sites

| ◄·Prev | Title Information | | Show Copies | Shelf Browse |

291 B871b	**TITLE:**	Bulfinch's mythology : The age of fable ; The age of chivalry ; Legenc Thomas Bulfinch.
Copies In: 1	**UNIFORM TITLE:**	Mythology
Copies Owned: 1		
📖 Book	**AUTHOR:**	Bulfinch, Thomas, 1796-1867.
	PUBLISHED:	New York : Modern Library, [19--?]
	PHYSICAL DESCRIPTION:	x, 778 p. : ill. ; 22 cm.
	NOTES:	Includes index.
	NOTES:	Bibliography: p. [v]
	NOTES:	Presents the myths of ancient Greece, Rome, Britain, and Scandinavia Arthur, Charlemagne, and Beowulf.
	SUBJECT:	Charlemagne, Emperor, 742-814--Romances.
	SUBJECT:	Charlemagne, Emperor, 742-814.
	SUBJECT:	Mythology.
	SUBJECT:	Chivalry.
	SUBJECT:	Folklore--Europe.
	ELECTRONIC ACCESS:	http://www.webcom.com/shownet/medea/bulfinch/welcome.html
	ELECTRONIC ACCESS:	http://Diogenes.Baylor.edu/WWWproviders/thorburn

in the creation of the cataloging record in school settings. The specialized needs of users, adherence to national standards, the constraints of local system capabilities, and the accounting needs of school districts and business offices are examples. The fact that records are closely tailored to needs of local users has implications for the usability of data in shared cataloging ventures.

Survey results revealed that 79% of LMCs purchase records from vendors along with materials (see Appendix). Clearly, greater cooperation from vendors and system designers would be desirable in helping LMC catalogs to meet the specialized needs of their users. System limitations can prevent users from finding the information they need. For example, Rottenbucher (Rottenbucher and Lamb 1994) discovered that the amount of space allotted for field 505 in her system was inadequate for the contents notes she needed to create. In those cases, she was forced to put the table of contents information in the Field 520 instead.

Though this solution proved feasible for the short term, the nonstandard use of the 520 field for table of contents information has significant drawbacks. When enhanced (with a second indicator value of 0 and subfield t),

Field 505 permits table of contents information to be retrieved by a title search rather than just a keyword search. This capability does not extend to data in field 520. Nonstandard use of the field could have implications for cooperative cataloging opportunities. The need for standardization will become increasingly important as opportunities for shared and cooperative cataloging increase, particularly with respect to Z39.50 access to other catalogs.

Nonstandard uses of MARC also reflect a need for better training and continuing cataloging education for LMSs. Solid knowledge of current cataloging standards would enable LMSs to produce high-quality records with confidence when original cataloging is necessary. More importantly, this knowledge would allow them better to evaluate the data they purchase from vendors and to demand higher-quality, curriculum-enhanced records that would help to connect the specialized needs of teachers and students with library materials.

SYNOPSIS OF RESULTS

Survey results show that direct-access electronic resources are being fully integrated into collections and services in the LMC, with 79% providing access to software and interactive multimedia through the catalog. On the other hand, 96% of respondents do not catalog Internet resources, suggesting that LMCs are only beginning to integrate access to Internet resources into library services. Catalog records for electronic resources, both remote and direct-access, strongly reflect nonstandard and local practices. Although many enhancements for curriculum materials have been added to the MARC format, with the potential to powerfully link curricula, users, and library collections, most LMC catalogs do not reflect the use of these enhancements either for electronic or other materials.

CONCLUSION

Literacy building partnerships between school library media specialists and other educators must be developed and enhanced. As society becomes increasingly technology-driven, the rift between those who have access to information and those who do not will continue to grow, with powerful economic and social implications. Martinez observed that "computer literacy may become the de facto prerequisite for citizenship in the next century" (1994, 395). As they, too, become increasingly technology-driven, LMCs are a natural gateway to the abundance of information resources. LMSs, in their role as information specialists, are natural gatekeepers, uniquely poised to take a pivotal role in promoting information literacy and equitable access to information.

This leadership role should include integration of new formats into library collections, programs, and services. LMC catalogs should continue to provide access to information in all formats, including electronic. Providing access through school library catalogs to both direct-access and remote-access electronic resources is a logical role and a desirable step in promoting information literacy. Including electronic resources in the library catalog will facilitate access and increase use of these important resources.

Despite the many challenges associated with cataloging Internet resources, they, too, should be included in the LMC catalog. Internet resources represent information that can complement resources already in the LMC (Everhart 1997, 166). LMSs, in their role as instructional partners, have the necessary skills and expertise to use these resources to their full potential and to evaluate and link them to the curriculum (Everhart 1997, 166).

A majority of respondents (62%) currently evaluate Websites for library access through alternative means. This is a small step away from evaluating them for inclusion in the catalog. Despite technical issues, evaluation is the key to the process and is where the real value of catalog access to these resources lies. Internet resources should undergo the same careful selection process as other items included in the catalog.

Web-based catalogs are desirable for the LMC for a number of reasons. First, they offer significant advantages to young users, who often have difficulty using traditional catalogs. Edmonds (Edmonds, Moore and Balcom 1990) found that children have difficulty with the alphabetization and filing skills necessary for catalog use, and that skill in using catalogs is developmental, with younger children searching less successfully than older. Borgman (Borgman et al. 1995) observed the need to reduce the keyboarding and alphabetization demanded of young users, and noted children's preference for a browsing interface in catalogs. These findings suggest that the graphical user interface of Web-based catalogs, with their point and click functionality, could be easier for children to use and may improve their access to information. Second, the use of electronic resources is enhanced in Web-based catalogs, since users can take advantage of catalog hotlinks directly to Internet resources. LMCs should begin to use Field 856, even if current catalogs are not Web-based, since they may be in the future.

Information Power also advocates the role of the LMS as an instructional partner, who "joins with teachers and others to identify links across student information needs, curricular content, learning outcomes and a wide variety of print, nonprint, and electronic information resources" (1998, 5). Library media specialists should plan for the implementation of the curriculum enhancements to the MARC format, if they are not already being used. These enhancements include use of fields 520, 521, 526 and 658 as described in this paper. These fields enable powerful connections to be made, linking the curriculum with library resources. They hold much potential for enhancing teaching and learning, and are particularly useful for describing electronic and nonprint resources, which are not as easily browsed as other formats.

But however desirable these innovations may be, the reality is that many school media specialists and even district catalogers face a severe lack of time, resources, funding, staffing, and administrative support. These are probably the biggest obstacles to providing quality access to electronic resources in LMCs and to creating curriculum linkages. One participant commented:

> Because our school district has very tight budgetary constraints, many library media specialists have no time to do original cataloging. Nor do most schools understand the value of adding information as you describe to the records provided by vendors. Therefore, the library media specialists do not have the time or opportunity to edit records providing such enhancements. Until administrators understand this work and its value to teachers and students, we will not be given opportunities to do it. Until we are given opportunities to demonstrate its value, administrators will not support us doing this work.

Clearly, the best solution to these problems lies in the development of cooperative ventures, whether at the district, state or national level. The United States is an incredibly information- and technology-rich society, with arguably the best model of national bibliographic control in the world. These resources could and should be harnessed to provide better access to digital resources in school library media centers. Further research is yet to be done on possible cooperative ventures that would involve libraries, vendors, national cooperative programs, and bibliographic utilities. The importance of standardization of cataloging data in successful cooperative cataloging ventures cannot be overemphasized, and better-quality vendor records, improved system design, and cataloging education for school media specialists are needed. The feasibility of developing a core record standard for curriculum materials (regardless of format), that would harmonize the needs of LMCs, the *Guidelines for Standardized Cataloging of Children's Materials,* and the curriculum enhancements to the MARC record, should be explored.

SOURCES

Anglo-American cataloguing rules. 1988, 2nd ed., 1998 rev. Chicago: American Library Association.

Borgman, Christine L., Sandra G. Hirsch, Virginia A. Walter, Andrea L. Gallagher. 1995. Children's searching behavior on browsing and keyword online catalogs:

The Science Library Catalog Project. *Journal of the American Society for Information Science* 46(9): 663-684.

Deyoe, Nancy and Nan Myers. 1999. Survey: Issues in cataloging URLs/PURLs. AUTOCAT [Online], Mar. 10. Available E-mail: AUTOCAT@acsu.buffalo.edu.

EBSS Curriculum Materials in the Online Catalog ad hoc Subcommittee. 1990. Curriculum materials in online catalogs: Standardized cataloging for curriculum centers. *C&RL News* 51 (6): 562-565.

Edmonds, Leslie, Paula Moore, and Kathleen Mehaffey Balcom. 1990. The effectiveness of an online catalog. *School Library Journal* 36: 28-32.

Everhart, Nancy. 1994. How high school library media specialists in automated and nonautomated media centers spend their time. *Journal of Education for Library and Information Science* 35 (1): 3-19.

_____ 1997. Internet access in school library media centers. *Internet Reference Services Quarterly* 2(4): 165-184.

Information power: Building partnerships for learning. 1998. Chicago: American Library Association.

Kranz, Jack. 1987. Cataloging of curriculum materials on OCLC: A perspective. *Cataloging & Classification Quarterly* 8 (2): 15-28.

Lewis, Roberta Welsh. 1989. Elementary school children express their need for catalog information. *Journal of Youth Services in Libraries* 2 (2): 151-156.

MARBI (Machine-Readable Bibliographic Information). 1997. Discussion paper no. 105: Reading program information. Http://lcweb.loc.gov/marc/marbi/dp/dp105.htm

_____ 1998. Proposal no. 98-17: Reading program information in the USMARC Bibliographic Format. Http://lcweb.loc.gov/marc/marbi/1998/98-17.htm

Martinez, Michael E. 1994. Access to information technologies among school-age children: Implications for a democratic society. *Journal of the American Society for Information Science* 45(6): 395-400.

Miller, Marilyn L. and Marilyn L. Shontz. 1998. Plug it in: The wired school library. *School Library Journal* 44 (10): 27-31.

Minier, Roger. 1994. Automated library systems add curriculum information. *Indiana Media Journal* 16 (4): 58-59.

Murphy, Catherine. 1991. Subject access in online systems: Enhancing the curriculum connection. *The Bookmark* (Fall): 24-26.

_____ 1994. Curriculum-Enhanced MARC (CEMARC): A new cataloging format for school librarians. In *Literacy: traditional, cultural, technological: selected papers from the 23rd Annual Conference, International Association of School Librarianship.* Kalamazoo, MI: International Association of School Librarianship.

_____ 1998. Curriculum-enhanced MARC. Chap. 15 in *Cataloging correctly for kids: An introduction to the tools*, 3rd ed. Sharon Zuiderveld, editor. Chicago: American Library Association.

(NCES) National Center for Education Statistics. 1999. Internet access in public schools and classrooms: 1994-98. Washington, DC: National Center for Education Statistics. Also available via the Internet at: http://nces.ed.gov/pubs99/1999017.html

(RTSD/CCS) Resources & Technical Services Division/CCS Cataloging of Children's Materials Committee. 1982. Guidelines for standardized cataloging of children's materials. In *Cataloging correctly for kids: An introduction to the tools*, Rev ed. Sharon Zuiderveld, ed. Chicago: American Library Association, 1991.

Rottenbucher, Adele, and Annette Lamb. 1994. Enhancing MARC records for better key-word searching of the online catalog. *Indiana Media Journal* 16 (4): 60-71.

USMARC code list for relators, sources, description conventions. 1997. Washington, DC: Cataloging Distribution Service, Library of Congress.

USMARC format for bibliographic data. 526 Study Program Information Note. Available via the Internet: http://lcweb.loc.gov/marc/bibliographic/bd526.html

Van Deusen, Jean Donham. 1996. An analysis of the time use of elementary school library media specialists and factors that influence it. *School Library Media Quarterly* 24 (2): 85-92.

Ward, David and Diane VanderPol. 1999. Survey on: Providing access to Internet resources. Unpublished. Available via the Internet at http://www.nevada.edu/~wardd/survey/

Wehmeyer, Lillian M. 1976. Cataloging the school media center as a specialized collection. *Library Resources & Technical Services* 20 (4): 315-325.

APPENDIX

Survey on the Cataloging of Electronic Resources in School Libraries
TABULATION
92 total responses

1. Do you provide WWW/Internet access in your library? *89* (96.74%)

2. Do you have an online public-access catalog? *73* (79.35%)

3. Is it possible to access your catalog through the Internet? *17* (18.48%)

4. Is your catalog Web-based (are "hotlinks" available?) *19* (20.65%)

5. Source of cataloging records (e.g., OCLC, purchase from vendor, Bibliofile, etc.) OCLC *22* (22.82%)

Purchase from vendor (e.g., Follett, B&T) *73* (79.35%) Other: 37 (40.22%)

Bibliofile:3 Original cataloging: 18; catalog cards: 1; CIP: 3; statewide system: 4

County-wide system: 1; Centralized district cataloging: 2; LC, 1; MARCIVE, 1. Z39.50, 1

6. What percentage of your collection do electronic resources (software, CD-ROMS, interactive multimedia) comprise?

7. Do you catalog electronic resources? *58 Y*(63.04%) *34 N* (36.96%)

A. Which formats do you catalog?

Software (including CD-ROMs): *58* (63.04%)

Interactive multimedia: *41* (44.57%)

Other (please describe): *12* (13.19%) (3, laser disk, 1, hardware, 9 videos)

B. Do you provide access to electronic resources through some other means besides your catalog (Library homepage, etc.) *67* (72.83%)

Library homepage: *30* (32.61%) Print guides: *34* (36.96%) On select workstations or separate lab: *57* (61.96%) Through bibliographic instruction: *47* (51.09%)

8. Do you currently catalog Internet resources (Websites)? *4* (4.3%)

Do you provide access to Internet resources through some other means besides your catalog? 67 Y (72.83%), 25 N (27.17%)

Through Library homepage: *32* (34.78%) Print guides: *37* (40.22%) Bookmark files on workstations: *56* (60.87%) Bibliographic Instruction: *51* (55.43%)

9. Do you use field 856 in your catalog records? *8* (8.7%)

A. For Internet resources *5* (5.43%)

B. For items that are versions or components of Internet resources *3* (3.26%)

C. For Internet resources that are related to the item you are cataloging: *3* (3.26%)

10. Do you/have you

A. Purchase/d 856 links from a vendor to enrich current holdings? *1*(1.08%)

B. Purchase/d records that are already enriched with 856 fields? *4* (4.35%)

11. Do you have any formal procedures for maintaining 856 fields? *1* (1.08%)

12. A. Do you actively seek and evaluate educational Websites for inclusion in the catalog? *9* (9.78%)

B. Do you actively seek and evaluate educational websites for inclusion through an alternate means (such as through a library homepage?) *57* (61.96%)

13. A. Do you use field 658 to correlate curriculum objectives with library resources? *1 Y* (1.08%): For print & AV

B. Do you correlate resources to (Check all that apply): 0 No responses

State standards ____ Y/N National standards ___ Y/N Local standards ____ Y/N

14. Do you use field 520 to record reviews (1st indicator value of 1)? *14* (15.22%)

If yes, do you record reviews for (Check all that apply):

Print materials: *12* (13.04%) Software: *7* (7.61%) Internet Resources: *2* (2.17%) Other A/V: *8* (8.7%)

15. For field 521, which of the following *first indicators* do you use, and for which kinds of materials (print, software, Internet resources, other AV)?

A. 0 (Reading grade level) *29* (31.52%) For Print: *8* (27.6%) For software: *1* (3.4%) For AV: *1* (3.4%) No specification: *19* (65.5%)

B. 1 (Interest age level) *20* (21.74%) For Print: *2* (10%); no specification, *18* (90%)

C. 2 (Interest grade level) *24* (26.09%) For print: *4* (16.7%); no specification, *20* (83.3%)

D. 3 (Special audience characteristics) *8 Y* (8.70%) Use for Special Education: *2* (25%); Use for Gifted: 1 (12.5%); no specification: *5* (62.5%)

E. *4* (Motivation/interest level)) *8 Y* (8.70%), no format specified

16. Do you use/plan to use field 526 (Study program information) *2 Y* (2.17%)

ALADIN:
An Example of Integrating Traditional and Electronic Services in the Digital Environment

Ursula Giere

Eva Kupidura

SUMMARY. This article provides an overview of ALADIN (Adult Learning Documentation and Information Network) and reports on a worldwide survey carried out by the Documentation Centre of the UNESCO Institute for Education and co-financed by the German Federal Ministry of Education, Science, Research and Technology. The survey served as a first step towards implementing international co-operation and cross-border networking between adult education documentation and information services as part of ALADIN's activities. The survey helped to identify a variety of networking procedures and important components of organizing and cataloguing traditional as well as electronic formats on the global scale. Overall, the survey helped to provide data so that adult education can benefit from worldwide exchange of information and bring about the democratic globalization of knowledge. (Full report and information on ALADIN members are available at: http://<www.unesco.org/education/aladin>.) *[Article copies available for a fee from The Haworth Document Delivery Service: 1-800-342-9678. E-mail address: <getinfo@haworthpressinc.com> Website: <http://www.HaworthPress. com>]*

Ursula Giere is Research Specialist and Head of the Documentation Centre at the UNESCO Institute for Education, Hamburg, Germany, UNESCO Institute for Education, PO Box 13, 10 23 20110 Hamburg, Germany (e-mail: U.GIERE@unesco.org).

Eva Kupidura is Head of the Resource Centre of the International Council for Adult Education (ICAE), 720 Bathurst Street, Suite 5000, Toronto, Ontario M5S 2R4, Canada (e-mail: icae@web.net).

[Haworth co-indexing entry note]: "ALADIN: An Example of Integrating Traditional and Electronic Services in the Digital Environment." Giere, Ursula and Eva Kupidura. Co-published simultaneously in *Journal of Internet Cataloging* (The Haworth Information Press, an imprint of The Haworth Press, Inc.) Vol. 3, No. 1, 2000, pp. 41-52; and: *Metadata and Organizing Educational Resources on the Internet* (ed: Jane Greenberg) The Haworth Information Press, an imprint of The Haworth Press, Inc., 2000, pp. 41-52. Single or multiple copies of this article are available for a fee from The Haworth Document Delivery Service [1-800-342-9678, 9:00 a.m. - 5:00 p.m. (EST). E-mail address: getinfo@haworthpressinc.com].

© 2000 by The Haworth Press, Inc. All rights reserved.

KEYWORDS. ALADIN, digital libraries, cataloging, indexing, Internet, UNESCO

THE RATIONALE OF ALADIN

Lacking adequate financial and human resources, adult education documentation and information centres cannot satisfactorily fulfil their tasks at a time of increasing demand for adult education and training. In many developing countries such documentation and information centres are hardly yet developed. New technologies have, if anything, widened the information gap between industrialized countries and developing countries, and even where efficient documentation centres or access to the World Wide Web are available, the centres often operate in an isolated way.

Against this background, the Documentation Centre of the UNESCO Institute for Education has taken the initiative to establish ALADIN, the *A*dult *L*earning *D*ocumentation and *I*nformation *N*etwork (http://www.unesco.org/education/aladin). ALADIN has become a network of so far 90 adult learning documentation and information services in all regions of the world and is coordinated by the Documentation Centre of the UNESCO Institute for Education (UIE), Hamburg, Germany. Initiated during the Fifth International UNESCO Adult Education Conference (CONFINTEA V), Hamburg, 1997, ALADIN has had strong supporters from the very first moment of its existence, including UNESCO Headquarters; the International Council for Adult Education (ICAE); the World Bank; the 'Centre de documentation sur l'éducation des adultes et la condition féminine,' Montreal; the Alexander N. Charters Library of Resources for Educators of Adults at Syracuse University; the Slovene Adult Education Centre; the ERIC Clearinghouse on Adult, Career and Vocational Education; ALICE , Information Centre on Non-formal Adult Education in Europe; the Rössing Foundation, Namibia; ACCU, the Asia/Pacific Cultural Centre for UNESCO; ASPBAE, the Asian/South Pacific Bureau of Adult Education; REDUC, Latin America; Damascus University; and the Ministry of Education of Nepal.

ALADIN, which has as its objective to counteract the imbalance in access to adult learning documentation and information, is committed to incorporate in its network also those services that are not yet online. It is a fundamental principle of ALADIN that the exchange of information through the WWW cannot completely replace the more traditional exchange of media. While working to create and to strengthen the technological capacity of its members, the network promotes the integration of new technologies with traditional means of communication, combining digital cataloging and organization of data with traditional ways of cataloging and data management.

Neither digital cataloging regulations nor any other prescriptions for data management exist within ALADIN. An attempt is made to include the whole spectrum of data management procedures. Not methodological, but content issues are priority concerns of ALADIN. Aiming at providing all members of the global adult education community–policy-makers, researchers, business, media, adult educators and everyone engaged in lifelong learning–with comprehensive and up-to-date high quality information of the contemporary adult education scene, ALADIN cannot limit itself to those few adult learning documentation and information services so far applying digital cataloging.

Any discussion of digital cataloging and organizing data in the global context of ALADIN would risk being somewhat detached from the reality if it failed to address the fundamental issue of access to electronic communications and new information technologies. Talking about co-operation and exchange of information in a globalizing world means dealing with increasing disparities. The accelerating use of new technologies and digitalization of documentation and information work contribute to the widening of the information gap between industrialized and developing countries. ALADIN's data sadly concur with those included in the latest *Human Development Report* of the United Nations Development Program (UNDP) (UNDP: Human Development Report 1999. Globalization with a Human Face. New York, 1999). UNDP's examination of trends in the use of new technologies in developing countries brings striking and far-reaching conclusions. Although it is widely acknowledged that the society of today is knowledge-based, and new communications technologies are among the main forces of the globalization, those who have often been deprived of information, and whom the new communications means might help in bridging the knowledge gap, are not able to benefit from global trends of declining cost and increasing availability of digital resources.

Information-poor countries are often poorly electronically connected. UNDP reports that 'in Cambodia in 1996, there was less than 1 telephone for every 100 people. In Monaco (. . .) there were 99 telephones for every 100 people. A widely accepted measure of basic access to telecommunications is having 1 telephone for every 100 people–a teledensity of 1. Yet as we enter the next century, a quarter of countries still have not achieved even that basic level. (. . .) At the present average speed of telecommunications spread, Cote d'Ivoire and Bhutan would take until 2050 to achieve the teledensity that Germany and Singapore have today' (p.62). Similarly, while it is estimated that by the year 2001 700 million people will be Internet users (UNDP p.58), UNDP also reports that 'in mid-1998 industrial countries–home to less than 15% of people–had 88% of Internet users. North America alone–with less than 5% of all people–had more than 50% of Internet users. By contrast, South Asia is home to over 20% of all people but had less than 1% of the world's Internet users' (p.62). Although the cost of hardware has been declining steadily, computers still remain out of reach for a big part of the world population. UNDP reports: 'Buying a computer would cost the average Bangladeshi more than eight years' income, compared with just one month's wage for the average American' (p.62).

Reflecting this reality, ALADIN's members' services vary immensely in size, information capacity and level of organization of resources. While some of them have to rely on some hundred books or documents in their information work and lack the means to apply technologically advanced documentation methods (as, for example, ROCARE in Cameroon with 150 books and documents), and others draw their information from several thousand computer-cataloged publications (as, for example, the Slovene Adult Education Centre with 2,900 books and documents), some other Network partners provide access to huge sophisticatedly organized electronic databases (like ERIC/ACVE, Columbus, Ohio) or even rely completely on the organization of data in the digital environment of the Internet (as, for example, the Global Information Networks in Education, GINIE, University of Pittsburgh, Pennsylvania). Involved in such fields as, for example, health, environment, agriculture, gender, adult literacy, work and employment, or democracy and citizenship, all services, whatever their size and level of organization, offer invaluable information work within their capabilities to their clientele and altogether build a comprehensive picture of contemporary global adult education policies, research and action. As diverse as the field and the clientele is also the cultural and linguistic variety of the ALADIN members: Out of 90 ALADIN members (September 1998), 49.5% are based in Europe (46.1% in Western Europe and 3.4% in Central/Eastern European and Baltic countries), 16.9% in Asia and the Pacific, 13.5% in North America, 11.2% in Latin America and the Caribbean, 7.9% in Africa and 1.1% in the Arab Region. (More services, especially within larger systems such as university libraries, certainly exist.)

MAPPING THE PRESENT SITUATION
OF ADULT LEARNING DOCUMENTATION
AND INFORMATION SERVICES

With financial support of the German Federal Ministry of Education, Science, Research and Technology UIE's Documentation Centre carried out a systematic survey in order to identify potential ALADIN members and in order to find out what exists "out there in the world of adult learning documentation and information" in terms of networking and cataloging activities. Out of the 148 persons/ centres contacted 105 responded (response rate = 71%), 90 of which were applicable for ALADIN membership. The data collected include: basic institutional data; size and type of collection/electronic resources; methods of data management; information and publications profile highlighting services and special activities; user profile; challenges and obstacles in carrying out the work; strategies and perspectives to improve services; the role envisaged within ALADIN. The results of the survey have been published in 1998 in the form of an analytical and annotated *Directory* of ALADIN members (Giere, Ursula: Developing a Network of Adult Learning Documentation and Information Services. Directory of Members 1998. Hamburg, UIE, 1998. 203 p.). Some of the findings (of September 1998) related to networking and cataloging activities in a digital environment are presented here, in particular, access to electronic communications, homepage in the Internet, externally accessible databases, methods of data processing, electronic database software, classification systems, indexing tools and cataloguing rules.

Networking

Access to Electronic Communications

All ALADIN members but one have access to telephone and fax, 87% have e-mail access. (See Figure 1.)

Homepage in the Internet

Seventy percent, a relatively high number of ALADIN members, have established homepages in the World Wide Web. (See Figure 2.)

Externally Accessible Databases

Among ALADIN members with access to the WWW, only 23% so far arranged for an online, external access to their databases, and out of those only very few have full text online search capacity (see Appendix 1).

FIGURE 1. Members with E-Mail Access by Region

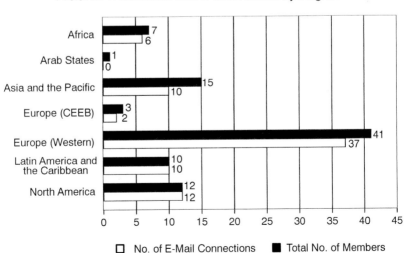

FIGURE 2. Members Having Their Own WWW Home Page by Region

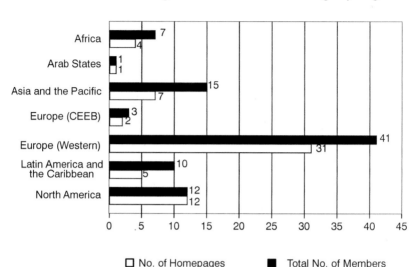

☐ No. of Homepages   ■ Total No. of Members

Methods of Data Processing (Computerized/Manual)

Seventeen percent of ALADIN members have not given any information on their way of data processing. This may imply that some of them do not process data at all. Thirteen percent of ALADIN members are processing their bibliographical data in a conventional manual way, and 70% process their data electronically.

Electronic Database Software

While the majority of ALADIN members, namely 28%, work with CDS/ISIS, a data processing software developed and distributed by UNESCO, 42% use a diversity of software programmes (ACCESS, ALLEGRO, LARS, LOTUS, ORACLE, etc.). (See Figure 3.)

Classification, Indexing, and Cataloging Activities Practiced Within ALADIN

Classification Systems

The classification systems most often used by ALADIN members are the Dewey Decimal Classification (17%), the Universal Decimal Classification (11%), and the Library of Congress Classification (6%). Seventeen percent of

FIGURE 3. Database Software Used by Members in %

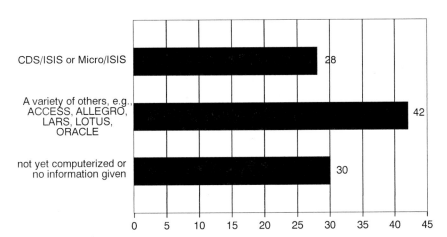

ALADIN members have developed their own classification systems, while 4% use a variety of national variations of the Decimal Classification or other systems. Forty-five of ALADIN members have not given information.

Indexing Tools

The *UNESCO Thesaurus* and the *UNESCO: IBE Education Thesaurus* are the indexing tools used by the majority of ALADIN members. Together, they represent almost 50% of all thesauri named. Other identified indexing tools named (in some cases ALADIN members reported that they use more than one indexing tool) include:

- national or regional standardized descriptors (e.g., *Australian Thesaurus of Education Descriptors, Tesauro Colombiano de Educación, European Education Thesaurus*): 17%;
- keywords lists/thesauri tailor-made for a specific institution (e.g., keyword list of the Institut für Arbeitsmarkt -und Berufsforschung der Bundesansalt fur Arbeit- Institute for Employment Research, Germany, *OECD Macrothesaurus, World Bank Thesaurus, Thesaurus of ERIC Descriptors*): 15%;
- thesauri specialized in a particular area (e.g., *Canadian Literacy Thesaurus, Multilingual Thesaurus of Vocational Training, Human Rights Thesaurus, Feminist Thesaurus*): 15%; and
- *Library of Congress Subject Headings* or *Sears List of Subject Headings:* 13%.

Forty-eight percent of ALADIN members did not specify their indexing tools, what may perhaps indicate that they do not use any, as for example explained by GINIE in the following way: 'Traditional education thesauruses are not helpful for subjects such as land-mine awareness education materials in GINIE.' Several ALADIN members report that they adopt thesauri to their needs. The J. Roby Kidd Resource Centre of the International Council for Adult Education (ICAE), for example, uses the *UNESCO: IBE Education Thesaurus* as its main indexing tool adding descriptors reflecting terminology specific to ICAE's work.

Cataloging Rules

AACR and AACR2 (Anglo-American Cataloging Rules) and their modifications are the most frequently used cataloging rules within ALADIN (about 40%). Around 10% use RAK, the cataloging rules originating from German-speaking countries or SAB, the Swedish cataloging system. Forty-nine percent of ALADIN members have not given any information about the cataloging rules applied, which may indicate that some of them may not use any rules at all, as, for example, expressed by one of the members: 'Human resources for cataloging are not available.'

Lack of human resources for cataloging and other information-related activities, lack of trained personnel, of funds, of electronic equipment, of technological know-how, even of reading materials or furniture are well known problems in the world of documentation and information in general and in adult learning documentation and information in particular. However, joining hands, networking within ALADIN, enlarges the information capacity of the individual adult education documentation and information services immensely: With 70% of its members having homepages in the Internet, with 23% of its members having externally accessible databases, with 70% processing their data electronically, with 55% applying some form of classification system and another more than 50% using thesauri for their indexing work and organizing their data with descriptive cataloging rules, ALADIN possesses–given the heterogenity of its members–a relatively high level of organization not only in conventional library but also in digital information standards. In particular the fact that a high percentage of ALADIN members apply professional indexing practices using controlled standardized language contributes to the quality of storage and retrieval of this specialized knowledge and information pool, accessible conventionally in print format via the *Directory* (since autumn 1998) as well as electronically via ALADIN's Website (since summer 1999).

THE ORGANIZATION OF ALADIN'S DATA
IN THE DIGITAL ENVIRONMENT

After surveying the situation of adult learning documentation and information services worldwide in 1997/98 the data collected about the individual services were harmonized and systematized for publication of the *Directory* in print form in such a way that the transfer of data into ALADIN's Website was already completely prestructured and preprepared. In summer 1999, with assistance of UNESCO HQ, the Documentation Centre of UIE has put up ALADIN's Website on the Internet. The ALADIN Website functions as a distinctive entity of both the larger Website of the UNESCO Education Division and the homepage of the UNESCO Institute for Education. Creation and management of the ALADIN Website are based on tools provided by Front-Page. The Website offers a dynamic and interactive navigation developed through JavaScript's applications avoiding multiple hyperlinks and long pages with many texts.

While the ALADIN Website follows the structure of data of the printed *Directory*, it enhances at the same time the organization of these data by profiting from technical advantages of the hypertext. As the printed *Directory* the ALADIN Website includes under distinctive sections: the analysis of the survey carried out by UIE's Documentation Centre, the profiles of the 90 ALADIN members, listings of their areas of specialization, the countries which are covered by their collections, the countries in which the services are located, the regions in which the services are located, their working languages. Other sections include listings of databases with external online access, homepage addresses of ALADIN members, interactive forum, a 'How to join section' with a questionnaire, and an internal search engine. The Website provides hot links to all Internet-based resources maintained by the ALADIN members–their Websites and, when available, externally accessible databases.

An interesting feature of the ALADIN Website organization is the variety of search options offered. The user interested in a particular piece of information has at his/her disposal several shortcuts allowing to search directly for ALADIN members' names, areas of specializations, geographical foci, location (region or country) or working languages. These search paths correspond to the indexes included in the book form of the *Directory*. A special search device of the ALADIN Website gives access to a comprehensive search engine allowing to search on a metalevel the entire ALADIN Website as well as all UNESCO Education Websites for desired information. The search engine is interfaced under UNESCO HQ cgi-bin and indexed with WAIS software. Whatever search strategy preferred, the user of ALADIN's Website will be led to relevant adult learning documentation and information services competent to supply information either by electronic databases or by traditional means of communication. Since only about 23% of ALADIN members so far have databases accessible via hot lines directly from the ALADIN Website, invaluable sources of so far often hidden and silent information would therefore be lost if the more traditional accessible information resources in all the other ALADIN bases would not be consulted.

The ALADIN Website is an example of innovative organization of data on adult learning. By the systematization of its content, it adds a structured and quality controlled pool of knowledge in the field of adult learning to the Internet. Before becoming a searchable entity on the Internet ALADIN's data are being harmonized and cataloged. Harmonizing as well as cataloging imply directed human activities requiring professional effort determining the relevance and reflecting the intellectual content of an item. This human intellectual effort of the global collectivity of ALADIN members makes the ALADIN Website distinctively different from programmed automated search engines like those developed by computer programmers at, for example, Alta Vista. Furthermore, ALADIN is an important and unique effort to organize digitally data originating in a largely non-digital reality of adult learning services of many regions of the world. This is the only way networking in the digital environment can bring about democratic globalization of knowledge. In view of the need for everyone to participate in the learning and information society of the future, a global network like ALADIN must also incorporate those who are not yet online and will not be so in the near future. Worldwide exchange of information means that everybody taking part in the exchange gives and takes, in accordance with their cultural background and level of technological development.

SOME FUTURE STRATEGIES OF ALADIN

While integrating traditional and electronic services in the digital environment, ALADIN strives at strengthening the technological capacity of its members, laying the groundwork for the establishment of new centres and linking them up with ALADIN. Funds have been raised for the implementation of a small scale three-year-programme of this kind in 10 low income countries in the African and in the Asian region: Cameroon, Kenya, Sierra Leone, Bangladesh, India, Nepal, Pakistan, Sri Lanka and Vietnam. In all these countries ALADIN has already at least one co-operating member ready to actively contribute to the institutionalization of adult documentation and information services and their electronic networking. In addition, UNESCO HQ has offered to host homepages of adult learning documentation and information services as long as they do not have their own access to the Internet. Although ALADIN may have lost the magic power to make dreams come true instantly by rubbing the oil lamp, the will power of ALADIN's members may bring about changes gradually and steadily.

APPENDIX 1.
ALADIN Databases with External Online Access

Adult Education Resource and Information Service (ARIS)
http://sunsite.anu.edu.au/language-australia/search/aris1.html

ALICE: Information Centre on Non-formal Adult Education in Europe
http://www.vsy.fi/alice

Basic Skills Agency Resource Centre
Institute of Education Library
telnet://library.ioe.ac.uk

Bundesinstitut für Berufsbildung
Library, Documentation and Information Services (K4)
via Modem

CEDEFOP–European Centre for the Development of Vocational Training
Library and Documentation Service
www.trainingvillage.gr

CENTRE INFFO–Centre pour le développement de l'information sur la formation professionnelle continue
Documentation Department
minitel 3617 FORINTER (accessible in France only)

CIDHAL–Comunicación, Intercambio y Desarrollo Humano en América Latina, A.C.
http://www.laneta.apc.org/cidhal/cidha13.htm

Coady International Institute
Marie Michael Library
http://www.stfx.ca/coady-library (start a NOVANET session, then click the link for Specific Collections to find Coady)

Council of Europe
EUDISED
http://www.bdp.it/banche/eudifor.html (via Bibliotheca di documentazione pedagogica in Florence)

ERIC Clearinghouse on Adult, Career, and Vocational Education (ERIC/ACVE)
http://www.aspensys.com/eric/searchdb/dbchart.html; for full-text document delivery
http://edrs.com

German Foundation for International Development (DSE)
Documentation Centre
http://www.dse.de/zd/

Global Information Networks in Education
via http://www.pitt.edu/~ginie follow link programmes/projects

The National Centre for Educational Resources
http://skolenettet.nls.no/fjernund

National Vocational Education and Training Clearinghouse
http://www.ncver.edu.au/voced.htm

Réseau Européen de Formation–Education des Adultes Ruraux
(R.E.F.A.R.)
via agreement

Slovene Adult Education Centre (SAEC)
Regional Information-Documentation Centre for Adult Education Research (RI-CAER)
http://izumw.izum.si/cobiss then follow link to special libraries

UNESCO
Documentation and Information Service/Education Sector
http://www.unesco.org/general/eng/infoserv/doc/library.html

UNESCO–International Bureau of Education (IBE)
Documentation and Information Unit
http://www.unicc.org/ibe/Inf_Doc/Nat_reps/natrep.htm

University of Alaska Anchorage
Consortium Library
telnet://sled.alaska.edu

The World Bank
http://jolis.worldbankimflib.org/external.htm

Cataloging K-12 Math
and Science Curriculum Resources
on the Internet:
A Non-Traditional Approach

Karen A. Plummer

SUMMARY. The Eisenhower National Clearinghouse for Mathematics and Science Education (ENC), a project funded through the Office of Educational Research and Improvement at the U.S. Department of Education, was created to collect and describe K-12 math and science curriculum resources and provide online access to the descriptive cataloging records (http://www.enc.org/rf/nf_index.htm). This article discusses methods of identification and selection of WWW sites for ENC, and addresses the cataloging and abstracting of these WWW sites utilizing non-standard cataloging guidelines. This article also discusses ENC's efforts to add value information through the identification of state frameworks or national standards appropriate to the resource, awards or third party reviews, and by linking to related collection items or Websites that support, enhance, or are required for use of the resource described. *[Article copies available for a fee from The Haworth Document Delivery Service: 1-800-342-9678. E-mail address: <getinfo@haworthpressinc.com> Website: <http://www.HaworthPress.com>]*

Karen A. Plummer is Catalog Coordinator, Eisenhower National Clearinghouse (ENC), Columbus, OH (e-mail: kplummer@enc.org).

The author extends her thanks to Dr. Kimberly S. Roempler, Dr. Terese Herrera, and Lynda C. Titterington for providing information on selection and abstracting of Internet resources and to Tracy Crow for editorial support.

[Haworth co-indexing entry note]: "Cataloging K-12 Math and Science Curriculum Resources on the Internet: A Non-Traditional Approach." Plummer, Karen A. Co-published simultaneously in *Journal of Internet Cataloging* (The Haworth Information Press, an imprint of The Haworth Press, Inc.) Vol. 3, No. 1, 2000, pp. 53-65; and: *Metadata and Organizing Educational Resources on the Internet* (ed: Jane Greenberg) The Haworth Information Press, an imprint of The Haworth Press, Inc., 2000, pp. 53-65. Single or multiple copies of this article are available for a fee from The Haworth Document Delivery Service [1-800-342-9678, 9:00 a.m. - 5:00 p.m. (EST). E-mail address: getinfo@haworthpressinc.com].

© 2000 by The Haworth Press, Inc. All rights reserved.

KEYWORDS. Mathematics, science, curriculum, Internet, Websites, cataloging, abstracting, selection, K-12 teachers, non-AACR2, education

BACKGROUND

The Eisenhower National Clearinghouse for Mathematics and Science Education (ENC), authorized by federal legislation (P.L. 101-589, Section 204) as part of the Excellence in Mathematics, Science and Engineering Education Act of 1990, was created with ambitious goals in mind. ENC was required by the United States Department of Education's Office of Educational Research and Improvement (OERI) to plan, develop, organize, and operate a national clearinghouse for science and mathematics education materials. Additionally, the Clearinghouse was to facilitate more effective identification of successes in mathematics and science education improvement and reform, as well as provide comprehensive information on support and materials for mathematics and science education developed or funded by federal agencies.

In order to meet these objectives, ENC began collecting curriculum resources and created an online database containing searchable bibliographic records with detailed descriptions of those curriculum resources. ENC's original statement of work was very specific about what types of information should be recorded in these bibliographic records. ENC also sought teacher input on the structure of the record through a series of focus groups across the country. The resulting record structure included a combination of standard cataloging and non-traditional, added-value features.

Many of the required fields can be found in accepted cataloging standards such as the *Anglo-American Cataloguing Rules*, 2nd edition, 1988 Revision, including title, statement of responsibility, edition, publication/distribution area, physical description, series, grade level, audience, general materials designator (GMD), and notes. Local practice has led to some data entry changes in these standard fields. For example, very little is abbreviated in the catalog record and all records are title main-entry. Non-traditional fields were developed to provide added-value data, including locally-defined subject identifiers, equipment specifications (software/hardware requirements), ordering information (vendor address, ISBN, order number, and pricing), links to supporting materials in the ENC collection, evaluation data (awards, citations, field tests, full-text reviews), 200-300 word abstracts, extended table of contents notes, pedagogical type, standards information, correlations to textbooks, geographical focus, and physical media type.

With record structure well in hand, ENC turned its focus to collection development. ENC initially focused on "real" (direct access) resources (print, software, videotape, optical media, etc.), housed in a repository at ENC's headquarters at The Ohio State University in Columbus, Ohio. As trends in the education community, particularly those represented in national math and science standards, continue to emphasize increased use of technology in the classroom, catalogers and content (subject) specialists began looking at the possibility of including "virtual" resources in the collection. The growth of the Internet in the 1990s and the proliferation of K-12 World Wide Web (WWW) sites have provided rich additions to the ENC catalog and collection.

SELECTION

The Content Support Working Group performs collection development and selection of resources at ENC. Two Resource Specialists (one in Mathematics Education, the other Science Education) bring years of classroom experience and professional expertise to the task of selecting resources, and Internet resources have brought real challenges to their task. Internet sites constitute a special category of resources: anyone can put together a Website. Often, there are no controls. A site may look exciting but contain no or invalid content. Alternately, a site may include excellent content but lack any sort of organization to use that content effectively. A site may be static, developed in the first rush of Internet growth but never updated to incorporate changes in technology. Or the site may have almost everything going for it: great content, easy to use, easy to navigate, highly respected authors, and all the recent technological bells and whistles, but never engage the intended audience.

The early days of simple selection when there were few K-12 specific Websites have long passed and critical evaluation of an ever-growing Internet is now the norm. Dr. Kimberly S. Roempler (Associate Director, formerly Science Education Resource Specialist) indicates that her early selection criteria were very simple: valid science content, respected authorship, and clean design that included "color or something that moved around on the screen."[1] Through talking with teachers, interacting with students in the classroom, and examining Websites on a daily basis, Roempler now recognizes five specific criteria[2] for selection for Internet resources:

1. Content validity
2. Navigation and usability
3. Authorship
4. Audience engagement
5. Exhibits the strengths of Web technology

By understanding and using these criteria, educators should be able to more effectively judge good vs. bad K-12 Websites.

Roempler states that as with "real" resources the single most important criteria in selecting Websites is content validity. Keeping in mind the lack of standardized review on Web content and a pervasive belief that if something is in writing it must be true, examination of accuracy is crucial. Is the information presented comprehensive or cursory? Is the information presented misleading or inaccurate? Is the site equitable in regard to culture, gender, and race? Does it promote one point of view or provide a balanced overview of a subject? Is the content current? Is the content supported by bibliographic references and suggestions for further research?[3]

Roempler's mathematics counterpart, Dr. Terese Herrera (Mathematics Education Resource Specialist) agrees. She adds that worthwhile content is more than just valid information, but also includes the idea that the site is of value to educators. As she examines each site, Herrera asks, "Can this site be used by teachers or students or parents to learn math or science? Does the site add to educators' professional development? Can the materials at the site be used easily as background for instruction?"[4]

Navigation and usability is a critical issue and in many ways, precedes content validity as selection criteria. Great content that is not easily accessible is very frustrating for the user. Overwhelming graphics or multimedia applications combined with a low-end computer and modem Internet access can discourage use of the site immediately. Timing also enters into consideration. Many sites, such as NASA SpaceLink (http://spacelink.nasa.gov/index.html), are heavily hit during the school day afternoon. Design of the homepage and clearly defined links from one section to another are also important to consider. Nothing is more frustrating in the classroom than to click on "Student activities" and then have to click six more levels down to actually reach a usable activity.

Authorship issues range from the initial URL listing to persons or organizations responsible for the intellectual content and design of the site. Is the server or sponsoring organization commercial (.com), non-profit (.org), educational (.edu), or governmental (.gov)? Are the identified authors credible? Are they associated with credible organizations? Are the authors identified at all? Roempler states that "high quality sites should enable the user to easily find out about the persons or organizations responsible for the contents of the page. What is their affiliation? What credentials make it appropriate for them to write about the topic. . . . Sites should also provide a way for users to get in touch with the authors, not only to ask questions but also to verify the legitimacy of the page's sponsor."[5]

Websites must also actively engage the intended audience. How can a Website "engage" the user? First of all, the reading level should be appropriate to the intended audience. A highly textual site intended for preschoolers or first graders will not engage the students because they will not understand the material. The content should also be appropriate to the age group. High-level technical specifications for computer design will not engage the typical elementary student. Many valuable sites also provide opportunities for students or teachers to communicate with others with "Ask a Scientist" or "Ask a Mathematician" sections to encourage interaction. Other sites foster joint projects between different schools in the study of a specific topic, such as water quality in a river. In her examination of Websites, Roempler asks some tough questions, "Does the content promote inquiry learning? Are students encouraged to think and reflect? Are critical thinking skills needed to analyze and synthesize information?"[6]

The Internet is a wonderful educational tool with great potential, but it is not the best tool in all situations. Some Websites contain an HTML version of a textbook or reference book. There is not much to it–you click to turn the page. No engagement, no interaction; it would be more useful to purchase the print version of the text. Other Web sites go much further and provide an interactive learning tool that may be based on the same textbook. Such sites may include high level graphics and video images, Java applets that allow the student to experiment with geometric figures or determine salinity levels of ocean water, links to realtime data sources, reorganization of text and hyperlinks to relevant related topics, quizzes, concept maps, etc. Instructional design and appropriate use of the available technology are critical issues.

After considering all the criteria above, a further selection category emerges. Each month, ENC staff select the ENC Digital Dozen (http://www. enc.org/classroom/dd/nf_index.htm). The Digital Dozen (DD) consists of 13 of the best K-12 math and science education Websites. These sites are featured prominently on ENC's Website and designated as DD award winners in the bibliographic record. How does selection of these sites differ from day-to-day selection? Herrera explains that DD sites are selected using all of the above criteria, with an emphasis on the site's "potential for learning . . . [and] the way of learning through this site should be unique; available only through this vehicle of the Internet."[7] Other criteria are also considered such as:

- Supports educational reform efforts and national standards
- Purposeful and attractive use of graphics and other multimedia
- Reflects cultural diversity
- Current and accurate information that is regularly updated
- Depth of coverage of specific topics
- Promotes cross-curricular learning
- Provides innovative or cutting-edge resources for educators

Many of these ideas are expansions of the original selection criteria, and Websites do not have to meet all of the criteria to be nominated for DD status. Manipula Math with Java (http://www.ies.co.jp/math/java/index.html), DD May 1998, is a good example of the best of the Web with engaging content that makes effective use of new technologies.

At the time of selection, the Resource Specialists assign preliminary subject identifiers, grade levels, and pedagogical type. Initial subject assignment is broad-based; generally an indication that it is mathematics or science content and often a secondary subject such as Geometry or Physical science may be assigned. The Specialists examine the site for intended grade level. They also identify the pedagogical types represented on the site. Pedagogical type includes: Activities, Bibliographies, Biographies, Calculator-active materials, Career guidance materials, Children's literature, Curriculum frameworks, Curriculum guides, Demonstrations, Games, Instructional tools, Laboratory manuals, Lesson plans, Literature, Math curriculum programs, Probeware, Professional development materials, Professional guides, Resource materials, Study guides, Teacher developed materials, Teacher guides, Teaching units, Tests and assessments, Textbooks, and Workbooks. ENC is looking to update this list in the near future to take into account differences between "real" and "virtual" resources.

CATALOGING

The basic description of K-12 math and science Internet resources presents a set of unique difficulties, particularly in comparison with print or other resources. There is often no rhyme or reason to how a site is set up–no identifiable title page, credits information, and publisher information. Sites range from highly organized and nearly book-like to total chaos and confusion and everything in between. ENC's Cataloging Working Group has met this difficulty by establishing some simple guidelines for their task.

Establishing the site's title is the first task for the catalogers. There are many places to look for this information: the "homepage," the browser's title bar, the HTML <TITLE> tag, running banners, index frames, etc. ENC has limited title information to that found inside the browser window; the actual HTML page display and not the associated browser's title, scroll, or status bars. The main title should be the predominant heading on that page and may be further verified through "About this site," credits, or other pages that refer back to the main title. A further complication with titles is the often used, prominently displayed heading "Welcome to the [name of site] homepage"–while this provides a friendly welcome to the site's newcomers, using this as the main title provides its own problems. Imagine the user browsing through a title list of 300 "Welcome to the . . . ." titles! To help decrease frustration levels, ENC generally eliminates the initial "Welcome" phrase and begins the title with the next significant word.

Next stop for the catalogers is establishing a statement of responsibility for the Website. Authorship for a Web site is akin to authorship for a CD-ROM or other software. It may involve great numbers of people (writers, animators, programmers, graphic artists, photographers, HTML coding, directors, etc.) or the only reference may be an anonymous Webmaster. Discovering the information often requires patience and detective skills! There may be a credits page linked directly off the homepage; it may be buried layers within the site; or it may not exist at all. Another consideration is looking at each site from the users' point of view–while many people may contribute to a Web page, what kind of information is the teacher looking for? ENC guidelines suggest that limiting authorship to a few primary contributors representing those responsible for the math and science content of the site. Professional organizations, federal agencies, or commercial producers as well as teachers, teacher/student collaborators, or students who have created or assisted in development of a site are added to the statement of responsibility.

Who is the publisher for a Website? Is it the person/Webmaster who posted the page on a server? Is it the Internet provider that maintains the server? Is it the organization that sponsored the site? ENC has simplified this issue to define publisher as the initial domain name for the site. For example, *The Sound of Chaos* site (http://www.discovery.com/stories/technology/fractals/ fractals.html), includes the publisher statement: Bethesda, MD : Discovery Channel Online, Discovery Communications, Inc.

As schools across the nation are gaining access to the Internet, connectivity and local hardware determine how much of the Internet can be reasonably accessed in the classroom or school library. ENC's records must also reflect the technology of the Web site. The Equipment field helps teachers determine whether they will be able to fully utilize a specific site. Catalogers list plugins required for site use, browser-compatibility issues, additional software/hardware requirements, and recommended connection speed for optimal use. When faced with low-end computers, old versions of browsers (Netscape 2.0, etc.) and slow modem connections, teachers cannot utilize many of the Java enriched, multimedia, frames-based sites that are common on the Internet today.

Does this mean that catalogers have to become Web technicians to list all these technical specifications? No, absolutely not! Most sites list technical specifications somewhere within the site. The sites may not have clear title, authorship, or publisher, but most will identify the lowest-end browser required, plugins required (often including a link to the download site for that plugin), and types of files which require additional software. Noting that a site is loading a Java applet or receiving a JavaScript error also are clear indicators of requirements for the site. If the information is not readily available on the site itself, the catalogers do not include the Equipment field in the bibliographic record.

Table of Contents information is very useful for making choices about whether or not to use a site in the classroom. The problem that catalogers face is determining what constitutes a Table of Contents on a Website. Many sites have nice, bulleted lists of topics on the home page. Other sites have an index list on one side (or frame) of the screen and headings on the other side (or frame). Some sites have some cutesy-funny links that serve as entry points to the site or broad headings that link to more substantial list breakdowns on a secondary page. Many sites also include major category breakdowns as navigation bars (text or graphic) somewhere on the Web page. From the catalogers' point of view, the most useful sites have text-based site maps that break down the content of the site into hierarchical outline format.

The purpose for the Table of Contents is to provide an overview of all the content on the site. The catalogers examine the site at length, focusing on recording the major topics covered on the site, as well as recording more in-depth information aimed specifically at teachers and students. When top level headings are vague, secondary headings from subsequent pages are added to the note. The goal is both to provide sufficient information about the content of the site and to reflect the organization of information on the site.

Additional information recorded in the bibliographic record includes Funding information. Many Websites are developed through funding from contracts, grants, or sponsorships. If this information is provided on the site, the full name of the funding agency is recorded, along with contract or grant numbers. While this information is probably less critical to many ENC users in terms of use in the classroom, funding agencies such as the National Science Foundation (NSF), the Annenberg/CPB Math and Science Project, etc., help to indicate the credibility of the site.

The final category of information recorded during the cataloging process is Physical Media (also known as Resource Type). ENC has developed an authority-controlled list of specific media types for searching purposes and each record includes a minimum of one media type. Terms appropriate for Internet resources include: Audio file, Bulletin Board Service (BBS), Data sets, Database, Electronic document, Email resource, FTP resource, GIF images, Gopher resource, Java applets, Journal, JPEG images, Listservs and list archives, Magazine, MPEG video images, MS Word file, Newsletter, PDF files, QuickTime video images, RTF files (Rich Text Format), TIFF image, Video image, Virtual reality model, WAV audio file, WordPerfect file, World Wide Web (WWW) resource.

An optional field in bibliographic records refers to supporting materials. Some Websites are designed to support specific print or other media curriculum resources. For example, Discovery Channel Online has designed a number of Websites geared to a single program or series of programs. These sites include lesson plans, activities, further information, and ordering information for the videotape versions of the programs. Supporting material links are added to the bibliographic record for the Web resource to direct teachers immediately to the bibliographic record of the specific videotape, textbook, etc.

ABSTRACTING

Once the basic description of the Website is completed, the Abstracting Working Group takes over to provide the most critical components of the ENC bibliographic record: a 200-300 word descriptive abstract and assignment of subject identifiers. The abstractors also examine the site to determine if it was designed to meet any state or national curriculum standards, verify grade level of the site, and verify pedagogical type.

Abstractors tend to approach Websites much more critically than "real" resources. There are no built-in controls on the Internet, nor is there peer or editorial review for many Websites. Sites are added to the Web by the thousands daily and existing sites grow, reorganize, and update frequently. It is not unusual for an entire site to change from Selection to Cataloging to Abstracting! Web sites present a different type of challenge for the abstractors.

Lynda C. Titterington, Science Education Abstractor, explains that abstractors need "to create an abstract that accommodates change . . . to strike a balance between a general but possibly uninformative abstract and a detailed abstract that can become obsolete."[8] When examining Websites, abstractors generally look for six types of information:

1. Mission statement for the site; information about the authors, intended audience, and the goals and objectives for the Website.
2. Credentials of the authors.
3. Content validity (accuracy, appropriateness).
4. Information that is presented in a way that cannot be duplicated in print or other media.
5. Opportunities to engage the student. Titterington points out that she especially likes "quiz forms that allow the student to pause and check their understanding. It's even better if they can get immediate feedback. Other neat things are animations and Java applets that demonstrate processes and relationships, and simulations that allow students to manipulate variables."[9]
6. Classroom, home, and other real life connections (hands-on activities that allow students to interact with real people and experiment with physical objects).

One other concern the abstractors face when examining Websites includes the range of quality of sites. Titterington explains that "Good sites have so much wonderful information that I have trouble deciding what to highlight in my abstract. These sites also draw me in and keep me there for more time than I can afford to spend on them. Poorly designed and written Websites are simply exasperating. Frequently the authors don't include a clear statement of the mission of the site, or a description of themselves/agency or their agenda and credentials."[10]

The abstractors examine the site in depth, and generally check all links throughout a site. The abstractor will focus on the original content of the site, rather than external links to other servers. A typical abstract begins with a general statement about the purpose of the site. The abstract for *Evidence: The True Witness* (http://library.advanced.org/17049/gather/) begins: "This World Wide Web (WWW) site, developed by an international team of high school seniors as part of ThinkQuest 98, features an interactive game and information about careers in forensic science. ThinkQuest is a worldwide competition that challenges students from around the world to collaborate and create educational resources for the Internet community."[11] This statement immediately identifies the grade level and audience (high school, generally grades 9-12), main topic of the site (forensic science), and establishes the credentials of those responsible for development of the site (high school seniors through the ThinkQuest competition).

The second section of the abstract describes specific features of the Website in more detail. From the abstract for *Evidence: The True Witness*: "The homepage features a clickable image map that invites visitors to take a tour of the site that introduces the game and the site's reference and career information sections. The interactive game encourages students to apply their detective skills and forensic knowledge as they assume the role of KC Rodgers, a detective without a clue, who must identify the kidnapper of Susie Van Konkel. The game features humorous video sequences of Rodgers as he bumbles about interviewing suspects and searching the house for evidence. Students also solve puzzles, gather evidence, and process it in a virtual laboratory. The reference section provides a content notepad with background information about specialties in forensic science such as anthropology, odontology (forensic dentistry) and pathology; ballistics, document, and fiber analysis; and fingerprinting and DNA analysis, as well as forensic entomology and toxicology. Each topic is covered through narrative text, photos, illustrations and animations."[12]

The next portion of the abstract provides a more in-depth description of a specific section of the site, such as sample articles, lesson plans, and activities as well as support materials provided. Again, from *Evidence: The True Witness*: "The DNA finger printing section, for example, includes an introduction to DNA structure, and explanations of protein synthesis, DNA replication, and restriction enzymes. Students can also do a simulation in which they isolate DNA from a hair follicle, then compare it to a panel of suspects. The career section contains job descriptions of some of the main specialties in the field of forensic science. It also includes full length interviews with forensic professionals and invites visitors to email their questions to the scientists."[13]

The final section of the abstract lists additional features found on the site. It also includes the abstracted date and authorship of the abstract. Authorship of the abstract includes the initials of the ENC abstractor(s). If the abstractor has also paraphrased some text from the author of the site, it is noted as well. From *Evidence: The True Witness*: "A glossary, site search engine, and an annotated reference list of books and related sites are also provided. Abstracted 04/99. (Author/LCT)."[14]

Construction of the abstract is a time-intensive task, performed by two full-time abstractors (both Master's degree level; one in math education, one science education) and two graduate research assistants (science). After examining the Web site in depth, the abstractors identify appropriate subject identifiers for the site. The math and science vocabulary has been developed in house, based originally on the ERIC identifiers and descriptors, simplified, enhanced through feedback from teachers, and reviewed against terminology used in curriculum standards documents.[15]

ENC follows a "one-fifth rule" and assignment of subject identifiers is generally limited to any topic that constitutes one-fifth of the total resource. Exceptions to the one-fifth rule are made on occasion for special features or emerging trends in the field. There are no other limitations to assignment of subject identifiers. Minimally, there must be at least one subject listed, and there is no maximum. On average, 10-15 subject identifiers are added to each record. Returning to the *Evidence: The True Witness* site, ten subject identifies have been assigned to the record including: Science, Biological and life sciences, Careers, DNA fingerprinting, Fingerprints, Forensics, Pathology, Integrated/interdisciplinary approaches, Social sciences, and Anthropology.

The abstractors also look for connections between the content of the site and national and/or state curriculum standards. If a site has been designed to create explicit connections between content and standards, it is generally evident from the first look at the home page. For example, the Exploring Data (ENC-013874) site (http://forum.swarthmore.edu/workshops/usi/dataproject/index.html) links to standards under each grade level range on the home page. A quick click on "Standards" under the "K-4" heading brings back a page with detailed information on the specific K-4 NCTM Standards (National Council of Teachers of Mathematics, *Curriculum and Evaluation Standards for School Mathematics*. Reston, VA: National Council of Teachers of Mathematics, 1989) met by activities contained on the site. California state and the school district of Philadelphia (PA) mathematics standards are also listed; all with links directly to the full-text of the relevant section of the standards document.

In the course of examining the Website, the abstractors look at the bibliographic record's assigned grade levels and pedagogical type terms and verify that the correct terms have been added or as needed, add terms that have not been assigned. Once these tasks are completed, the record is completed as well. Each record is reviewed by the appropriate Resource Specialist for content information, as well as by a cataloger before the record is uploaded for public viewing.

CONCLUSION

The ever-changing nature of the Internet presents catalogers and abstractors with many problems for description. Most of these problems have relatively simple solutions. An ongoing problem of great concern is how do we keep the bibliographic record current? As records for Websites are completed and uploaded to the public search engine at ENC Online (http://www.enc.org), the data within the record may already be obsolete.

Change on the Web takes many forms: a site can change addresses (URLs); the content can be reorganized, updated, or deleted; or content, images, applets, etc., can be added to enhance the site. Any change from content to authorship should be reflected in the bibliographic record. URL changes are the easiest to identify. Verification software exists to automatically check URLs and report bad links. Users and other ENC staff often report problems with URLs when visiting Websites described in bibliographic records. All other changes must be monitored by human interaction.

Like other agencies describing the dynamic Web, ENC has no easy solutions but initial thoughts are to use two methods to deal with the currency issue. First, the abstract must be dated ("Abstracted 5/99") so there is some indication as to when the information was current. This provides the user with a point of reference. ENC is also in the process of establishing annual review schedules for Website records. As the number of records grows within the ENC database, the problem of review and currency will continue.

NOTES

1. Kimberly S. Roempler, "Using the Internet in the Classroom: Becoming a Critical Consumer of the Web," *ENC Focus*, forthcoming.

2. Roempler.

3. Roempler.

4. Terese Herrera, interview with author, 18 May 1999.

5. Roempler.

6. Roempler.

7. Herrera.

8. Lynda C. Titterington, interview with author, 17 May 1999.

9. Titterington.

10. Titterington.

11. Abstract segment from ENC-014314

12. Abstract segment from ENC-014314

13. Abstract segment from ENC-014314

14. Abstract segment from ENC-014314

15. Sharon Zuiderveld, ed., *Cataloging Correctly for Kids: An Introduction to the Tools*, 3rd ed. (Chicago: American Library Association, 1998), 97. "It may become a practice in applying curriculum headings [. . .] to use national standards where they are available (for example, mathematics) or to use thesauri, such as ERIC for educational terms or the Eisenhower National Clearinghouse for mathematics and science vocabulary, where regular subject headings are inadequate."

Dewey Applications
for the Simple Arrangement
of a Link Library:
The Case of Science Net

Cheryl Martin
Wayne Daniels

SUMMARY. This article focuses on *Science Net*, a project that uses the Dewey Decimal Classification (DDC) for ordering a set of large files of links for K-12 science curriculum resources for Canadian schools. The project aims to provide an alternative to the rigours of sorting through search engine results by providing what are in effect virtual library shelves, which support online browsing that is similar to conventional browsing of library shelves. The article also discusses the adaptation of the Dublin Core data elements to fashion a template for cataloguing not simply the records that will appear in *Science Net*, but those that will also comprise the *Virtual Reference Library* project. The cataloguing and indexing procedures developed for both projects are described. *[Article copies available for a fee from The Haworth Document Delivery Service: 1-800-342-9678. E-mail address: <getinfo@haworthpressinc.com> Website: <http://www.HaworthPress.com>]*

Cheryl Martin is Director of Bibliographic Services, McMaster University Library, Hamilton, Ontario, Canada (e-mail: martinc@mcmaster.ca). Ms. Martin was formerly employed by the Toronto Reference Library, Toronto, Ontario, and was a member of the Science Net project team.

Wayne Daniels is Science Net Project Coordinator, Toronto Public Library, Toronto, Ontario, Canada (e-mail: wdaniels@tpl.toronto.on.ca).

[Haworth co-indexing entry note]: "Dewey Applications for the Simple Arrangement of a Link Library: The Case of Science Net." Martin, Cheryl, and Wayne Daniels. Co-published simultaneously in *Journal of Internet Cataloging* (The Haworth Information Press, an imprint of The Haworth Press, Inc.) Vol. 3, No. 1, 2000, pp. 67-77; and: *Metadata and Organizing Educational Resources on the Internet* (ed: Jane Greenberg) The Haworth Information Press, an imprint of The Haworth Press, Inc., 2000, pp. 67-77. Single or multiple copies of this article are available for a fee from The Haworth Document Delivery Service [1-800-342-9678, 9:00 a.m. - 5:00 p.m. (EST). E-mail address: getinfo@haworthpressinc.com].

© 2000 by The Haworth Press, Inc. All rights reserved.

KEYWORDS. *Science Net*, Virtual Reference Library, metadata, Dublin Core, cataloguing of Internet resources, Toronto Public Library

INTRODUCTION

The skills that librarians bring to the task of ordering of information are too seldom thought of beyond the confines of the library, and sometimes fail to receive due emphasis within it. Libraries are of course composed of their collections, as a house is built of individual bricks. But a heap of bricks no more makes a house than a mass of books, periodicals, and so forth makes a library. It is in the task of arranging and indexing this abundance, in such a way as to allow users to find what they are after, that librarians add enormously to the value of what is on offer.

Libraries typically order their collections by means of some recognized classification scheme and, via the subject catalogue, give users access to more detailed subject matter which may cross the boundaries of the classification. But for many library users a trip to the library often consists chiefly of browsing library shelves in search of material of interest to them. However unsystematic this may be, it is evidently congenial to those who prefer it. While such users might not have much interest in the details of the system that supports their favourite activity, librarians are aware that it is the classification that creates individual collocations of related material, while also establishing a hierarchical relation among the various groupings.

In the largely unmediated environment of the Internet, there is a case to be made for exploiting the power of classification to create order within large collections of Internet links, treating them as if they were objects populating a virtual bookshelf. This makes an attractive alternative to the tedium of sifting through endless irrelevant search engine results. The subject hierarchy of the classification furnishes a variety of built-in search pathways, one which may be brought out through a series of nested menus. And, if it were possible to combine the classification with a subject search via a dedicated search engine, then the user would have a highly effective means of refining search results within a pre-coordinated offering of relevant material. Similar to a method suggested by Stuart Weibel in a recent article:

> Many disciplines support classification systems that promote better access to their literature. Prior to the Web, the use of classification systems was justified on the basis of making a given body of literature more coherent and, hence, more useful for scholarship. These benefits continue and are augmented by the possibility of using classification systems as browsing structures that can enhance the immediacy and utility of online discovery. The machine-processing of classification

data has the potential to amplify the intellectual reach of the searcher and sharpen the ability to discriminate among resources in the vast store of knowledge that is increasingly digital.[1]

Using classification schemes to organize subject-specific and audience-specific Internet resources has been under investigation at the Toronto Reference Library (now part of the Toronto Public Library) since 1996. Most recently this work has taken the form of a Website called *Science Net* <http://sciencenet.tpl.toronto.on.ca/>. The aim is to provide teacher and student access to a large collection of K-12 science resources freely available on the Internet. We shall present an outline of this project, touching also on its immediate predecessor, by way of introducing a more detailed discussion of how the Dublin Core metadata elements were selected and adapted as the basis for a template that would enable the creation of individual, searchable records to comprise a relational database supporting both *Science Net* and the larger structure of the *Virtual Reference Library (VRL)* <http://vrl.tpl.toronto. on.ca/>. The cataloguing process is described, including the procedures involved and a description of the standards used. Although the *Science Net* project coordinator is a cataloguer, and could be expected to understand and follow appropriate description and indexing standards, access to the *VRL* sites is almost exclusively provided by collection development librarians working in public service departments. The fact that most of the cataloguing would be done by non-cataloguers influenced some of the decisions we made about how to catalogue the sites, and what kind of information they needed to make effective use of the metadata template.

EXPANDING UNIVERSE: THE PILOT PROJECT

The forerunner project to *Science Net* was a Website called *Expanding Universe: A classified search tool for amateur astronomy* <http://www. mtrl.toronto.on.ca/centres/bsd/astronomy/index.html>. Details of this site have been reported in an earlier paper.[2] As the name suggests, it was aimed at a specific target audience. *Expanding Universe* comprises a number of standard HTML pages that are linked in a file structure that replicates the Dewey hierarchy implicit in their formation. Users are able to search via menus which allow them to delve ever deeper into the classification until they reach the desired specificity. Access is also provided through an alphabetic menu consisting of the Dewey and Dewey-like terms used to identify each "shelf." Some liberties were taken with the Dewey nomenclature on the ground that this was an adaptation for a particular audience, not a reproduction faithful at all points to the original. Because the progression from general to specific terms is for the most part logical, the user can move through a series of screens with ease.

Expanding Universe contains over 1700 astronomy links. By subdividing these into smaller groupings within a structured whole, the user is saved the tedium of scrolling down excessively long lists of links that otherwise would be only loosely related. Moreover, in this way the collection can be grown coherently by extending or introducing classification numbers, according to need. As mentioned, this provides an alternative to (though hardly a replacement for) the usual search engine approach–one which can have considerable advantages for the user. And so, despite the simplicity of its design and functionality, *Expanding Universe* has been enthusiastically received by its target audience. In fact, about a quarter of the contents of *Expanding Universe* consists of sites suggested by amateur astronomy enthusiasts. Project feedback proved invaluable and has led to various alterations in the structure as suggested by the site's users. This last have been of enormous importance since restrictions on available staffing have meant that the growth and viability of the site has been necessarily, and in part, the work of its users.

ON TO EDUCATION:
THE GENESIS AND STRUCTURE OF SCIENCE NET

The possibility had been suggested, some time before the initial project, of creating a site that would provide access for students and teachers to subject curriculum resources in support of online learning in Canada. A detailed account of both the ensuing *Science Net* project and the broader one of the *Virtual Reference Library* has been given elsewhere.[3] Briefly, we first approached a number of school boards to test for interest in such a service. The result was encouraging. Teachers often expressed the view that, while interested in exploring the Internet as a classroom resource, the prospect of spending hours in search of useful sites was daunting; increasingly, time is in short supply among teachers, and they expressed some enthusiasm at the thought of librarians providing them (and their students) with a large, easy-to-use, pre-selected offering of resources.

Next, the challenge of funding the project was met when the Library received a generous gift from Atomic Energy Canada Limited, as they expressed an interest in supporting efforts that encouraged science education in Canada, and decided that the proposed *Science Net* would serve this goal. With financial support, work began in earnest. A number of off-site meetings were held with teachers as to their preferences and criteria and the resulting input was funnelled into the design process. This latter activity extended over several months and was carried out by the Library and by the multi-media firm Digital Renaissance (name since changed to Extend Media). The task, as we saw it, was to create a site that incorporated both a lively and engaging design for students as well as the required functionality, which was to be similar to that of *Expanding Universe*. Since teachers had stated a wish for us to segregate sites intended for them from those meant for students, and moreover to distinguish the latter into, at the minimum, grades K-6 and 7-12, we incorporated these features into the finished product.

The user of *Science Net* can call up a page, at any point in the classification, which will display the sites for the respective groups. This amounts to a cross-classification of sites. Hence, while sites that come under the DDC number for physics (530) appear on one page, with menu access to the subdivisions of that subject expressed by the numbers DDC 531 to 539, each level is effectively cross-classified by the intended audience group.

Initially, the result has been to choose a somewhat shallow hierarchy to contain the results. This is because of the discovered imbalances among the three groups in terms of available resources: if extended to greater depths, the classification would result in numerous gaps which would give an unfinished look to the whole, as well as perhaps discouraging users from proceeding to a deeper level–where a resource is to be found–from the shallower level at which, it might be, there is nothing. However, as with *Expanding Universe*, the classification can be extended as warranted by subsequent growth. It is a relatively straightforward task to change the class numbers of records that appear at a general level for a more specific level, unlike the arduous business of relabelling physical objects like books. For now, the existing collocations provide greatly improved subject specificity over the disciplines covered. Furthermore, with additional funding, we hope to provide, contingent on funding, a number of enrichments, such as brief annotations to assist users in deciding which resources look promising, and added indexing to enable search engine access to the subject contents of the sites (see below).

Science Net divides science into eight subjects that roughly correspond to three established curriculum categories: physical sciences (physics and chemistry); life sciences (biology, botany, and zoology); and earth and space sciences (geology and earth sciences, paleontology, and astronomy). These can be seen as a group by selecting the "subject" option from the second splash screen. (The first gives the option of proceeding in either English or French.) At time of writing, physics and chemistry have been completed, offering some 1200 links between them, while geology is in process. Just as in *Expanding Universe*, *Science Net* offers an "a-z" search option, although, since this index will contain terms from all eight subjects, it remains somewhat thin at present. We have also included an e-mail form for encouraging feedback, as it proved useful with the work done on the astronomy site. Initial response to *Science Net* has indeed been encouraging, and we expect that, once the remaining gateways have been opened–by April of 2000 if all goes according to schedule–the site will become a highly useful tool for students and teachers in Canada and elsewhere.

As mentioned above, *Science Net* has been planned as part of a larger structure: the *Virtual Reference Library* (*VRL*). This will be grown on a modular basis as funding is provided for each of its elements. In order to adequately support the *VRL*, it was decided that a relational database was needed that would contain records for the entire structure. Not only must these records be made available within various modules of the *VRL* and dynamically generated, in some cases, according to specified formats, but they must also be searchable by means of a dedicated search engine. For these reasons it seemed desirable to look into ways in which records, of varying lengths, might be created, incorporating a prescribed set of searchable fields that, while less detailed than full MARC cataloguing, would nevertheless be flexible enough to bring out desired features of a resource, expressing relationships between one resource and another where appropriate. Record creation was to be the responsibility of designated staff, widely dispersed throughout a large library system. The idea was to enable the library to support the *VRL* by making optimal use of its available staff expertise through a simple and uniform administrative interface. In the next section we describe the process by which all this was accomplished.

DECISIONS ABOUT ACCESS

As we began discussions of how to provide access to the *Science Net* sites, we also had to consider how the decisions we made would affect the *VRL*. Although the *VRL* is not arranged using DDC, we needed to make choices regarding indexing, access, and the design of a metadata template that would apply to both projects. We also had to consider the implications of the fact that non-cataloguers would be cataloguing most of the sites for the *VRL*. The method for entering metadata had to be reasonably simple, and we had to provide clear and easily understandable instructions for using the template and for determining what information to enter in each field.

Science Net is a link library providing organized access to other Websites, and the metadata is stored separately from the Websites in an Oracle database. An administrative interface is used by the Gateway Administrator to set up access to the database and to establish categories and classification levels; the interface is then used by the cataloguers to add WWW sites to an individual bookmark file, and to enter the metadata about each site. For *Science Net*, the Gateway Administrator and cataloguer are presently the same person. Due to the size and scope of the project, the function of Gateway Administrator for the *VRL* is shared by a team, who cooperatively provide user support and problem solving, in addition to establishing categories and quality control standards for keywords and other access points. Each cataloguer has a logon id and password to access the administrative interface. Cataloguers cannot change or add categories; that responsibility has been given to the Gateway Administrators, to ensure consistency and some degree of control over the form and type of access points. A Project Manager oversees and administers the entire project.

Early in the development process, we decided to use the Dublin Core Metadata Element Set.[4] A large number of projects were already using Dublin Core, and it was the most developed element set to date. There was a great deal of documentation available, and the "academic" Internet community had strongly endorsed Dublin Core. We were also guided by the work of the Nordic Metadata Project,[5] especially their HTML-based form for metadata entry. We decided that entering cataloguing information using a form was a good way to ensure consistent entry of elements, without asking librarians (who may or may not have cataloguing experience) to learn and remember Dublin Core rules and syntax. Example 1 shows the beginning of the form we developed, as it appears in the administrative interface.

Decisions also had to be made about what information was necessary to provide access, and how each element would be displayed and indexed. We held extensive discussions with our database designer, Digital Renaissance,

EXAMPLE 1. Form for Metadata Entry for the *Science Net* Project

This form is based on the Dublin Core element set that was current at the time of implementation. Any changes to the element set or to the interpretation of fields since then are not reflected in the element set used for this project.

about what information we would be entering into the database, and how we wanted to display and access it. This was a difficult and time-consuming process for all members of the project team, both from the Library and from Digital Renaissance. Because of our varied backgrounds and levels of knowledge, we sometimes made assumptions about what others on the team meant when a particular concept was being discussed. As an example, we wanted to exclude initial articles from the title index, so that the indexing would begin at the first significant word. MARC coding, of course, provides this type of control over the indexing, but we couldn't expect non-librarians to necessarily understand that this is a normal feature in a library database, or for them to anticipate this type of request. We also found that the database was being developed with limited facility to deal with diacritics and special characters outside of the French interface for *Science Net*. We knew that the *VRL* would have sites in several languages other than English, and wanted to be able to use diacritics and special characters as necessary. This problem made all of us aware that we needed to have much more in-depth discussions about issues of this type so that we all understood the requirements, and so that we all made sure we understood what each other meant by a particular term or phrase.

We had to decide first what we wanted to be able to display and index, and whether this information could be provided using the Dublin Core element set. Most of the data that we wanted was easily accommodated, such as title, DDC number, author and publisher. Because *Science Net* was developed to support the school curriculum, we also needed to be able to search and display information about the intended audience of the material at the site. An extra tag was developed called "Properties" in which the cataloguer could indicate the level of the site: K-6, 7-12, and Teachers. An Advanced category was also provided, mainly to create a separate listing of university department sites for each subject, intended for the information of students wanting to pursue their studies at the post-secondary level. We also wanted to indicate if a site was graphics-intensive or was slow to download, given that many educational institutions use basic equipment. We likewise thought that it was worthwhile to flag sites that were created by students. Canadian focus is of particular interest, given the site's primary audience; this is indicated using the Coverage tag, with MARC as a type and MARC geographic codes for Canada and the provinces.

If the Gateway to Educational Materials (GEM)[6] metadata standard had been developed at the time we were working on *Science Net*, we might have decided to use it instead of Dublin Core, since it provides a structure to describe educational resources. But at the time, Dublin Core was the best choice for this project since we were developing standards to be used in both *Science Net* and the *VRL*.

CATALOGUING OF SITES

Sites for *Science Net* are selected and catalogued by the Project Coordinator, who also functions as the Gateway Administrator. The Project Coordinator uses a browser to search for sites, and bookmarks them using the Administrative Interface. The resource form is then used to enter information about each site. Because *Science Net* is designed to approximate the user's view of a shelf of books, the sites are accessible primarily by DDC classification number and title. There are no keywords added in the Subject element, except one or two terms which form the classification description. Additional indexing may be provided at a later date, contingent on funding. The terms used in the description are taken directly from DDC schedules in most cases. This has made the process much faster; as in most cataloguing, the greatest amount of time and effort is usually put into classification and subject analysis.

The *VRL*, on the other hand, does not include a classification scheme, but offers keyword access. The Toronto Reference Library had already developed a controlled-access link library for WWW sites which was only accessible within the library. In this link library, called *World Vue*, sites were originally arranged hierarchically with a series of menus. In 1997 a project added keywords to *World Vue*; these keywords were based on Library of Congress subject headings. The information contained in *World Vue* became the foundation of the *VRL*. When the project team evaluated the transfer of information from *World Vue* to the *Virtual Reference Library* database, we considered a programming solution, but it was not cost-effective. The sites were transferred manually, each selector taking his or her area and working from a printout and text file of the sites in that area. Most of the transfer involved "cutting and pasting" information from the text file into the resource form.

During the transfer of information, the selectors evaluated the keywords that had been assigned to each site and decided if any needed to be added or deleted. We developed a list of terms that should and should not be used, based on LCSH. For example, when "Canada" was to be included as a keyword, the selector was requested to enter "Canadian" as well, but not "Kanada" or "Dominion of Canada," which are both cross-references to the approved term. *World Vue* had included all of the terms and cross references. Selectors also had to adjust to the idea that the *VRL* had a keyword index, so each individual word was indexed separately. This has implications for information retrieval. For "databases," one of the LCSH cross-references is "data banks." If this was included in the keywords for a database, anyone searching for bank information who entered the word "bank" would also retrieve databases. This adjustment took some time and effort for the selectors; it was a challenging task to evaluate all of the possible meanings that a word might have, and what kind of sites it might retrieve. We wanted to produce a high-quality database in which users would retrieve material that was appropriate to their information request, as much as possible. Therefore, the emphasis was on quality of indexing, not necessarily on quantity. We hope that future enhancements will include a small "authority file" of terms which can be used and updated by the cataloguers so that they are using terms consistently throughout the database.

Our metadata template includes all of the Dublin Core elements that existed at the time of its development, although not all are presently in use. The elements that are used regularly include Title, Author/Creator, Subject and Keywords, Description, Publisher, Other Contributor, Format, Resource Identifier, Language, and Coverage. The training material provided to each selector indicates what information is to be entered in each field, the format to be used, and how and where it is indexed. Most of the fields that are not used were ruled out, either because they would not be indexed or displayed, or because the amount of time it would take to enter the information made the procedure cost-ineffective. We decided that only one title would be entered in the "Title" field; all other titles are entered in the "Description" field, which is also keyword indexed. The Description field is used to provide a short description of the site when the title is not self-explanatory; this description displays in the results list and is keyword indexed. *Science Net* may eventually add similar annotations, again depending on available funding. The Date field is used in *Science Net* to enter the date that the site was last modified, as a way of generating an indication for the user that the site may have been revised. It is not used in the *VRL*.

CONCLUSION

The success of *Science Net* depends upon its provision of a rich selection of Internet resources for its user group, resources that are clearly arranged in an accessible, easy-to-use manner. In this way it should prove possible to demonstrate the continued relevance of those skills which have long been at the disposal of the users of traditional libraries. So, too, as its parent, the *Virtual Reference Library*, continues to add one "room" after another, the coherence of the whole will be ensured by the determination to capture something of the essential order present in a conventional library. A case of old wine in new bottles, then, since providing some kind of systematic access to the rapidly growing, yet still essentially chaotic, world of Internet resources is more vital than ever, not to mention the need for establishing ordered access to those digitized collections that will form an important part of the *VRL*. Surely it is no more than sensible to exploit, in necessarily adapted form, the organizational expertise gained from the refinements that have accrued over centuries of library practice. This is apt to take a variety of forms, of course, as optimal means come to be identified and exploited. But first there is need for a workable framework.

No project can succeed without providing the means of carrying out essential tasks in an efficient manner. The practical success of the project is certainly due in part to its administrative interface. It is easy and relatively fast to use the resource form to enter data about sites, without having to fully understand the complexities of the underlying metadata. The guidelines for using the resource form include elements of traditional cataloguing practice (such as using the title on the home page as the title of the site), but in general it has been possible to train non-cataloguers to catalogue sites without exposing them to a large number of rules. The project provides an example for others who might need to organize an undertaking of this type. If the sites were being catalogued in the traditional way for inclusion in the library's catalogue, our approach would not work because of the enormous body of rules and codes that must be considered, interpreted, and applied on a daily basis by traditional cataloguers. However, it is certainly possible to catalogue sites using a resource form such as the one we developed for *Science Net* and the *VRL*, provided that appropriate training and support are available. The increased value to the user will assuredly justify the outlay.

NOTES

1. Stuart Weibel, The State of the Dublin Core Metadata Initiative, *D-Lib Magazine* 5, no. 4 (April 1999). (http://www.dlib.org/dlib/apri199/04weibel.html).

2. Wayne Daniels, Browsing Your Virtual Library: The Case of Expanding Universe (sidebars by Jeanne Enright and Scott Mackenzie), *Library Hi Tech* 15, nos. 3-4 (Consecutive issues #59-60, 1997): 119-126.

3. Wayne Daniels and Kathy Scardellato, Past into Future: Capturing Library Expertise in a Virtual Library, *Library Hi Tech*. Forthcoming.

4. The Dublin Core Metadata Set: Reference Description (http://www.oclc.org/oclc/projects/core/about/element_set.htm).

5. The Nordic Metadata Project's website can be found at: (http://renki.lib.helsinki.fi/meta/nm2/index.htm).

6. GEM: The Gateway to Educational Materials (http://www.geminfo.org/).

Straining the Standards:
How Cataloging Websites
for Curriculum Support
Poses Fresh Problems
for the *Anglo-American Cataloging Rules*

D. Grant Campbell

SUMMARY. This paper discusses two primary issues that arose from cataloging educational sites as part of the Cataloguing Internet Resources Project in Canada. First, the complex hierarchies in which many education-related resources are found is discussed–along with the need for new policies to determine "extent" for documents embedded in the interlinked bibliographic universe. Second, the concept of and the need to re-evaluate the definition of the "edition statement" in the Web environment are discussed. Overall, further communication is needed between the educational and cataloguing community to provide access to educational resources in the electronic environment. *[Article copies available for a fee from The Haworth Document Delivery Service: 1-800-342-9678. E-mail address: <getinfo@haworthpressinc.com> Website: <http://www.HaworthPress.com>]*

D. Grant Campbell is Assistant Professor, Faculty of Information and Media Studies, University of Western Ontario (e-mail: gcampbel@julian.uwo.ca). Mr. Campbell was Coordinator of the Cataloguing Internet Resources Project, January-June, 1997.

The author wishes to acknowledge the assistance of Joseph P. Cox, the staff at the Inforum in the Faculty of Information Studies, and the members of the Cataloguing Internet Resources Project for their assistance and support.

[Haworth co-indexing entry note]: "Straining the Standards: How Cataloging Websites for Curriculum Support Poses Fresh Problems for the *Anglo-American Cataloging Rules*." Campbell, D. Grant. Co-published simultaneously in *Journal of Internet Cataloging* (The Haworth Information Press, an imprint of The Haworth Press, Inc.) Vol. 3, No. 1, 2000, pp. 79-92; and: *Metadata and Organizing Educational Resources on the Internet* (ed: Jane Greenberg) The Haworth Information Press, an imprint of The Haworth Press, Inc., 2000, pp. 79-92. Single or multiple copies of this article are available for a fee from The Haworth Document Delivery Service [1-800-342-9678, 9:00 a.m. - 5:00 p.m. (EST). E-mail address: getinfo@haworthpressinc.com].

© 2000 by The Haworth Press, Inc. All rights reserved.

KEYWORDS. Cataloging, Internet resources, educational resources, digital genres

INTRODUCTION

The library community has taken two distinct approaches to the challenge of organizing and describing remote-access computer files. The "non-traditional" approach explores emerging metadata sets for describing Web resources, new techniques of harvesting and indexing them, and new databases in which to place them. The "traditional approach" attempts to bring many decades of cataloguing experience to bear on these new documents, to describe them according to standard cataloguing rules and to integrate them with descriptions of other media in a library online catalog.

While both methods have their attractions, the traditional method is especially alluring in educational environments. Educational institutions have always depended heavily on their libraries and library catalogs to support their various instructional programs and to train students and instructors in information searching. Integrating Web documents into an online catalog, therefore, is highly desirable in many cases: it draws selected resources of the World Wide Web into a learning environment which benefits from a tradition of rich, detailed cataloging procedures.

School, college and university libraries, therefore, have taken active roles in the creation of bibliographic records for Web resources. Canada, for instance, witnessed the Cataloguing Internet Resources Project, a joint venture between A-G Canada and the Faculty of Information Studies at University of Toronto. The project produced a collection of records for Websites selected by various libraries in Canada, including the Peel Board of Education, Ryerson University, and the Universities of Alberta and Manitoba. The policies and practices developed from the project are described in the forthcoming publication *Cataloguing the Chameleon*, by Joseph P. Cox and Jennifer Dekker. This paper seeks to explore some of the theoretical and methodological issues that arose from the project, and to suggest ways in which cataloguing Internet resources for educational institutions creates new challenges for the *Anglo-American Cataloging Rules*.

THE EDUCATIONAL PROCESS, THE LIBRARY CATALOG AND THE WORLD WIDE WEB

In an educational setting, a library catalog is both a vital support to curriculum-based learning, and a means of learning in its own right. On the one hand, it provides access to "a wide range of materials related to the instructional programs in the school" (IASL, 1999). On the other hand, it provides a medium whereby students can learn one of the most vital skills of all: to search for information. This skill, as Kulthau reminds us, is a complex process which involves multiple stages and requires that searchers "reflect and become aware of their own process" (Kulthau, 1998). For Miksa, the library is crucial to the educational process because it facilitates a lively interaction between the user and information (Miksa, 1998).

The library catalog of an educational institution, then, must fit this interactive and iterative process of information searching and processing. In particular, it must

- provide access to resources that have been selected to support the school's curriculum;
- provide bibliographic descriptions that are sufficiently detailed to enable the searcher to evaluate the document's relevance to the search;
- describe resources consistently, within the standard bibliographic model, so that searchers can build on their previous search experiences and gain efficiency; and
- provide a clear, unambiguous and stable link between the bibliographic record and the document it represents.

The growth of the World Wide Web has increased the importance of the library use in educational institutions, and this importance arises both from the Web's opportunities and from its limitations. The Z39.50 protocol enables libraries to mount their catalogs on the World Wide Web, and enables users to search multiple catalogs through a common Web interface. The library catalog, therefore, is more accessible than ever before: it can be reached easily from a great distance by anyone with an Internet connection. In addition, the hyperlinks in a Web-based library catalog enable the Web searcher to move directly from the bibliographic record of a Web resource to the resource itself. The catalog, therefore, is more than an organized list of documents: it provides a gateway to the electronic documents themselves.

This gateway has the added advantage of being a discriminating gateway: more discriminating than many Web-based search tools. The Web documents in a library catalog were not gathered by bots, spiders or other automatic harvesting and retrieval devices. They were not retrieved because of some accident of word frequency or through careless or deliberately misleading metatags. The library catalog, by its nature, is a product of the collection development process, and this process is just as important for documents freely mounted on the Web as it is for documents acquired by payment through publishers and distributors. The Web documents described in a library catalog have been selected according to the institution's criteria of quality and relevance; as such, they represent the shape, scope and dimensions of the library's educational purpose.

Furthermore, the Web resources in a library catalog appear alongside resources in other media as well. The student or researcher derives from the catalog an integrated tool of information delivery: one which gathers all media types into a common exercise of inquiry, rather than isolating Web information as an entity with different search techniques, different qualities, and different standards of authority. The library catalog, then, "implements the library model for providing access to [Internet] resources," combining the power of the Web with the value-added features of authority control and subject analysis (Dillon and Jul, 1996). Cataloging Web resources in a library catalog enhances the role of the school library and the school librarian as a "'knowledge navigator' . . . [who is able to] relate the objectives of the school and classroom curriculum to the rich variety of learning resources assembled in the school" (IASL, 1999). By including Web resources in its library catalog, the educational library is extending its rich traditions of support and guidance into the arena of the World Wide Web.

The *Anglo-American Cataloging Rules* form a major part of this rich cataloging tradition. They provide an information model and a set of principles that began with Panizzi and Cutter, and continued on through the Paris Principles and the development of the International Standard Bibliographic Description. When we describe Web resources with these rules, therefore, we are casting those resources within a model which has three important characteristics.

First, a surrogate for the record is created: a brief, accurate, standardized description which can be integrated into the catalog with records for all other information resources. By manipulating the surrogates, rather than the documents themselves, the searcher can find information more easily and more efficiently. Second, the *Anglo-American Cataloguing Rules* make a distinction between the *content* of a work and its *carrier*. Access points are determined largely by the intellectual content of the item, while the bibliographic description is based on the physical qualities of the bibliographic unit: the physical item that contains the content (*AACR2R*, 305). Recent studies (Howarth, 1998, Delsey, 1998) have suggested that this distinction is by no means clear and consistent throughout the rules, and the IFLA Study Group on the Functional Requirements for Bibliographic Records has recently suggested a four-tiered model that moves from "work" to "expression" to "manifestation" to "item" (IFLA, 1998). Nonetheless, the guiding principle is clear: a bibliographic record describes a physical item that "holds" or "contains" the intellectual content.

In its commitment to the "bibliographic unit," library cataloging traditionally centers on the discrete physical object, rather than on sections or parts of the object. While rules exist for providing analytics in special cases, libraries can generally afford to catalog only the monograph and the serial, and not the individual chapters or articles. Access at this sub-monograph level has traditionally been provided by subject bibliographies, commercial periodical indexes and online databases; the searcher uses the index to locate a citation for an article, and uses the catalog to locate the physical copies of the serial within a library's holdings.

Finally, *AACR2R* is committed to media-independence: theoretically, the rules can describe a computer file or a diorama as effectively as they can describe a printed book. The various chapters of *AACR2R* provide "a comprehensive, media-neutral descriptive framework" that can be applied to all types of documents (Gorman and Oddy, 1998). The description of an Internet site, therefore, is based on Chapter 9, "Computer Files," combined with rules from other chapters as necessary (particularly Chapter 13, "Serials"), and then assigning access points according to Chapters 21 through 25.

THE EVOLUTION OF DOCUMENT TYPES ON THE WORLD WIDE WEB

To understand how far these assumptions hold true with digital resources, we need to understand what happens to traditional document types when they migrate to the World Wide Web. Is an electronic journal the same as a printed journal? Is a printed topographic map the same as the display from a geographic information system? If they are different, are those differences significant in terms of bibliographic description and access?

The answers to these questions lie in Miksa's concept of the school library as a place of dynamic interaction between user and document. If interaction is a key element in document acquisition and use, then the library catalog, in providing its descriptions of Internet resources, should anticipate how users will interact with these resources. With electronic documents, part of this interaction involves questions of functionality.

Recent research in digital genre has discussed the migration of traditional text-based genres to the Web, and how their nature has changed (Crowston and Williams, 1996). Shepherd and Watters (1998) suggest that when a document type, or "genre," migrates onto the Web, its traditional content and form are augmented by a new element of functionality, defined as the capabilities which the electronic medium affords for manipulating and interacting with the document. They suggest four primary types of "cybergenres," all defined by the degree to which they incorporate the new functionalities into the traditional document form:

- *Replicated Genre:* in which a document born in a print or other non-electronic medium appears in electronic form much as it did in its original form.
- *Variant Genre:* in which a document remains largely faithful to its print counterpart, but changes its form and content somewhat to accommodate new functionalities.
- *Emergent Genre:* in which the genre has evolved to the extent that it now constitutes an entirely new genre, with its own characteristics, its own form and content, and its own functionalities.
- *Spontaneous Genre:* a genre which has no counterpart in another medium.

Educational resources selected by libraries for cataloging and integration into online catalogs come from all four categories. And all four types of resource present fresh challenges that strain the cataloging rules in unexpected ways.

REPLICATED GENRES

Some educational resources are clearly "documents" in the traditional sense: government reports, discussion and background papers, task force reports, and papers from conference proceedings. These are self-sufficient, clearly-demarcated works which would not look very different on paper. Indeed, most of them originated in paper form, and often appear on the Web either as an HTML document or as a downloadable file in a page-fidelity format such as PDF. Very little functionality has been added to these documents in their electronic form, although hyperlinks often enable the user to move through the document, and to link to Web-based items in the bibliography. Typical of this type is the Final Report of the CARL-AUCC Task Force on Academic Libraries and Scholarly Communication, titled *The Changing World of Scholarly Communication: Challenges and Choices for Canada* (1996). For such documents, the cataloging is fairly straightforward; the document has reached a final form which will not allow for further revision, and its status as an electronic document makes no difference to the main and added entries. As the sample record below indicates, a "System Requirements" note can be added to specify any hardware or software requirements. And an 856 field will provide a link directly to the resource itself (See Figure 1).

The problems involved in cataloging this type of document are common to cataloging all Web resources, the greatest of which involves using the Uniform Resource Locator (URL) to link to the document. Linking to an address is a dangerous business, as Web catalogers have discovered through bitter experience. As Alan Emtage warns us, "having [a URL] does not mean the object being looked for will exist . . . URLs are transient and can become

FIGURE 1

110	2		$a AUCC/ABRC Task Force on Academic Libraries and Scholarly Communication.
245	1	4	$a The changing world of scholarly communication $h [computer file] : $b challenges and choices for Canada : final report of the AUCC/ABRC Task Force on Academic Libraries and Scholarly Communication.
256			Computer data
260			$a [Canada] : $b Association of Universities and Colleges of Canada : $b Canadian Association of Research Libraries, $c 1996.
538			$a Mode of access: available on the World Wide Web in both HTML and PDF format.
538			$a System requirements: a text-based World Wide Web browser or a PDF viewer.
650		0	$a Scholarly publishing $z Canada.
710	2		$a Association of Universities and Colleges of Canada.
710	2		$a Canadian Association of Research Libraries.
856	4	0	$u http://www.aucc.ca/english/sites/aucccarl.htm

invalid at any time" (1994). Even a finished document can move from one place to another on the World Wide Web, as organizations responsible for the document change names, memberships, or server locations. This creates the need for using tools for URL maintenance, such as link checking software or a PURL resolution service (Tyler, 1999). Furthermore, a document itself can be replaced, with its successor occupying the same location and filename, and consequently the same address. This is particularly common when preliminary drafts of a report are mounted, and then subsequently replaced with updated versions. Educational institutions that catalog Web resources, therefore, will need to exercise vigilance. Links from a bibliographic record to a remote-access file are unstable, and the failure of that link will prevent students from replicating and building on their searches.

VARIANT GENRES

Some documents are variant genres; while they retain a strong connection to their print origins, the possibilities inherent in both Web authoring and Web use create significant differences in the electronic version. This occurs most frequently with serials, where the *Anglo-American Cataloguing Rules* need to be interpreted very broadly. Many electronic journals have achieved the credibility and status accorded to print journals, and warrant cataloging and integration into the online catalog. Many are peer-reviewed, and make important contributions to their fields; many have print counterparts, or are continuations of printed journals. E-journals, however, have their own publishing contexts, and are unevenly developing their own characteristics. Some journals have dispensed with the traditional serial designations, numbering each article in sequence within a given timeframe. In some cases, even the publisher has become a problematic concept; *InterJournal*, for instance, provides a central location for indexes and abstracts to articles that pass its referees; the articles themselves, however, are distributed throughout the Web.

Inconsistent methods of presentation are all too familiar to long-suffering serials catalogers. In addition, however, the very methods used to minimize inconsistency in catalog records need updating, particularly in deciding the Chief Source of Information. According to the *Anglo-American Cataloguing Rules* Chapter 13, the Chief Source of Information for a serial is the title page of the first issue; in the absence of the first issue, the cataloger selects the first available issue (*AACR2R,* 276). This rule makes perfect sense for printed journals, whose issues appear in regular sequence. But the rule makes less sense on the World Wide Web. Many electronic journals have a central Web-site, containing links to all issues of the serial; this makes an ideal place for depositing important bibliographic information, such as the publisher, the ISSN and the editors-in-chief. Similarly, many e-journals that migrated from print versions began mounting issues in the middle of a sequence. Furthermore, earlier issues are retrospectively mounted as time and resources permit. The cataloger therefore has a number of viable candidates as the chief source of information:

- *The first issue mounted:* the first issue which the publisher has placed in electronic form. It often has minimal information, and has very little of the functionality of later issues; indeed, many earlier issues of e-journals are in ASCII text.
- *The earliest issue available:* This may well have been mounted later, and may well be superseded by a still earlier issue in the future as retrospective conversion to electronic form proceeds.
- *The journal home page:* This may well be the most informative source; however, it can sometimes be difficult to locate in a hierarchy of pages, and the cataloging rules provide no precedent for using it.

The description of an electronic journal, therefore, can vary depending on which source of information is selected for the description, a decision which is currently up to individual catalogers and cataloging agencies to decide.

EMERGENT GENRES

In some cases, the added functionality has created an entirely new genre, one which both educators and students can easily confuse with a familiar genre. The Web page of *Discover Magazine*, for instance, could easily be mistaken as the electronic version of the printed magazine: it is linked to specific issues, and contains substantial segments of each issue. In fact, however, it is a resource page which links selected stories from the magazine to Web resources which support and enhance the reading of the print magazine, including a photo gallery, a sequence of Web links, an e-mail connection, and a list of science news stories.

In such cases, the cataloger must provide links to the print version with which the resource is associated, while making it clear that this is a totally "new" document. In most cases, this involves placing a link to the resource page in the bibliographic record for the print magazine. The MARC 856 field has therefore been revised, with the second indicator indicating the relationship of the electronic resource to the resource in the record (Library of Congress 1997). The URL for the resource page for *Discover* Magazine, therefore, appears in the record for the print magazine, and the second indicator of the 856 field would have a value of "2," indicating that it is related to the resource being described, rather than being the resource itself:

```
245        0 0     $a Discover $h [text]
.....


856        4 2     $u http://www.discover.com
```

SPONTANEOUS GENRES

In addition to these transformations of print-based document types, the Web is abounding with educational resources which have, for all intents and purposes, no analogues in the print world. Some of these types, such as the home page, clearly result from the Web's power as an "electronic bulletin board": its ability to post relatively informal and easily-updated information related to an organization. In addition, the Web is a repository for large collections of material, in many cases multimedia material: electronic text repositories, databases, archives of images. These sites are not "documents" so much as libraries, with their own collections, their own search engines, and their own procedures for access. Finally, the Web also contains numerous programs which can be used to manipulate and present data, such as geographic information systems.

Many of these spontaneous genres are unfamiliar outside the Web environment, and their relationship to other items in the library collection is not always clear. The bibliographic description, therefore, carries a heavy burden of explaining the nature of the site. In a study of library catalog use at the

University of Florida, graduate students picked the summary field as one of the most popular and heavily-used fields in bibliographic description for Web resources (Lundgren and Simpson, 1999).

CONSEQUENCES

What, then, are the consequences to students and educators of these new cybergenres? How does this new functionality, and its consequent trans-formations of traditional document types, affect the library's effort to provide accurate, consistent descriptions of resources across all media types, along with clear and stable links to those resources? I would argue that these objectives are often frustrated by two primary disruptions of our cataloging assumptions: the assumption of clear, hierarchical boundaries between docu-ments, and the assumption of stable intellectual content.

Web resources do not have the physical distinctiveness and "separate-ness" that other information objects have, and as a result we are losing the traditional hierarchical distinctions which enabled catalogers to distinguish between the "monograph" level and the "sub-monograph" level, both in theoretical and practical terms. With printed objects, the distinction is clear: the catalog enables us to locate the object, while the bibliography, index or online database helps us locate what is within the object. On the Web, there is not much difference between searching for either; indeed, the individual article is often located prior to any recognition that it belongs to a serial, or some other larger collection of works. For the cataloger, copy-cataloging becomes a confusing process. If no consensus exists on the optimal level of cataloging, multiple records could exist, based on different parts of the same Web page. And for the user, there is no clear understanding of what to expect from the catalog, and how consistent and thorough its coverage should be.

Michael Gorman has revealed a central paradox of modern information media: "each new form of communication is at once more portable (that is, good at conquering space) and less durable (that is, less good at conquering time) than its predecessors" (1997). The plight of the edition statement in Internet cataloging shows us how transient and mutable content has become. In traditional bibliographic scholarship, the "edition" is defined as "the whole number of copies of a book printed at any time or times from substan-tially the same setting of type pages" (Bowers, 1986). In the context of serial publications, the edition statement is used to distinguish separate but parallel streams in the production of discrete, sequential issues of a journal. The edition statement distinguishes between different language editions, different formats, and local editions. In all cases, the edition statement sets a meaning-ful, easily-identified boundary, within which all instances of a document can be *assumed* to be the same: "what matters, bibliographically, is the possibility of change" (Stokes 1989, 98).

The ease with which Web documents can be revised and updated has made the edition statement problematic. OCLC's *Cataloging Internet Resources* takes a position that is consistent with the transcription of edition statements in other formats: "If there is any change in the intellectual content of the file, or any change in the programming language or operating system, or any change to make the computer file run more efficiently, the item is considered to be a new edition" (1997). In practical terms, however, an active, popular, heavily-used Web resource is apt to be updated far more frequently than catalogers can handle. The guide produced for the Cataloguing Internet Resources Project in Canada, basing its interpretation on the *ISBD(ER)*, states simply that "edition refers to substantial changes within an item. It does not include the frequent or minor updates made to electronic resources" (Cox and Dekker 1999, 17). The frequent practice is to provide a note which expresses some sense of the frequency, with or without the date of the most recent update.

In educational situations, the edition statement has always been of the utmost importance. Both learners and educators need clearly-defined boundaries around manifestations of a work. These boundaries avoid misconceptions, and ensure that all readers are reading the same thing. But in a bibliographic universe where the content is mutable, this notion of "fixity" has to be redefined in a way that is meaningful to both students and educators. What, in an educational setting, constitutes a "substantial change"?

CONCLUSIONS

Cataloging Internet resources continues to be a popular and useful activity for educational institutions. But very little consensus currently exists as to what level of cataloging libraries should follow, and how it can be ensured that all users are linking to the same content in the same documents. What, then, are the implications for this process?

To begin with, full cataloging is expensive, and always has been. This forces libraries to be selective about the sites they catalog, and to seek out cataloging copy whenever possible. Copy cataloguing will no doubt increase, as more and more Websites are cataloged and added to library catalogs and to bibliographic databases such as the INTERCAT database at OCLC. In addition, selection of venue will be very important. Some sites are clearly more appropriate in other contexts: a library home page, or a course support Web page, which provides a series of hypertext links to a set of resources chosen specifically for a particular occasion. As Web authoring and Website maintenance becomes easier, these resource pages are emerging as a viable place to put time-sensitive course-related information which is tailored to the specific needs of a course, an instructor, or a school.

The rise of metadata standards also suggests ways in which Internet resource cataloguing can become more efficient. Metadata sets such as the Dublin Core were developed in part by the library community, and their individual fields map to MARC records with at least partial accuracy. As meta-tags are used with greater frequency and regularity on the World Wide Web, it may be possible to generate minimal MARC records from these meta-tags, to make Web resources accessible, at least in some preliminary form, very quickly.

Nonetheless, the harsh truth is that bibliographic descriptions of Web resources require more, not less, detail in their cataloguing records, particularly in learning environments. If the school library catalog is to retain its role as a means of knowledge navigation and a site of dynamic interaction between users and documents, the bibliographic records must support the iterative process involved in learning to search for information. It has traditionally done so by presenting information in regular, consistent way which encourages rapid movement from one record to another and efficient identification, collocation and evaluation. Indeed, David Levy has argued that the order and consistency of catalog records is the output, not the input of catalogers: the exercise of painstaking effort and careful thought to produce records that are consistent with each other, while remaining true to the variety of the resources they describe (1995). For searchers in a school environment, learning from previous searches as they navigate through the stages of a complex quest for information, the need is doubly great for bibliographic records that provide full, consistent and informative descriptions, as well as accurate and stable links.

To integrate these bibliographic records successfully into online catalogs, complex decisions have to be made regarding their relationships to records for print resources, and descriptive notes have to be constructed to explain anomalies in designation, publisher statements, and system requirements. Summary fields must be accurate and helpful. Above all, the successful integration of Internet resources into library catalogs will depend on the active participation of educators and reference librarians, who can set the policies and select the resources which will enable Web resources to enhance the learning process.

REFERENCES

Anglo-American Cataloguing Rules. 1998. Prepared under the direction of the Joint Steering Committee for Revision of AACR; edited by Michael Gorman and Paul Winkler. 2nd ed., 1998 revision. Ottawa: Canadian Library Association, 1998.

AUCC-CARL/ABRC Task Force on Academic Libraries and Scholarly Communication. 1996. *The Changing World of Scholarly Communication: Challenges and Choices for Canada*. [Canada]: Association of Universities and Colleges of Canada. [Online] *http://www.aucc.ca/english/sites/aucccarl.htm*

Bowers, Fredson. 1986. *Principles of Bibliographical Description*. Princeton, NJ: Princeton University Press.

Cataloging Internet Resources: A Manual and Practical Guide. 2nd ed. Ed. Nancy B. Olson. Dublin OH: OCLC Online Computer Library Center, 1997. [Online] *http://www.purl.org/oclc/cataloging-internet*

Cox, Joseph P. and Dekker, Jennifer. 1999. *Cataloguing the Chameleon: A Guide to Electronic Resources*. Toronto: Faculty of Information Studies, University of Toronto. In Press.

Crowston, Kevin and Williams, Marie. 1996. "Reproduced and Emergent Genres of Communication on the World-Wide Web." In *Proceedings of the Thirtieth Hawaii International Conference on System Sciences. Volume II: Digital Documents Track*. Los Alamitos: IEEE Computer Society.

Delsey, Tom. 1997. "Modeling the Logic of AACR." In *International Conference on the Principles and Future Development of AACR, Toronto, Canada, October 23-25, 1997*. [Online] http://www.nlc-bnc.ca/jsc/confpap.htm

Dillon, Martin and Jul, Eric. 1996. "Cataloging Internet Resources: The Convergence of Libraries and Internet Resources." *Cataloging & Classification Quarterly* 22 No. 3/4: 197-238.

Emtage, Alan. 1994. "The Why and What of URLs and URNs." *Serials Review*. Winter 1994: 32-34.

Gorman, Michael. 1997. *Cataloguing, Chaos, and Cataloguing the Chaos*. Denton, Texas: School of Library and Information Studies, Texas Woman's University.

Gorman, Michael and Oddy, Pat. 1997. "*The Anglo-American Cataloguing Rules, Second Edition*: Their History and Principles." *International Conference on the Principles and Future Development of AACR, Toronto, Canada, October 23-25, 1997*. [Online] http://www.nlc-bnc.ca/jsc/confpap.htm

Howarth, Lynne. 1997. "Content versus Carrier." In *International Conference on the Principles and Future Development of AACR, Toronto, Canada, October 23-25, 1997*. [Online] http://www.nlc-bnc.ca/jsc/confpap.htm

International Association of School Librarianship (IASL). 1999. *School Libraries for Tomorrow: Summary Statement from Forging Forward: National Symposium on Information, Literacy and the School Library in Canada*. [Online] *http:// www.hi.is/~anne/forging.html*

IFLA Study Group on the Functional Requirements for Bibliographic Records. 1998. *Functional Requirements for Bibliographic Records: Final Report*. Munchen: K.G. Saur.

Kulthau, Carol Collier. 1998. "The process of learning from information." In *The Virtual School Library: Gateway to the Information Superhighway*. Ed. Carol Collier Kulthau. Englewood: Libraries Unlimited: 95-104.

Levy, David. 1995. "Cataloging in the Digital Order." *Digital Libraries '95*. [Online] *http://csdl.tamu.edu/DL95/papers/levy/levy.html*

Library of Congress, Network Development Office, and MARC Standards Office.

Guidelines for the Use of Field 856. Rev. August 1997. [Online] http://
lcweb.loc.gov/marc/856guide.html

Lundgren, Jimmie and Simpson, Betsey. 1999. "Looking Through Users' Eyes:
What Do Graduate Students Need to Know About Internet Resources via the
Library Catalog?" *Journal of Internet Cataloging* 1 (4): 31-44.

Miksa, Francis. 1998. "Basic Issues Regarding the Establishment of a National
SME&T Digital Library." In *Developing a Digital National Library for Undergraduate Science, Mathematics, Engineering and Technology Education: Report
of a Workshop.* Washington: National Academy Press: 94-100.

Shepherd, Michael and Watters, Carolyn. 1998. "The Evolution of Cybergenres." In
*Proceedings of the Thirty-first Hawaii International Conference on System
Sciences. Volume II: Digital Documents Track.* Los Alamitos: IEEE Computer
Society, 60-67.

Stokes, Roy. 1989. *A Bibliographical Companion.* Metuchen, NJ: Scarecrow Press.

Tyler, Tom. 1999. "URLs, PURLs & TRULs: Link Maintenance in the Web-accessi-
ble OPAC." In *Computers in Libraries '99.* [Online] http://www.du.edu/~ttyler/
ci199/proceedings.htm

Democratizing Education
at the Schomburg:
Catalog Development and the Internet

James Briggs Murray

SUMMARY. This article documents the development of the catalog at the Schomburg Center for Research in Black Culture (NYPL), from its early beginnings up through digital access as is now evident in its Internet presentation, *The Digital Schomburg*. The role of this unique library as educator and producer is discussed, as well as the cataloging decisions and processes required in mounting *The Digital Schomburg*. Links to a number of *Digital Schomburg* resources are provided. *[Article copies available for a fee from The Haworth Document Delivery Service: 1-800-342-9678. E-mail address: <getinfo@haworthpressinc.com> Website: <http://www.HaworthPress.com>]*

KEYWORDS. Cataloging history, digital libraries, Internet cataloging, Dublin Core, Schomburg Center

EDUCATIONAL ROOTS

Born in 1874 of African and European blood, in Santurce, Puerto Rico, young Arturo Alfonso Schomburg, for whom The New York Public Library's

---

James Briggs Murray is Founding Curator of the Schomburg Center's Moving Image and Recorded Sound Division. Mr. Murray has directed two major Center-wide NEH-funded cataloging projects. He also serves as the Center's Assistant Director for Media Productions and Theatre Operations, leading the Center's efforts in a variety of areas from video oral history to Webcasting.

[Haworth co-indexing entry note]: "Democratizing Education at the Schomburg: Catalog Development and the Internet." Murray, James Briggs. Co-published simultaneously in *Journal of Internet Cataloging* (The Haworth Information Press, an imprint of The Haworth Press, Inc.) Vol. 3, No. 1, 2000, pp. 93-108; and: *Metadata and Organizing Educational Resources on the Internet* (ed: Jane Greenberg) The Haworth Information Press, an imprint of The Haworth Press, Inc., 2000, pp. 93-108. Single or multiple copies of this article are available for a fee from The Haworth Document Delivery Service [1-800-342-9678, 9:00 a.m. - 5:00 p.m. (EST). E-mail address: getinfo@haworthpressinc.com].

© 2000 by The Haworth Press, Inc. All rights reserved.

Schomburg Center for Research in Black Culture is named, believed that his education should include the history and culture of both his European and his African ancestry. So, when an "educator" proclaimed that the absence of African studies in their curriculum was an indication that Africans have no history, the disbelieving young Schomburg determined to devote his life to giving the lie to that proclamation. There were no online catalogs for him to peruse–indeed he could find no manual catalog through which he could readily search Africana. Eventually, therefore, he traveled the globe in search of documentation of Africa and its peoples, gathering all that he could find that was either by or about the global Black experience. He dreamed of disseminating that documentation to anyone and everyone thirsting for knowledge of the glory of Africa's past, as well as the accomplishments of her descendants in the African Diaspora, dispersed throughout the globe largely via the business of enslavement.

BIRTH OF A LIBRARY

By the time of the Harlem Renaissance, Black America's 1920s and 1930s cultural and intellectual explosion, writers, scholars, performers, etc., literally camped out at Schomburg's new home in Harlem to drink from the fountain of knowledge his collection offered in continuous streams. His residence became no less than an educational research center, jubilantly, but distress-ingly, bursting at the seams with manuscripts, monographs, newspapers, periodicals, photographs, art objects and a steady flow of researchers. Many feared that the educational opportunities experienced by the fortunate few able to get into the Schomburg home, would not be accessible to the growing numbers of local, national, and international potential researchers who began to hear of these treasures. The Carnegie Corporation responded to the distress calls from the Harlem community by acquiring Schomburg's collection and donating it to The New York Public Library (NYPL). Thus was born what today has become the world's most prominent and comprehensive center for the study and presentation (via exhibitions and performance programs) of the history and culture of peoples of African descent. A manual card file was established and the public was invited in to study the Schomburg treasures.

AN EARLY CATALOGING DILEMMA

It would seem that Schomburg's dream of educating a broad population on the history and people of Africa could now quickly begin. But as library professionals know so well, acquisition is only one step in the process. Full democratic access to the collection requires both acquisition and appropriate cataloging. This was hampered somewhat by an administrative dilemma–although the Schomburg collection had been developed both for scholarly research and local community access, the collection had been placed administratively and physically under the jurisdiction of NYPL's Circulation Department, rather than its Reference Department. Schomburg's books (and many other materials) were cataloged and shelved in accordance with the Dewey Decimal System. The Cataloging Office of the NYPL Circulation Department, located some five miles downtown from the Schomburg, which was in Harlem, reported numerous difficulties within a year of undertaking the cataloging of the Schomburg Collection. Among those that they reported and those that might be deduced were:

- The experience of the Circulation Department's catalogers was with relatively small in size, general subject, open-shelf circulating collections. The Schomburg Collection was a large, subject-focused, closed stack, non-circulating collection.
- The Circulation Department's catalogers had their greatest familiarity with contemporary imprints, both monographic and serial, the bibliographic data for which required no extraordinary or specialized training to discover or decipher. The Schomburg Collection holdings consisted largely of rare titles requiring substantial time and effort to establish appropriate subject and descriptive cataloging.

GROWING THE CATALOG

By 1939, the year after Arturo Alfonso Schomburg's death, the collection had doubled in size and the cataloging records were found to be seriously inadequate. Numerous titles previously lumped together under the Dewey number for *slavery* required redefining to more appropriate intellectual locations. For example, large groups of books on such subjects as *race relations in the United States* had to be redefined from the Dewey classification for *slavery* to 323.173; and, works on African ethnology, economics, anthropology and history had been cataloged in the travel section of Dewey. This suggests perceptions of Africa, more as a tourism adventure than as a land of people, culture and history.

Dr. Lawrence Reddick, succeeding Mr. Schomburg as Curator, determined that the re-cataloging of the collection would be among the highest priorities of his administration. During the full decade of his tenure, much of the re-cataloging work focused upon revising and expanding the Dewey classification designations for the collection. Under the administration of Jean Blackwell Hutson, the next Curator of significant impact and longevity

(1948-1980), it was determined by the Cataloging Office that *see* and *see also* references should be added. This was the beginning of subject heading access to the Schomburg collections; and, it took still another ten years (some twenty years after the death of Arturo Alfonso Schomburg) before the re-cataloging of the full collection was substantially completed.

THE GROWING CATALOG'S IMPACT ON THE WORLD STAGE

By 1960 Schomburg patrons stood a fairly good chance of finding the materials they sought simply by browsing the card catalog and its *see* and *see also* references. But it was necessary for them to make a physical visit to the Center to access the catalog and the collections. The next significant stop along the Schomburg cataloging road came in 1962 when G. K. Hall published *The Dictionary Catalog of the Schomburg Collection of Negro Literature and History* in nine volumes. These nine volumes, filled with pages of photographic images of the actual catalog cards created in the previous couple of decades, were able to inform a national and international audience of the rich Schomburg holdings that told the story of peoples of African descent. It was just in time for the 1960s explosion of interest in Black Studies that resulted from the modern Civil Rights Movement, the rise of Black militancy, and the expansion of Black consciousness and cultural identity. Not since Arturo Alfonso Schomburg and his contemporaries were living in the world of the Harlem Renaissance, in the 1920s and 1930s, had there been such a flurry of library patrons seeking and demanding information on Black literature, history, culture and the arts. The dissemination of the dictionary catalog greatly assisted librarians and educators who were beginning to develop Black collections, Black Studies departments and Black Studies curricula throughout the world in response to the demand. Many based their acquisitions lists directly on the Schomburg holdings, as published by G. K. Hall. Simultaneously, copies of many Schomburg books, newspapers, periodicals, etc., captured via microfilm, the preservation medium of the day, were acquired by those academicians and librarians to build their collections and to support their curricula.

Affirming the leadership role of the Schomburg collections in the growing world of Black Studies scholarship, The New York Public Library transferred the Schomburg Collection from the Branch Libraries (formerly the Circulating Department) to the Research Libraries (formerly the Reference Department) in 1972. This was yet another significant step along the cataloging road. Effective 1 January 1972, all Research Libraries titles, with an imprint date of 1972 or later, and all other materials being added to the collections for the first time, irrespective of publication date, would be included in a new computer-generated dictionary catalog known as the *Automated Book Cata-*

log (ABC). Fast forwarding for a moment nearly a quarter century later (in 1995), G. K. Hall published a CD-ROM containing the existing holdings of the Schomburg Center. And early in 1997, through National Information Services Corporation (NISC), the Schomburg Center published *Black Studies Database: Kaiser Index to Black Periodicals*, both in CD-ROM and in a Web version, providing access to more than 170,000 citations drawn from significant and influential journals, magazines, newspapers, newsletters, pamphlets and reports relevant to the Black experience from 1948-1986. But back in the 1970s, even while G. K. Hall published the *Dictionary Catalog* and the *ABC* was making international users more and more aware of the Schomburg Center's holding, in-house users were having an increasingly difficult time grappling with the logistics of identifying and gaining access to the exponentially growing collections.

THE DILEMMA OF RAPID GROWTH

In 1978 the Schomburg was departmentalized in order to manage better the growing collections. The Black Studies boom had not only exponentially increased collection usage at the Schomburg Center, but the collections themselves had grown exponentially, reflecting the increased presence of Black people, issues and events in publishing, broadcasting and other media. The General Research and Reference Division took charge of the books, newspapers and periodicals in both print and microform. The Art and Artifacts Division became responsible for sculpture, paintings, artifacts, works on paper, prints, material culture, etc. Personal papers, organizational records, rare books, playbills, typescripts, sheet music and other historic documents went to the Manuscripts, Archives and Rare Books Division. The Photographs and Prints Division became home for 18th and 19th century photomechanical prints as well as 19th and 20th century photographs. And the Moving Image and Recorded Sound Division continued to build the collections of motion picture films, videos, radio and television broadcasts, dramatic readings and productions, recorded music and oral histories. With this departmentalization came divisional curators, increased staffs and a greater concentration on collection development in non-print formats than had ever before existed at the Center. Not only did the books and serials begin a new growth spurt, but the special collections also experienced significant increases in acquisitions funding. This growth and expansion also coincided with preparations for moving the collections from the original 1905 McKim, Mead and White New York City Landmark and National Register of Historic Places building, to a much more modern facility in 1980. Divisional curators, lacking the cataloging support to match the collections' growth, began developing local finding aids and databases so that collection management could be maintained at least within their respective divisions. The collection development, administrative and physical growth and expansion of the Center in the late 1970s and early 1980s also meant that no single librarian or curator had an in-depth knowledge of the full collection, as had been the case in previous decades. Once again the Center faced a cataloging crisis, but this time on a much larger and more complex scale, as cataloging standards and rule interpretations for several formats were only in developmental stages.

THE CATALOG GOES ONLINE

Departmentalized into five collection divisions under individual curatorial guidance and management, the Schomburg Center, in the fall of 1984, brought on board its first Director. Even while speaking of an expanded program of outreach and interpretive educational and performance programs, historian Howard Dodson emphasized the urgency of bringing the growing collections under bibliographic control in an online environment. The next year NYPL's Research Libraries instituted its first OPAC, CATNYP (Catalog of the New York Public Library). Dodson recognized the possibilities afforded by the Preservation and Access program of the National Endowment for the Humanities. In the late 1980s and early 1990s NEH funded two major Schomburg Center cataloging projects, through which we computerized cataloging records for tens of thousands of items in all five collection divisions. Also during this time, the MacArthur Foundation funded a retrospective conversion project, through which data from those catalog cards created during the 1940s and 1950s were incorporated into CATNYP.

Since most library users seek to find available materials in all formats on their particular subject of interest, the NEH cataloging projects and the MacArthur retrospective conversion project provided, for the first time, patrons' ability to learn of the Center's holdings in all five divisions at a single computer terminal. No longer was it necessary to visit each division in order to determine what each had on a subject of interest. A Web-based version of CATNYP went online in 1995, coinciding with the centennial celebrations of The New York Public Library, and making it possible for global audiences to conduct subject and other searches of the Schomburg Center's cataloged multi-formatted holdings.

Although not as problematic as the Dewey classifications used to categorize the Schomburg collections in the 1920s, we paid great attention in the 1980s and 1990s to expanding subject access to the collections and to issues of form and genre. Since the days of Arturo Alfonso Schomburg, we have collected materials in nearly every conceivable format as they emerge–from centuries-old rare books to early photographic processes like daguerreotypes; from African art objects to Caribbean sound recordings; from manuscripts to motion pictures; and from music videos to CD-ROM databases. Although the Library of Congress Subject Headings (LCSH) structure allowed for our building adequate subject headings, the Library of Congress Name Authority File (LCNAF) left much to be desired because so many people, places, organizations, etc., simply had not been established. Fortunately, NYPL became a NACO member during this time, facilitating our ability to establish access points significant to our collections.

THE LIBRARY AS EDUCATOR

Just as Arturo Alfonso Schomburg prepared for educational access to a people's history and culture, at the last turn of the century, so too has today's Schomburg Center staff been positioning itself for its educational role via collection access. Our era's symbolic calendar transition–the coming of the new millennium–arrives with unforeseen and unprecedented technological activity and opportunity. Our passion is identical to Schomburg's, even if the form, the processes and the methods of access are drastically different. Schomburg could not have known of the technological revolution that has given birth to the information age upon which we now depend. He and his colleagues focussed on collecting, preserving and making accessible historic and cultural treasures within a physical building. They, and their immediate successors, continued to collect and publish book catalogs that were dispersed throughout the world. Our work today must be fueled with Schomburg's collection, preservation and access passions. But the information age in which we live also dictates that we consider, in our educational access strategies, not only the audiences in our physical buildings, but the global audience that sees us via the Internet.

Teachers, librarians, curators and other educators have often sought to supplement their students' diets by suggesting that they tune in to television and radio broadcasts, as well as a variety of audiovisual products available in their local libraries. But today's environment offers the interactivity and the time flexibility of the Internet, a 24/7 "broadcast system." One need not sit and await a broadcaster's schedule. One may choose to visit a site at 3:17 a.m. on a Sunday morning, rather than waiting for some network or theatre to rerun the piece of interest. Of course, finding the specific item sought may lead to some frustrating and disappointing moments plowing through the often numerous hits returned by the major search engines because of misuse of metadata tags.

THE LIBRARY AS PRODUCER

Even while the core function of the Schomburg Center remains its research library operations, exhibitions and public programs are sharing center stage as means of educational dissemination. Jazz and dance concerts are as familiar to our audiences as are theatrical and film productions. And, of course, as an educational institution, academic forums are a must. In January 1995, the Center presented a two-day symposium entitled: *Africana Libraries and the Information Age*. We wanted to explore where we've come from, where we are and where we need to go as information providers and as educators. Presentations were made by a virtual who's who of renowned African American librarians, and a strong representation of professional librarians in the prime of their careers. Building upon these presentations on historical and contemporary library operations was a final panel of cutting-edge professionals, demonstrating everything from traditional library methods and materials in new technology formats (searching periodicals text on CD-ROM) to a live Internet session introducing the Black presence on the World Wide Web. (Remember, this was January 1995.) Having the opportunity to conduct the live Web session, this writer took the opportunity to advocate for more assertive librarianship. This is to suggest that it is no longer enough for curators to limit their collection development juices to the process of collecting the products of others. As we inch closer to the day of global online access to books and periodicals, today's librarian and curator must consider themselves not only as passive educators, but also as active producers, educators and providers of content. This might be manifest in videotaping oral histories and public forums and/or mounting exhibitions and multimedia works on the Internet.

THE DIGITAL SCHOMBURG–A LIBRARY WITHOUT WALLS

As a library becomes an Internet producer (and thereby becomes an active educator), among the first critical steps is to determine which collection materials to make accessible. Copyright law becomes a virtual "associate producer," as we seek to avoid becoming an intellectual property rights test case in the courts. Perhaps the most obvious materials to mount are those falling outside of copyright restriction, or otherwise deemed in the public domain. At the Schomburg Center, oral histories and public programs that we've produced ourselves since 1980 are also excellent candidates. We generally have participants execute release agreements, which give us full rights to their testimonies. Exhibitions are also strong candidates. From the moment we mount an exhibition in our physical exhibition hall, that exhibition is educating (and is generating critical feedback from) our patrons. So much original creative work goes into an exhibition, that converting it into a Web presentation is no more complex than scaling it down, if necessary, editing and/or reformatting the text, digitizing some images and/or audio-visual clips, and re-designing the exhibition hall installation for the Web environment.

FROM DEWEY TO DIGITAL:
IF YOU CATALOG IT, THEY WILL COME

If You Catalog It, They Will Come! A cataloger's adaptation from a popular motion picture. So read the sign on the door of our late 1980s cataloging office, which was occupied by a series of dedicated young catalogers I had the privilege of selecting to begin the process of cataloging the special collections at the Schomburg Center under two major NEH grants. I remember standing and contemplating that sign upon my arrival one morning. I remember thinking that these young folks, relatively fresh out of library school, would bring a warm smile to the face of Arturo Alfonso Schomburg. He would applaud the fervor and energy with which they devoted themselves to assuring that the world would learn of the collections of the Schomburg Center. Working with them made cataloging more of a focal point of Schomburg Center operations than at any time in the institution's history. And we knew then that we were on the threshold of an information technology explosion. We were both challenged and energized by our position on the timeline between Dewey Decimal System cataloging and global digital online access. We anticipated that the inevitable changes would come increasingly faster and in exponentially more efficient ways–ways that we could not even imagine, just as Mr. Schomburg could not have imagined our end-of-century cataloging environment. What was clear, though, was that, whatever we did, it needed to be done in as consistent and open an architecture as possible. It was also clear that we needed to do as much of it as possible.

By the time we began talking of mounting an online digital library, it was also clear to us that we needed to remain ready to evolve our cataloging strategies and methods just as collection formats and technologies continue to evolve. This required an almost unprecedented collaborative work effort among information technology staff, administrators, catalogers, curators, conservation and preservation staffs and public service librarians. It wasn't long before one issue led to another, another and another, resulting in a full agenda of issues from many perspectives to be resolved. But they were no longer administrative, cataloging, curatorial, etc., issues–they were *library* issues; they were all of our issues. Our mission was both to succeed at the projects at hand and to establish institutional standards and procedures that would facilitate and guide, rather than trap and handcuff, those working on similar projects later. For example, what appeared to many among us initially to be a fairly straightforward process for the Website mounting of monograph texts, quickly evolved into an ongoing series of meetings for months upon months among staff unaccustomed to such collaborative planning sessions. Following all of these meetings and months came the determination to encode the text in accordance with the TEI (Text Encoding Initiative) DTD (Document Type Definition) of SGML. Using the SGML tags would present the text while preserving the literary structure of the original work. But, the administrative decision to include a broad range of staff in the discussions led to our awareness that the SGML markup we were planning would require that end users acquire a viewer plug-in. We searched for a solution–a way in which end users would have immediate and simple access to the texts. Ultimately we settled upon Inso's DynaWeb electronic publishing software. Installed on our Web server, DynaWeb converts the SGML files to HTML on the fly, completely transparent to the end user. It is most unlikely that so appropriate a solution would have been identified, acquired and implemented without the collaborative efforts of representative staff from the aforementioned groups.

From these group representatives, we formed a new group–the Web Access Group. It is this group that reviews each online digital library project and finds solutions for the many obstacles and various problems that present themselves. We agreed that global Internet users would need to be pointed to our digital collections through the popular Internet search engines. But, in the case of our *African American Women Writers of the 19th Century,* described more fully below, the textual data resided in SGML files, and the search engines would never find them. Our solution was to create an HTML page as a launching point for each digital collection. The HTML pages for the women writers collection (see Appendix A) and the African American images collection (see Appendix B) contain many appropriate Dublin Core metadata elements through which the search engines can direct global users to those 19th Century treasures. Upon arriving at the women writers' Website, a user is free to conduct keyword searches within a particular volume or across the full collection.

In the case of our *Images of African Americans from the 19th Century* Web presentation, the problem was quite different but the solution was similar. Using a software product called Cold Fusion, we stored some five hundred images in an online database. As a request is made, the system calls up the images and presents them in an HTML page. With no way to give Internet searchers a clue to the images in the database, we again created an HTML home page for the collection, which includes several Dublin Core metadata elements (see Appendix B) to direct searchers to the collection. As with the collection of 19th Century women writers, the user interface was designed for the navigational ease and visual comfort of everyone from the academic scholar to the casual Internet surfer.

Currently many eyes are on XML as a major contributor to the resolution of many of these problems. In one of my SGML training sessions a few years ago, the instructor remarked that XML will never replace SGML, but that SGML gives XML something to chew on. Indeed our coming online manuscript finding aids, encoded in SGML, will be modified for XML, simplifying the process of making those finding aids accessible on the Internet.

THE 21st CENTURY LIBRARY

I recall discussions in the mid-1990s in which people rushed to announce that the birth of the Internet, with its capacity for virtually infinite expansion, meant the death of the finite CD-ROM. It didn't take long for the producers of CD-ROM products to announce that the next incarnation of CD-ROMs would include hyperlinks through which users would get the latest updates to various resources by launching a concurrent Internet session. In the 21st Century library, our Internet resources must be viewed as digital extensions of our core collections and operations.

The convergence of technologies and collection formats in a single medium, the computer workstation, must not be viewed by educators and information providers as the destruction of tradition–indeed the Gutenberg Press has only recently had its five hundredth birthday, only an instant on the timeline of human history. We must view the developing information technology age as an opportunity for a new and extraordinary step–The Internet Step–in our ability truly to democratize education. So long as we mount rich resources and provide the appropriate cataloging and metadata entry and access points, our resources will educate global populations, from the Mississippi Delta to Soweto, from Appalachia to Kosovo. As they are guided to our resources, so too will they be guided to the resources and awareness of each other. True democracy in education depends not only upon those politicians and corporate leaders with the wherewithal to purchase computers; it depends also upon those in a position to gather educational materials, to produce them in an accessible manner, and to mount the cataloging guideposts that will draw audiences to those resources. Perhaps the next great challenge to the cataloging community–at least one of the great challenges–is to change the current state of Internet "cataloging." The world is becoming dependent upon Yahoo, Lycos and other search engines to determine what information exists on a subject, and therefore, the only information users will consider. So long as any and everyone can add metadata tags to their Web pages, the search engines will continue to return literally hundreds or thousands of hits on various topics, with no intelligent and easy way to narrow the search. The challenges to catalogers in the digital age are clearly more complex and of greater scale than those faced by earlier generations. But producers and educators alike truly need the assertive guidance of the cataloging community in simplifying the digital maze in which we find ourselves.

CONTENT OF THE DIGITAL SCHOMBURG

Following are current examples of rich collection materials (text, graphics, sound and video) that have been reformatted and redesigned in a variety of ways for Web presentations under our overall banner, *The Digital Schomburg*. All are accessible from the Schomburg Center's home page *(http://www. nypl.org/schomburg)*.

September 1994

Gallery of Voices and Images

(http://www.nypl.org/research/sc/scl/MULTIMED/voicegal/voicegal.html)
A collection of audio clips of historic figures such as scientist/educator George Washington Carver and social activist/educator Mary McLeod Bethune.

May 1995

Past Programs on Videotape

(http://www.nypl.org/research/sc/scl/pastevnt.html)
A listing of important videotaped academic forums and performance programs, produced in the Center's Langston Hughes Auditorium, which are available for research.

February 1997

The Schomburg Legacy: Documenting the Global Black Experience for the Twenty-First Century

(http://www.nypl.org/research/sc/WEBEXHIB/legacy/legacy2.htm)
The Schomburg Center's first Internet exhibition is drawn from a major physical exhibition of the same name.

January 1998

Gallery of Video Oral History

(http://www.nypl.org/research/sc/scl/MULTIMED/JAZZHIST/jazzhist.html)
Unveiled at the January 1998 meeting of the International Association of

Jazz Educators, this Web presentation includes twenty-one selected Quick-Time files of video clips from the Schomburg Center's *Louis Armstrong Jazz Oral History Project*, in which musician educators interviewed other prominent musicians. Using the MARC 856 field in the OPAC provides a direct hyperlink from the cataloging record to the video clip on the Website.

June 1998

African American Women Writers of the 19th Century

(http://digital.nypl.org/schomburg/writers_aa19/)
The very foundation of African American literary tradition is in this collection. Included are the first book of poetry by an African American (Phillis Wheatley's 1773 *Poems on Various Subjects, Religious and Moral*); the first book of essays by an African American (by Ann Plato in 1841); and, the first novel published by an African American in the United States (Harriet Wilson's 1859 *Our Nig*).

June 1998

Images of African Americans from the 19th Century

(http://digital.nypl.org/schomburg/images_aa19/)
As a companion piece to the digitized texts of nineteenth century African American women writers, the Schomburg Center also mounted a selection of nineteenth century photographic images of African Americans.

APPENDIX A. Dublin Core Record for The Digital Schomburg's *African American Women Writers of the 19th Century*

```
<HTML>
<HEAD>
<TITLE>NYPL Digital Schomburg African American Women Writers the 19th
Century </TITLE>
<META NAME="DC.Title" CONTENT="Digital Schomburg Images of African
Americans from the 19th Century">
<META NAME="DC.Creator" CONTENT="Pamela Ellis">
<META NAME="DC.Creator.Address" CONTENT="pellis@nypl.org">
<META NAME="DC.Subject" CONTENT="Schomburg Research Center, Center
for the Humanities, NYPL Library for the Performing Arts, African-American
Culture, Civil War, Labor, Family, 19th-Century, Autobiograpy, Amanda Smith,
Behind the Scenes, Elizabeth Keckley, Biography of an American Bondman,
Josephine Brown, Brand Plucked From the Fire, Julia A.J. Foote, Contending
Forces, Pasuline E. Hopkins, Driftwood, Olivia Ward Bush, Essays, Ann Plato,
Ethiope Lays, Priscilla Jane Thompson, From the darkness cometh the light,
Lucy A. Delany, Gleanings of Quiet Hours, Goodness of St. Rocque, Alice
Dunbar-Nelson, Hazeley Family, A.E. Johnson, History of Mary Prince, a West
Indian slave, Mary Prince, Homespun heroines, Hallie O. Brown, House of
Bondage, Octavia V. Rogers Albert, Incidents in the life of a slave girl, Harriet A.
Jacobs, Infelicia, Adah Isaacs Menken, Iola Leroy, Frances E.W. Harper, Life
and Public Services of Martin R. Delany, Frank [Frances] A.Rollin, Loew's Bridge
A Broadway Idle, Mary E. Tucker, Louisa Picquet, the Octoroon, Hiram Mattison,
Magnolia Leaves: Poems, Mary Weston Fordham, Megda, Emma Dunham Kelly,
Memoir of Old Elizabeth, a coloured woman, Anonymous, Memories of
childhood's slavery days, Annie L. Burton, Morning Glories, Josephine D. Heard
(Henderson), Narrative of Bethany Veney, slave woman, Bethany Veney,
Narrative of the life and travels of Mrs. Nancy Prince, Eloise Bibb, H. Cordelia
Ray, Phillis Wheatley, Phyllis Wheatley, Productions, Maria Stewart, Religious
Experience, Jarena Lee, Reminiscences of my life in camp, Susie King Taylor,
Rhymes from the Cumberland Effie Waller Smith, Songs From the Wayside,
Clara Ann Thompson, Songs of the Months, Effie Waller Smith, Twenty Year's
Experience of a Missionary, V.W. Broughton, Violets and Other Tales, Alice
Dunbar-Nelson, Virginia Dreams, Maggie Pogue Johnson,Work of Afro-American
Women, N.F. Mosell">
<META NAME="DC.Description" CONTENT="Published works by the African-
American women.">
<META NAME="DC.Publisher" CONTENT="The New York Public Library, Astor,
Lenox, and Tilden Foundation">
<META NAME="DC.Contributor" CONTENT="Pegasus, Inc.">
<META NAME="DC.Date" CONTENT="1998-04-03">
<META NAME="DC.Type" CONTENT="Text">
<META NAME="DC.Format" CONTENT="text/html">
<META NAME="DC.Identifier"
CONTENT="http://digital.nypl.org/schomburg/writers_aa19/">
<META NAME="DC.Language" CONTENT="English">
<META NAME="DC.Relation" CONTENT="http://www.nypl.org">
<META NAME="DC.Coverage" CONTENT="1998-">
<META NAME="DC.Rights" CONTENT="The New York Public Library">
</HEAD>
```

```
<FRAMESET ROWS= "*,350,*" framespacing=0 border=0 frameborder=0>
<FRAME SRC="blank.html" NAME="intop" frameborder=0 marginwidth=0
marginheight=0 scrolling="no" border="no">
<FRAME SRC="inmain.html" NAME="content" frameborder=0 marginwidth=0
marginheight=0 scrolling="no" border="no">
<FRAME SRC="fineprint.html" NAME="intop" frameborder=0 marginwidth=0
marginheight=0 scrolling="no" border="no">
</FRAMESET>
<NOFRAME>
<BODY BACKGROUND="images/background.gif" BGCOLOR="WHITE"
TEXT="BLACK" LINK="darkred" VLINK="indianred">
<IMG SRC="images/hinge.gif" BORDER=0 HSPACE=0 VSPACE=5>
<IMG SRC="images/headtext.gif" BORDER=0 HSPACE=25 VSPACE=5><BR>
<IMG SRC="images/women.gif" HSPACE=155 VSPACE=5><BR>
<IMG SRC="images/images.gif" HSPACE=155 VSPACE=0><BR>
<IMG SRC="images/aa19cent.gif" HSPACE=155 VSPACE=0><BR>
<IMG SRC="images/hinge.gif" BORDER=0 HSPACE=0 VSPACE=0>
</BODY>
</NOFRAME>
</HTML>
```

APPENDIX B. Dublin Core Record for The Digital Schomburg's *Images of African Americans from the 19th Century*

```
<HTML>
<HEAD>
<TITLE>NYPL Digital Schomburg Images of African Americans from the 19th
Century </TITLE>
<META NAME="DC.Title" CONTENT="Digital Schomburg Images of African
Americans from the 19th Century">
<META NAME="DC.Creator" CONTENT="Pamela Ellis">
<META NAME="DC.Creator.Address" CONTENT="pellis@nypl.org">
<META NAME="DC.Subject" CONTENT="Schomburg Research Center, Center
for the Humanities, NYPL Library for the Performing Arts,
African-American Culture, Civil War, Labor, Family, 19th-Century">
<META NAME="DC.Description" CONTENT="Visual images from the
Schomburg Center and the Center for the Humanities.">
<META NAME="DC.Publisher" CONTENT="The New York Public Library, Astor,
Lenox, and Tilden Foundation">
<META NAME="DC.Contributor" CONTENT="Pegasus, Inc.">
<META NAME="DC.Date" CONTENT="1998-04-03">
<META NAME="DC.Type" CONTENT="Text">
<META NAME="DC.Format" CONTENT="text/html">
<META NAME="DC.Identifier"
CONTENT="http://digital.nypl.org/schomburg/images_aa19/">
<META NAME="DC.Language" CONTENT="English">
<META NAME="DC.Relation" CONTENT="http://www.nypl.org">
<META NAME="DC.Coverage" CONTENT="1998-">
<META NAME="DC.Rights" CONTENT="The New York Public Library">
</HEAD>
```

```
<FRAMESET ROWS= "*,350,*" framespacing=0 border=0 frameborder=0>
<FRAME SRC="blank.html" NAME="intop" frameborder=0 marginwidth=0
marginheight=0 scrolling="no" border="no">
<FRAME SRC="inmain.html" NAME="content" frameborder=0 marginwidth=0
marginheight=0 scrolling="no" border="no">
<FRAME SRC="fineprint.html" NAME="intop" frameborder=0 marginwidth=0
marginheight=0 scrolling="no" border="no">
</FRAMESET>
<NOFRAME>
<BODY BACKGROUND="images/background.gif" BGCOLOR="WHITE"
TEXT="BLACK" LINK="darkred" VLINK="indianred">
<IMG SRC="images/hinge.gif" BORDER=0 HSPACE=0 VSPACE=5>
<IMG SRC="images/headtext.gif" BORDER=0 HSPACE=25 VSPACE=5><BR>
<IMG SRC="images/women.gif" HSPACE=155 VSPACE=5><BR>
<IMG SRC="images/images.gif" HSPACE=155 VSPACE=0><BR>
<IMG SRC="images/aa19cent.gif" HSPACE=155 VSPACE=0><BR>
<IMG SRC="images/hinge.gif" BORDER=0 HSPACE=0 VSPACE=0>
</BODY>
</NOFRAME>
</HTML>
```

GEM:
Design and Implementation
of a Metadata Project for Education

Carrie Lowe

SUMMARY. The Gateway to Educational Materials (GEM) is a project funded by the Department of Education's National Library of Education and a special project of the ERIC Clearinghouse on Information & Technology. GEM catalogs and organizes educational materials on the Internet using metadata technology. This article focuses on the development of the GEM metadata profile, a key step in the development of the GEM project. Research activities contributing to the development and the refinement of the GEM metadata profile are presented, as well as two case studies that apply the GEM metadata profile. *[Article copies available for a fee from The Haworth Document Delivery Service: 1-800-342-9678. E-mail address: <getinfo@haworthpressinc.com> Website: <http://www.HaworthPress.com>]*

KEYWORDS. Metadata, educational resources, Dublin Core, Gateway to Educational Materials, cataloging

INTRODUCTION

In its inception, the Internet was a far more organized entity. Although the interface (Gopher, FTP) was less "friendly" than the Web, information was,

Carrie Lowe, MLS, is Assistant to the Director, School of Library and Information Science, University of Washington (e-mail: calowe@u.washington.edu). Prior to this position, Ms. Lowe was GEM Project Representative, Information Institute of Syracuse.

[Haworth co-indexing entry note]: "GEM: Design and Implementation of a Metadata Project for Education." Lowe, Carrie. Co-published simultaneously in *Journal of Internet Cataloging* (The Haworth Information Press, an imprint of The Haworth Press, Inc.) Vol. 3, No. 2/3, 2000, pp. 109-126; and: *Metadata and Organizing Educational Resources on the Internet* (ed: Jane Greenberg) The Haworth Information Press, an imprint of The Haworth Press, Inc., 2000, pp. 109-126. Single or multiple copies of this article are available for a fee from The Haworth Document Delivery Service [1-800-342-9678, 9:00 a.m. - 5:00 p.m. (EST). E-mail address: getinfo@haworthpressinc.com].

© 2000 by The Haworth Press, Inc. All rights reserved.

for the most part, organized and accessible. Searching was mostly left to professionals (such as librarians) well-versed in the technology of the Internet.

Times have changed. The Web has become a tangle of resources. Traditional searching technologies (such as large robot-driven search engines) are typically unable to meet the needs of many users, especially those searching for very specific or narrowly-defined information. An example of this kind of user is a teacher, who might be searching for an educational resource designed for use with a certain grade level, or which meets state or national standards. A search engine which returns thousands of resources on a single search is not helpful for a user.

One way that this problem is solved is through the use of Internet directories, such as Yahoo (www.yahoo.com) or Looksmart (www.looksmart.com). These services bring human intelligence to the Web, employing people to categorize and organize resources, making it easier to find them. It is clear that asserting bibliographic control over Internet resources, even in the most rudimentary sense, makes it easier to find and use them. Another technique which makes it easier for users to find resources on the Internet is the use of metadata to classify items. Metadata allows catalogers to describe a resource with precision, and when searched, these metadata records act in a way similar to library catalog records. Metadata cataloging allows users to get a glimpse of the content of resources before actually connecting to the resource itself, thereby saving time and effort.

Metadata is often cited as the technological development that may someday help information professionals to make sense of the Internet. The Gateway to Educational Materials (GEM) provides an example of the challenges and successes presented by a wide-scale metadata effort; challenges for the project's developers, the collection holders, and the end-users. The GEM Project uses metadata to make resource discovery easier for educators. The Gateway, GEM's online catalog of Internet based educational materials (www.thegateway.org), allows users to search or browse for resources. GEM uses a defined set of metadata elements to organize resources. These metadata elements are based on the Dublin Core element set and were refined through research.

THE GATEWAY TO EDUCATIONAL MATERIALS PROJECT

The GEM project, a consortium effort funded by the U.S. Department of Education's National Library of Education and a special project of the ERIC Clearinghouse on Information & Technology (which also runs the AskERIC project, a well-known question and answer service for educators), seeks to make finding educational materials on the Internet faster and easier. The GEM Consortium includes both user groups and collection holders.

The GEM Project has several components. The term *GEM* (www.geminfo. org) refers to the project itself, including all of its parts. *The Gateway* (www.thegateway.org) is the catalog of educational resources, the final product of the GEM project (see Figure 1). The *GEM Profile* refers to the metadata elements which have been chosen to describe the resources in The Gateway. *GEMCat* is the software developed by the GEM research team, which is used to create and imbed metadata elements. Each of these terms will be explained and explored in more detail below.

GEM's goal is to provide easier access to the distributed collections of lesson plans, activities, and other education resources found on commercial, nonprofit and government Internet sites. Organizations join GEM as collection holders or user groups. Collection holders are trained to "catalog" their collections (create and imbed metadata), and are responsible for maintaining their collections and publicizing the project. User groups are also responsible for publicity, and provide the GEM team with feedback which it uses to improve the tools. It is important to note, however, that it is not necessary to join the GEM Consortium to use The Gateway to access educational materi-

FIGURE 1. The Gateway Homepage (www.thegateway.org)

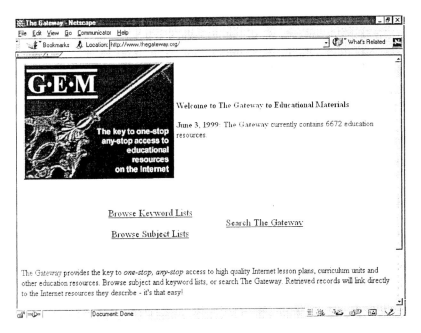

als. Consortium membership is only for user groups who would like to take part in governing the project and for collection holders who would like to make their collections available through The Gateway.

User groups and collection holders benefit from joining the GEM Consortium in several ways. For user groups, making members aware of The Gateway means helping them in their quest to pinpoint the types of educational materials they seek. User groups are also able to participate in governance activities to influence the development of GEM. For collection holders who make their educational materials available through The Gateway, this means their target audience is able to find their resources more easily. This is especially true for organizations with small collections of educational resources, which may not be well publicized, such as those belonging to museums.

There are several technologies in the GEM Workbench, which have contributed to its success (Figure 2). The first is GEMCat, the GEM metadata cataloging software. With GEMCat, catalogers create metadata records (the individual packets of metadata which describe and point to objects, something like a catalog card) for Internet resources. The metadata is imbedded in the resource itself, or saved to a separate file if necessary. GEMCat is available free of charge from the GEM Developers' Workbench; support and training materials are also available.

Whether or not GEM metadata can be imbedded directly into a resource depends largely on what type of resource it is. If the resource is an HTML document, then imbedding is possible, since metadata tags can be put into the document's header without altering the resource. However, if it is a visual or sound resource, then it may not be possible to imbed metadata without chang-

FIGURE 2. GEM Project Tools

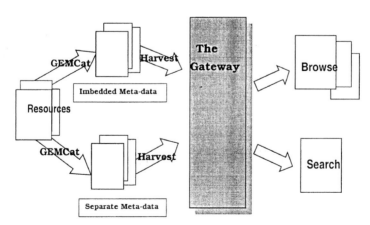

ing it in some way. In this case, is it necessary to create a separate metadata record which points to the resource.

After the metadata is imbedded or saved to a separate file, the harvest program is run to gather and compile each metadata record at a particular site and add the list to The Gateway. This step in the process is essential; harvest makes a copy only of the metadata record, not of the resource (lesson plan, curriculum unit) itself. Harvest collects all of the GEM records together at a central location, forming The Gateway.

The third GEM tool is Browse Builder. Browse Builder uses the metadata records collected by the harvest program to create simple HTML pages, which are the individual records in The Gateway (Figure 3). Browse Builder also creates the Subject and Keyword browse environments of The Gateway. Users of The Gateway can search for educational materials to meet their needs using the PL Web searching software, or they can browse The Gateway by keyword or subject.

The Internet is host to a growing number of large-scale information resources, including those providing access to educational resources. Many of these projects make HTML resources available through a database, which makes them easier for the Webmaster to modify and the user to retrieve.

FIGURE 3. An Example of a GEM Record

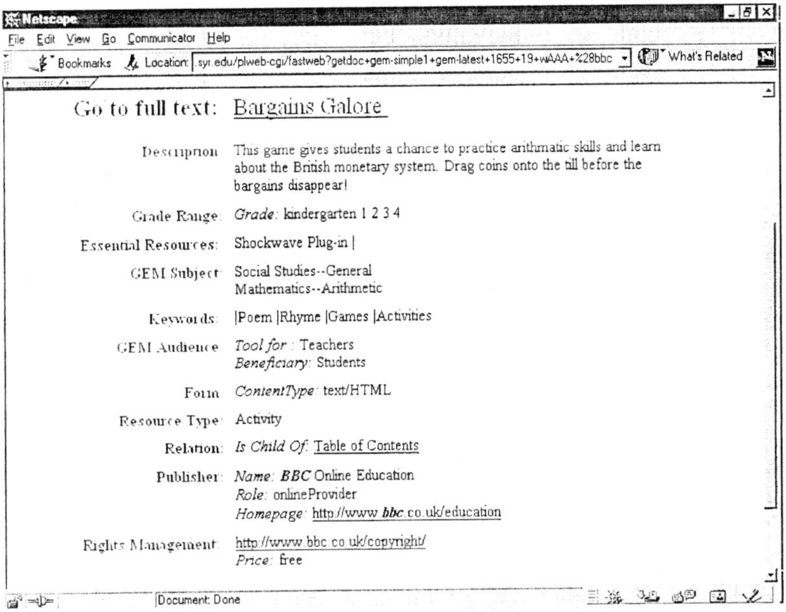

Organizations with collections of resources housed in a database who wish to make their resources available through The Gateway do not need to catalog each item individually using GEMCat. The first step in adding these resources to The Gateway is to map the database's fields to the GEM element set. After the fields are mapped, programmers with the collection holder organization write a script for the database which allows it to directly output GEM metadata records, which are then harvested and added to The Gateway. This preliminary work allows for automatic cataloging of very large collections.

One aspect of GEM that sets it apart from similar projects is the emphasis on training and support. The GEM team includes training specialists who conduct training sessions with the catalogers of collection holders to help them prepare to catalog efficiently using GEMCat. GEM has also prepared training materials which are available online. Users of The Gateway and collection holders have access to a toll-free support line, as well, which they can use to get help with any part of the GEM Project.

THE IMPORTANCE OF METADATA

Metadata is structured information that describes, manages, and organizes Internet resources. The easiest way to understand this concept is to think about a library catalog card. The card describes a resource (it may be a book, videotape, or CD), listing its title, author, location, and other information. Catalog cards can then be filed, and used to locate resources throughout the library. Metadata works much the same way. It can be used to describe an object on the Internet (such as an HTML document), and much like in a card catalog, can be used to pinpoint information on the Internet (Lowe, 1999).

Not all metadata is the same. Metadata description lies upon a continuum, ranging from the very detailed to the simple and bare. One example of highly detailed metadata is MARC (MAchine Readable Catalog). MARC allows catalogers to create a complex and complete portrait of an item. Cataloging in MARC requires trained professionals who are familiar with the scheme's standards and syntax. Miller (1996) describes MARC as "expert" metadata, requiring special knowledge to create and use.

Metadata can also be simple. Many Internet search engines, including the extremely popular AltaVista, are able to read metadata tags that some Web authors include in their resources. These metadata tags, which are imbedded into the header of the document, give only a partial portrait of the document they describe. Many search engines recognize the KEYWORDS metadata tag, and can use these keywords to rank a search.

In order to organize the vast Internet, a new approach to metadata was needed. Clearly, the overly simplistic approach to cataloging taken by many search engines would not give a complete picture of the document being described. Conversely, it is unreasonable to expect Web authors untrained in cataloging to use a complex approach like MARC. What was needed was a metadata cataloging scheme that would allow untrained catalogers to create useful cataloging records for an endless variety of documents. Besides being a more useful tool for authors and catalogers of Web documents, a new metadata approach would also need to provide enough information to be useful for people searching for information; it would need to allow them to access enough information about a document to make an informed decision about whether or not they should retrieve the item.

The solution to the problem of metadata on the Internet arrived in the form of a fifteen element set known as Dublin Core. Says Clarke (1997), "The Dublin Core's purpose is to enable searching in a more sophisticated manner than mere free-text indexing and search engines can support, without requiring professional cataloging effort to be invested." Dublin Core was created at the 1995 OCLC/NCSA Metadata Workshop by a group of interested stakeholders, and subsequent Dublin Core meetings have refined and further developed the element set.

The Dublin Core was designed to be useful for "document like objects" from nearly any subject area (Heery, 1996). The Dublin Core allows for materials of a range of formats (PDF files, sound files, HTML documents); it is also general enough to accommodate nearly any intellectual topic. The Dublin Core is:

- Coverage: The spatial and/or temporal characteristics of the resource
- Creator/Author: The person or organization responsible for the resource's content
- Date: The date the resource was made available
- Description: A description of the resource's content
- Format: The format of the resource
- Identifier: The resource's unique identifier
- Language: Language of the resource
- Contributors: Other contributors to the resource's content
- Publisher: The person or entity responsible for making the resource available
- Relation: The relationship of a given resource to other resources
- Resource Type: The category of the resource
- Rights Management: Copyright or restriction information
- Source: Identifies a resource from which a given resource was derived
- Subject: The topic of the resource
- Title: The resource's name, as specified by the creator

The Dublin Core has been identified as the emerging resource description standard for the Internet. This made it an excellent starting place for the GEM Project. GEM uses the Dublin Core as the foundation for its metadata set.

The Dublin Core itself is too general to describe resources in many subject areas, including education, in a useful way. Miller (1996) writes:

> The [fifteen] elements of the Dublin Core are not capable of describing all eventualities. If the core element set were extended to attempt this, it would rapidly become large and unwieldy, and ultimately one of the incomprehensibly complex metadata schemes that Dublin Core was created to avoid.

This represented a problem for the creators of Dublin Core. They needed to find a way to allow Dublin Core to adequately describe resources in a variety of subject areas, while retaining its essential simplicity.

The solution to this problem came in the form of the Canberra Qualifiers, released after a subsequent Dublin Core meeting. The Canberra Qualifiers allow other elements to be added to the core elements, and its existing elements to be expanded to better describe information resources from various subject areas (Sutton, in press). The GEM Project utilized the flexibility added to the Dublin Core through the Canberra Qualifiers in the creation of its element set. GEM added eight metadata elements to the Dublin Core which are tailored to the information needs of teachers. The elements include description elements, evaluative elements, and a meta-metadata element (Sutton, in press). The five descriptive elements include information which is important to educators in finding and evaluating educational resources, but is not included in Dublin Core. The descriptive elements are:

- *Audience.* Audience is a controlled-vocabulary element. There are two different dimensions of Audience–first, for whom is the resource created? Second, who is the ultimate beneficiary of the resource? A lesson plan, for instance, was created for teaching professionals, but the ultimate beneficiaries are the students. Audience gives a multi-dimensional description of the author's intention when creating the resource.
- *Duration.* This is an important piece of information for educators when they are deciding whether or not to use a resource. This free-text element allows catalogers to specify how much time to allot to use the resource. For instance, a simple lesson might have a Duration of "30 minutes," whereas a longer unit might take "10 one-hour class sessions."
- *Essential Resources.* Often, educational resources require special equipment. This can range from scissors and glue to microscopes and prepared slides. The Essential Resources element can help an educator decide whether or not they can use a particular resource.
- *Grade Level.* Grade level is a controlled-vocabulary element. It describes the grade or range of grades of students with which the resource works best.

- *Pedagogy.* Pedagogy allows the cataloger to describe teaching methods and student groupings which the resource necessitates. This is a controlled-vocabulary element.

While the GEM description elements fill in the gaps existing in Dublin Core for educational information, the evaluation elements add another dimension to cataloging Internet resources.

- *Quality Indicators.* The Quality Indicators element allows a collection holder to include evaluative information about a resource in its metadata record. GEM does not evaluate the resources in The Gateway; instead, GEM encourages collection holders to employ an independent third party to evaluate its resources. The evaluation scheme used can be built into the GEMCat cataloging software.
- *Academic Standards.* Many states are implementing standards as a way to increase accountability in schools. The Academic Standards element allows catalogers to map resources to referenced standards, making it easier for educators to find resources that fulfill a given standard.

The final GEM element is a meta-metadata element. This element gives overview information about the metadata itself. This element answers what some believe to be a shortcoming in the Dublin Core (Clarke, 1997). The element, *Cataloging Agency,* tells the user who created the metadata that they are reading. This element builds in accountability; it allows users to make a decision about whether or not they consider the metadata to be trustworthy or accurate. By combining the Dublin Core element set and the GEM elements, a tool is created which allows catalogers to create a complete description of an educational resource on the Internet–the GEM metadata profile.

RESEARCH FOUNDATIONS OF GEM

From its genesis, GEM has been a project grounded in research. The GEM elements that were added to the Dublin Core element set were chosen as a result of research conducted by the GEM team. In order to create a useful Internet resource for educators, several basic questions needed to be answered. These were (Small et al., in press):

- In general, what types of educational resources currently may be found on the Internet?
- What types of resources do educators find most useful for instructional design?

- What types of information are included in Internet-based educational resources and which types are essential for instructional design?
- Are there unique characteristics of information-seeking patterns and behaviors of educators searching for instructional design information?

These questions were explored in three different research studies. The first sought to determine the scope of educational materials that could be found on the Internet. The second explored how educators search for relevant educational materials. The third identified the types of information found in educational materials, and which of these educators consider the most important.

To explore the question of what types of educational resources are available on the Internet, the research team began with a sample of 95 teaching resources. A content analysis was then performed on these resources to identify the types of educational materials found on the Internet, and the information elements they contain. Despite the small sample size, the results of this study gave the researchers a general idea of the scope of educational materials on the Internet. The researchers found that 76% of the teaching resources were *lesson plans*, 23% of the resources were classified as *unit plans*, and 1% were *activities*. Although the researchers realized that this sample did not represent the full scope of educational materials on the Internet, lesson plans appear to be one of the most common types of instructional materials available. This gave the researchers an idea of how to describe the types of educational materials available on the Internet.

Identifying the information elements of the sample of Internet-based education resources was an important part of the development of the GEM project. Before it is possible to classify resources by the information contained within them, the kinds of information present within them must be known. This content analysis allowed the researchers to get a picture of the types of information found in educational resources on a wider scale.

To explore the information needs of teachers and the ways they satisfy those needs, the researchers turned to one of the most widely-used sources of educational information–the AskERIC question and answer service for teachers. AskERIC is the preeminent source of educational information on the Internet; on average, it receives over 900 questions per week. AskERIC provided the researchers with a way to unobtrusively observe the information-seeking behaviors of teachers.

The AskERIC service receives questions via e-mail from teachers looking for educational information. The researchers performed a content analysis of 161 AskERIC questions to get an idea of the information needs of K-12 educators. The research revealed that the queries posted by teachers contained two different types of information; *asked-for* information and *known* information (Small et al., in press). The content analysis revealed that the most frequently asked-for information is *resource type*, with lesson plans being the most frequently sought in that category (33% of the time). The most frequently known elements were *subject area*, *grade*, and *topic*. Grade appeared as both a range and as a specific level. This information was extremely significant to the GEM research team, since it informed them that, to meet the information needs of teachers, GEM would have to provide access to lesson plans.

The way that users of the AskERIC service formulate their questions (the pieces of information that they consider important in meeting their query) gives an indication of the way that they search for information in general. Teachers feel that the most important pieces of information they have in satisfying their need are resource type, subject area, grade, and topic. This information contributed directly to the creation of the GEM metadata elements.

The GEM team also gathered information by interviewing educators. These consultations occurred in two phases; the first, a series of semi-structured interviews, and the second, an on-line questionnaire. Five educators were interviewed about their information-seeking strategies. They were asked about the ways that they search the Internet, the resources that they rely upon online, the elements within resources which they consider to be most important, and whether the list of elements produced by the content analysis are complete.

The results of the interviews were also used to develop an online questionnaire for AskERIC users. The questionnaire consisted of 32 items, with 21 multiple choice and Likert scales (questions that ask subjects to evaluate an item on a sliding scale) and 11 open-ended questions. The questions covered many of the same topics as the interviews and content analyses: demographic information, Internet access, preferred sources of information for planning curriculum, information search processes, and important elements of lesson-planning resources.

The questionnaire was e-mailed to a sample of people who had used the AskERIC service in a particular three-month period. AskERIC users were chosen because they are likely to be involved in some way with K-12 education, and are also somewhat familiar with technology. Of the 2,135 people questioned, 260 were returned and judged by the research team to be valid (23 were found to be invalid because the respondent was not a K12 educator).

The results of the questionnaire create an interesting portrait of educators in the information age. Teachers reported that they most often used *non-human channels* (databases, textbooks, Internet resources, magazines) for lesson planning, followed by *human channels* (librarians, colleagues, family and friends). Teachers rely on *group forums* (bulletin boards, listservs, workshops) less often than other sources. It is important to remember that these results may not give an accurate picture of the use of technology by K-12 teachers, since the recipients of this questionnaire were chosen through their use of AskERIC, an online service.

The majority of the respondents reported experiencing a moderate degree of difficulty in the Internet search process. Math/science and social studies instructors experience the greatest ease in their search experiences, while pre-K teachers have the most trouble. Teachers in all subject areas were able to find at least some of what they were looking for on the Internet, with social studies teachers experiencing the greatest success.

The final section of the questionnaire asked teachers for feedback on the metadata elements selected through the content analysis. Respondents replied that the elements they consider to be most important when they are evaluating a resource are *topic* and *subject*, with *author description* and *publisher* considered the least important (Small et al., in press). The researchers used the ranking of metadata elements as a guideline in creating the GEM metadata profile. Many of the elements in the list correspond to Dublin core elements; those that do not became the GEM elements which were added to the Dublin Core to enable it to better describe educational materials.

Besides being the guiding force behind the creation of the GEM meta-profile, the preliminary research also helped the GEM team to design user-friendly interfaces. The Gateway currently has one simple search interface; through the research, the GEM team determined that it is most important to allow users to search using free-text terms and grade level. The simple search interface has so far produced satisfactory results. In addition to the simple search interface, The Gateway also allows users to browse the collection by keyword and subject.

CASE STUDY: ED'S OASIS

Ed's Oasis (http://www.edsoasis.org) is an educational Website based in California. ED's Oasis is funded by AT&T's Education Foundation, and sponsored by the California Instructional Technology Clearinghouse. According to the Ed's Oasis Website, the mission of the organization is "To help teachers use the Internet as an integral tool for teaching and learning" (http://www.edsoasis.org/About.html). Ed's Oasis accomplishes this through the provision of excellent resources, such as links to high-quality Websites and stories of teachers successfully using information technology in the classroom. Ed's Oasis also encourages communication between teachers all over the world: they run an information and technology mailing list, and also run a mentor program which gives expert teachers the opportunity to provide leadership to teachers just beginning to use technology in the classroom. Through its MasterSearch contest, Ed's Oasis gives teachers an opportunity to compete in a contest to choose the best Web-based lesson plans, which are then published on the Website.

The first step toward GEM Consortium membership is application; user groups and collection holders must submit the online application form which provides the GEM team with contact information and directs them to resources to be evaluated. In February of 1999, GEM contacted Terrie Gray, Director of Ed's Oasis, and invited the organization to apply to the GEM Consortium. After asking a few questions about the cataloging process, Terrie submitted the application.

GEM evaluates all collections submitted for inclusion in The Gateway. The evaluation criteria is based upon the roles and responsibilities for GEM members, as outlined in the GEM Consortium document (http://www.geminfo. org/Participation/gov.html). The evaluation form (Appendix A) allows the GEM team to get a sense of the collection, from its size to its authoritativeness. GEM does not assess resources for quality; instead, it insures that collections avoid statements of bias and demonstrate authoritativeness.

After Ed's Oasis was accepted into the GEM Consortium, the next step was to plan for cataloging. Since Ed's Oasis's resources are individual resources (rather than pages created dynamically through a database), it was necessary to catalog the resources individually. As a special service to new Consortium members, GEM agreed to do the introductory cataloging for Ed's Oasis. A style sheet (Appendix B) which was approved by Ed's Oasis was created for their 65 resources.

Once the resources were cataloged by the GEM team, the metadata records were shipped to Ed's Oasis. In order for the resources to appear in The Gateway, the metadata records had to be imbedded in the HTML of the resources. This is essential for metadata integrity. If the metadata is not kept within the document and is instead saved as a separate file pointing to the resource, any location change will not be reflected in the GEM metadata records. This means that users attempting to access the resource through The Gateway will be unable to do so. Ed's Oasis promptly added the metadata records to their resources. Once this process was complete, GEM was able to run harvest on the Ed's Oasis site. Ed's Oasis indicated to GEM the directories in which harvest should be run, and at what directory level it should search to capture the all of the metadata records. The harvest program made a copy of the metadata on the Ed's Oasis site and added those records to The Gateway.

Ed's Oasis and GEM have enjoyed a very successful relationship. Both have the goal of providing teachers with quality educational resources, which Ed's Oasis achieves through creating excellent content, and GEM achieves by simplifying access for a broad audience. Terrie Gray has reported that working with GEM was a positive experience:

First of all, I'd like to say it is an honor to have resources from our site included in GEM! Every step of the process was well-explained, and I really had to do very little. Everyone who has contacted me from GEM *has* been a gem. . . . very positive, congratulatory, and helpful. Working with them made all of us at Ed's Oasis feel special.

CASE STUDY: UTAH EDUCATION NETWORK

The Utah Education Network (UEN) is an ambitious project of the Utah State Office of Education, the Utah State Office of Higher Education, schools and universities, and several other organizations. UEN (www.uen.org) is a comprehensive educational resource for educators and students in the state of Utah. It provides online instruction, access to resources, and communication channels so that educators can discuss and share ideas. The UEN states their goal as to:

Provide the citizens of Utah access to the highest quality, most effective instructional experiences, administrative support services, library services, student services, and teacher resources regardless of location or time. These services will be delivered through seamless, technology rich, communications networks linking schools, world information networks, business, industry, and homes (http://www.uen.org/uen/about.cgi).

One essential component of UEN is UtahLink, which provides access to educational resources, such as a large database of lesson plans which map to Utah's state education standards. After an initial meeting at a conference, UEN and GEM staff decided to pursue a relationship which would include cataloging the UtahLink resources for inclusion in The Gateway.

UtahLink is a very large database-driven collection. The resources are housed in a Sybase database. The first step in making the resources GEM compliant was to match their database fields with the GEM metadata elements. UtahLink supplied GEM with their database fields, so that GEM could match them up with the appropriate elements and make recommendations for adding elements. An example of a recommendation that was made to UtahLink relates to the element Keywords. Although Keywords is not a required element in the GEM profile, The Gateway indexes metadata records by Keyword. This means that any records missing Keywords will not be included in the index. UtahLink included Keywords in some of their resources, but after a discussion about the importance of Keywords with members of the GEM team, they agreed to add them to the database. Once the database fields were aligned with the GEM metadata elements, Utah Education Network's programmers modified their single lesson plan template by adding the GEM meta tags and corresponding database queries. This process ensured that all new and existing lesson plans using that template output GEM metadata tags automatically. After completing this task, the programmers supplied GEM with a sample record to check for accuracy. The final step in cataloging the UtahLink resources was running the metadata harvesting program. It was able to move efficiently through the database, and the process resulted in the metadata records of nearly 800 UtahLink resources being added to The Gateway.

The UtahLink resources demonstrate the flexibility of the GEM profile and its technical tools. The GEM records for the UtahLink resources are rich and complete, particularly so in that they include the Utah State Education Standard to which they are aligned. This is an excellent way for teachers to get an immediate sense of the lesson and how it fits in to their curriculum. UtahLink is, in many ways, the future of GEM; a growing number of collections of educational materials on the Internet are including standards–both educational and national–and in the future, users of The Gateway will be able to search by educational standard.

CONCLUSIONS

The Gateway to Educational Materials Project is, collection by collection, taming the Internet for teachers. This ambitious goal is achieved through the creation of standards and the development of technical tools to implement those standards. As helpful as GEM might be for users seeking educational information, it does not to address information in other disciplines. In the din of many conversations about metadata on the Internet, the name Dublin Core is heard over and over again. Dublin Core provides the kind of flexible, extensible framework necessary to describe the broad range of information resources on the Internet. The GEM project provides a working example of the promise that metadata holds–it makes thousands of educational resources from many different collections available and easily retrievable. GEM proves that metadata–Dublin Core metadata–can deliver on its promise to make document retrieval easier and more efficient for users.

Metadata promises to be the technology capable of untangling an Internet that many users find bewildering. Whether or not organizations and individuals producing resources choose to employ metadata to make their documents more retrievable is their own choice; some doubt the ease of convincing them to do so, but most agree that metadata is necessary to make the Web usable.

GEM continues to make improvements on the project infrastructure and its product, The Gateway. Users are not always comfortable with the intermediate step that the GEM record represents; GEM continues to work on the interface of The Gateway, in an effort to make it as user-friendly as possible. Dialogue between users and developers in the form of the project's e-mail account, a feedback form, and usability tests allow users to submit their own ideas for improvement.

In the next year, the World Wide Web will experience another period of exponential growth. As the number of Web resources increases, it will be increasingly difficult for users to find what they need. GEM will also continue to grow over the next year; we expect the number of resources in The Gateway to double in year three. The strengths of metadata will ensure that it will remain easy to find resources in The Gateway.

WORKS CITED

Clarke, R. (1997). *Beyond the Dublin Core: Rich Meta-Data and Convenience-of-Use Are Compatible After All.* Consulted January 5, 1999. Available: http://www.anu.edu.au/people/Roger.Clarke/II/DublinCore.html.

Heery, R. (1996). "Review of Metadata Formats." *Program* 30(4): 345-373.

Lowe, C. (1999). "The Gateway to Educational Materials: Meeting the Needs of Teachers in the Information Age." *Meridian: A Middle School Computer Technology Journal.* Available: http://www.ncsu.edu/meridian/.

Miller, P. (1996). *Metadata for the Masses.* Consulted January 6, 1999. Available: http://www.ariadne.as.uk/issue5/metadata-masses/.

Small, Ruth et al. (1998). "Information-Seeking for Instructional Design: An Exploratory Study." *Journal of Research of Computing in Education* 31(2).

Sutton, Stuart (in press). "Conceptual Design and Deployment of a Metadata Framework for Educational Resources on the Internet." *Journal of the American Society for Information Science.*

APPENDIX A

Evaluation for Collection Holders Membership:

Authoritativeness/Quality:

Does the collection have institutional support or sponsorship?   Yes   No

Comments: _____

Are the materials educational?   Yes   No

Comments: _____

Do the materials avoid statements of bias and stereotyping concerning women and ethnic groups?   Yes   No

Comments: _____

Does the site apply stated standards for authoritativeness and quality?   Yes   No

Comments _____

Size/Significance

What is the size of the collection?   _____

Comments: _____

Is the collection database driven?   Yes   No

Comments: _____

Do the materials correspond to state or national standards?   Yes   No

Comments: _____

Cost/Availability

Cost of the resource:

Free   Partially free   Fee

Comments: _____

Accessibility:

Registration required   Not online

Comments: _____

===

GEM Administrative Group Recommendation

Accept

Do Not Accept

Reason: _____

APPENDIX B

Cataloging Lesson Plans Using GEMCat
Ed's Oasis Style Sheet

Title: Enter the title as it appears on the document.

GEM Subject: Choose at least one Level One combined with a Level Two.

Keyword: Proper nouns and words that describe the subject of the resource, but are not in the controlled subject vocabulary, are good choices for keywords. Keywords are meant to supplement the subjects.

Description: Cut and paste the description submitted by the creator(s). Edit as necessary. Use complete sentences and proper English.

Standards: Fill in information for standards as needed.

Resource Type: Lesson plan, Primary Source

Grade Levels: Select those that apply.

Audience: **A tool for whom?** Teachers
Who is the ultimate beneficiary? Students, Teachers

Identifier: **SID:** EdsOasis

Rights: **Cost:** Free

Format: Text/HTML or Text/PDF (1 resource)

Cataloging Agency: **Name: GEM**
Email: geminfo@geminfo.org
URL: http://www.geminfo.org

Online Provider: **Organization/Person Name:** ED's Oasis
URL: http://www.edsoasis.org/

Instructions: **Catalog the 43 lesson plans located at**:
http://www.edsoasis.org/TGuild/Lessons/TGuildTOC.htrnl

Catalog the 20 Spotlight on Effective Practice Teacher Interviews (primary source) located at:
http://www.edsoasis.org/Spotlight/Spotlight.html

Catalog the 8 Articles and Handouts (primary source) located at (only catalog the ones on the site, not ones that link off the site): http://www.edsoasis.org/Treasure/treasTa.html
Save within the resource and also as a separate file.

Metadata for a Digital Library of Educational Resources

Jane Greenberg

Karen Fullerton

Edie Rasmussen

SUMMARY. PEN-DOR (the Pennsylvania Education Digital Object Repository) is a digital library providing access to atomic Web-based objects for lesson plan construction, a set of fully constructed lesson plans, and curriculum standards for the state of Pennsylvania. PEN-DOR supports lesson plan construction and enhancement activities. Through a community-based memory documentation process, PEN-DOR plans to provide access to the collective experience of teachers, students, and public school administrators working with the repository's resources. The diverse activities supported by PEN-DOR present a series of challenges in organizing and accessing Web-based objects, lesson plans, and other PEN-DOR re-

---

Jane Greenberg is Assistant Professor, School of Information Sciences, University of North Carolina at Chapel Hill.

Karen Fullerton is a Consultant for Celeron Consultants.

Edie Rasmussen is Professor, School of Information Sciences, University of Pittsburgh.

The following PEN-DOR team members have played significant roles in metadata development and implementation within the context of the larger PEN-DOR project: Darin L. Stewart, Project Director and Principal Architect, who is currently a Senior Systems Architect/Senior Software Engineer at Advanced Technologies and Architectures; Maureen W. McClure, Director of the GINIE (Global Information Network in Education) project, Associate Professor, Department of Administrative and Policy Studies, and Senior Associate with the International Institute for Studies in Education (IISE), School of Education, University of Pittsburgh; and Sujata Banerjee, Associate Professor, School of Information Sciences, University of Pittsburgh.

[Haworth co-indexing entry note]: "Metadata for a Digital Library of Educational Resources." Greenberg, Jane, Karen Fullerton, and Edie Rasmussen. Co-published simultaneously in *Journal of Internet Cataloging* (The Haworth Information Press, an imprint of The Haworth Press, Inc.) Vol. 3, No. 2/3, 2000, pp. 127-144; and: *Metadata and Organizing Educational Resources on the Internet* (ed: Jane Greenberg) The Haworth Information Press, an imprint of The Haworth Press, Inc., 2000, pp. 127-144. Single or multiple copies of this article are available for a fee from The Haworth Document Delivery Service [1-800-342-9678, 9:00 a.m. - 5:00 p.m. (EST). E-mail address: getinfo@haworthpressinc.com].

© 2000 by The Haworth Press, Inc. All rights reserved.

sources for use. This article focuses on the development and implementation of the PEN-DOR metadata scheme, and discusses a number of metadata-related challenges that have emerged as a result of the project. *[Article copies available for a fee from The Haworth Document Delivery Service: 1-800-342-9678. E-mail address: <getinfo@haworthpressinc.com> Website: <http://www.HaworthPress.com>]*

KEYWORDS. Metadata, digital library, educational resources, Internet

INTRODUCTION

Today, the information and library science literature is full of discussions about planning, implementing, testing, and enhancing digital library projects. By the same token, education literature, primarily that with a K-12 focus, regularly carries lead articles and special features that emphasize the need to successfully incorporate computer-based technology into educational curricula. Related to these two nodes of progress (the digital library and computer-based educational technology) is the development of a number of educationally focused digital library projects functioning as technologically advanced curriculum development tools and innovative centers of student learning–offering, in both cases, a greater diversity of resources and a greater degree of access than the traditional library.

Among some of the digital library projects that help define this framework are the American Memory: Historical Collection for the Digital Library at the Library of Congress, which focuses on American history;[1] the University of Michigan's Digital Library, which focuses on earth and space sciences and supports middle school and high school science education;[2] and the Informedia Digital Video Library at Carnegie Mellon University, which focuses on biology, math, and physics, and also supports high school science education.[3] PEN-DOR, the digital library discussed in this article, addresses general educational curriculum needs for K-12 and also focuses on local and regional history for the state of Pennsylvania.[4]

The success of any educationally-focused digital library project relies heavily on instructors' and students' willingness to work with a new tool, effective project management, and available state-of-the art technology–not only in terms of computers, but classroom wiring, space, lighting, and other structural features that help provide an environment that is conducive to working with digital resources. In addition to these factors is the need for a metadata scheme that facilitates resource discovery and use of the objects, lesson plans, and other resources residing in the digital library.

As one may expect, there are a number of parallels between the evolving education-oriented digital library and the traditional school library or media center. In fact, even when servicing the best teachers–with an excellent project management team and a state-of-the art structural setup, the traditional education-based library (or any library for that matter) requires an effective metadata system, or multiple-metadata systems, in order to function. In other words, a consistent and stable metadata scheme is a critical component of a traditional library operation, and is also revealed as a necessary component of a digital library.

Along these lines, defining and implementing a suitable metadata scheme has been a central consideration for PEN-DOR. This article begins by introducing PEN-DOR and providing an overview of general topic of metadata and educational-based metadata. The article then focuses on PEN-DOR's metadata initiative. Finally, the article addresses a number of metadata-related challenges that have emerged as a result of the project.

THE PEN-DOR PROJECT

The Pennsylvania Education Network Digital Object Repository (PEN-DOR) system is a digital library developed by the University of Pittsburgh School of Information Sciences and School of Education to serve the Pennsylvania Education System and its 120,000 educators and their students. PEN-DOR is a component of a much larger education technology endeavor funded by the state of Pennsylvania, Link-to-Learn (L2L), which has as its goal the establishment of a statewide network, linking every Pennsylvania education facility to every other, the Internet, and the world at large.

PEN-DOR is both a digital library and an authoring environment, so that teachers can search for images, text and video on a topic in their curriculum, and use the materials they find to build a project for use with their students. It is hoped that teachers will also contribute their own digital resources for use by others. Teachers can also find and use projects submitted by other teachers, and document their use by contributing to a community memory associated with that project. Completed lesson plans are also included in the repository for teachers' use. Important resources which cannot be added to the repository because of copyright restrictions are linked to the site via an "educational resources" page, as are administrative resources and information on Pennsylvania's educational standards.

PEN-DOR contains a growing number of atomic objects, ranging from textual documents, graphic images, moving image clips, and sound pieces to multi-media lesson plans composed of a variety of objects. PEN-DOR began to actively capture Web-based atomic objects during the summer of 1998, when two school librarians (media specialists) and approximately 20 school teachers, representing a variety of subject disciplines and Pittsburgh area schools, participated in a number of object collecting sessions at the University of Pittsburgh. During these sessions, participants learned how to capture and upload atomic objects into the PEN-DOR database.

In an effort to seed the repository, PEN-DOR also obtained a number of educational-based learning collections from various other educational digital library and electronic resource initiatives. PEN-DOR's subject collection strengths from this activity include coverage of the planetary science as a result of objects obtained from the NASA; U.S. history as a result of objects/film clips obtained from the Baltimore Learning Community,[5] and maps and data about the countries of the world from the CIA World Factbook.[6] PEN-DOR also contains a collection of over 1,000 elementary and middle school lesson plans that were developed via the Link-2-Learn Initiative.[7] Lesson plans consist of three segments:

- *plans* that assist educators in structuring and organizing a lesson;
- *activity sheets* that guide students in working through an activity, which can also be used as online or as a printed handout; and
- *branching out tips* that direct instructors to other Web-based resources, which can be integrated into the classroom learning environment.

The lesson plan segmentation permits teachers to present material at a variety of depth levels, and provides a number of ways that students can learn via Web-based technology (e.g., as a group, an individual, and through various levels of connectivity with Web resources). The Link-2-Learn lesson plans available via PEN-DOR cover a range of subjects. The PEN-DOR metadata scheme is flexible enough to support access to both atomic objects and lesson plans, and also supports lesson plan enhancement and modification activities.

METADATA

Metadata in the networked world is "structured data about data."[8] Metadata is significant because it supports both the discovery and the use of objects and lesson plans (which are essentially objects in the broader sense). Metadata elements such as "creator," "title," or "subject" support discovery, and metadata elements such as "platform requirements," "rights use," or "grade level" support object or lesson plan use. Metadata helps to establish the parameters of distinct digital library environments by adding value through descriptive activities in order to assist search engines and users in discriminating, selecting and using resources. Metadata may be viewed as a quality control device in that it helps to filter non-relevant materials and produce retrieval results that have more precision than the results generally obtained via most of today's commercial Web search engines and indexes.[9]

With the exponential growth of the Internet, particularly the Web, members of various communities with a vested interest networked resource discovery have developed metadata standards. Among one of the most often noted metadata schemes is the Dublin Core, which is a general standard comprised of 15 core elements that can be used to describe resources in any community.[10] The goal of the Dublin Core standard is to support the creation of a quality metadata record that exists somewhere between the sophisticated catalog records found in library catalogs and the type of data-extracted records produced with most Web search engines.[11] The Dublin Core has served as a foundation and stimulus for the development of metadata standards that support the unique descriptive needs of specialized information communities. Examples of specialized metadata standards include the Encoded Archival Description (EAD)[12] for archival materials and Government Information Locator Service (GILS)[13] for government documents.

METADATA FOR EDUCATIONAL RESOURCES

Metadata schemes designed specifically for educational resources in the pre-digital environment were mainly limited to institutional and consortium level implementation. One reason for this is that historically educators have worked with an array of media formats, such as maps, kits, games, filmstrips, and so forth. Traditional cataloging methods, although accommodating on a basic level, are not suited for providing access to the noted variety of formats and their specified pedagogical placements. Over the course of time, however, librarians and teachers have worked together and devised effective organization systems to service both teachers and students.

Today, even in this digital era, it's *not* uncommon to find a local card catalog, printed or computer generated list, logbook, or other locally created metadata system that describes an item and identifies its designated location in a school media center or other type of repository. While these local developments have worked within selected environments, they have seldom supported aspects of interoperability and data exchange that are found with metadata structures and content standards used for cataloging monographs, serials, and other traditional library materials.

MAchine Readable Cataloging (MARC), developed initially for printing library catalog cards for books, but now the underlying communication standard in most online public access catalogs (OPACs) and bibliographic utilities, has provided school media specialists and users of these collections with a standardized metadata scheme. The development of the Curriculum-Enhanced MARC format (CE-MARC)[14] has resulted in the implementation of the following MARC fields to assist with the cataloging of educational resources: MARC field 520 "Summary Note," MARC field 521, "Target

Audience," MARC field 526, "Study Program," and MARC field 658, "Curriculum Objective."

The CE-MARC format, combined with the introduction of MARC field 856, "Electronic Location and Access," permits networked educational resources to be directly accessible in the Web-based OPAC environment. CE-MARC fosters collocation of educational resources with other educational and general library materials that have been cataloged in a system where MARC is the underlying communication format. Overall, the use of MARC for educational resources supports interoperability, data exchange, and other benefits that have not always been within the province of custodial activities surrounding educational resources.

Coinciding with the development of educational digital libraries has been the development of a number of metadata schemes to specifically support resource discovery and use of educational resources in the networked environment. Two of the more popular and widely deployed educational-based metadata standards are the Gateway to Educational Materials (GEM)[15] and the EDUCAUSE Instructional Management Systems (IMS) schemes.[16] Both of these metadata systems are a part of larger projects that focus on Web-based education and technology, and are supported by teams of persons with expertise in the areas of education in general, educational-technology, text-encoding, and resource discovery and description. Extensive efforts have taken place recently to harmonize the GEM and IMS metadata standard.[17] While the GEM and IMS standards are among the most widely deployed, there are a host of other metadata standards developed for educational resources— a number of which are discussed in other articles in this volume. Many of these other schemes work with or build on the GEM or IMS schemes. The PEN-DOR metadata scheme is based on the GEM scheme.

DEVELOPING THE PEN-DOR SCHEME

Developing the PEN-DOR metadata scheme involves three main steps: (1) scheme research and evaluation; (2) metadata design; and (3) advisory board feedback.

Scheme Research and Evaluation

The first step in designing the PEN-DOR metadata scheme involved research on and an evaluation of existing educational resource-related metadata schemes. The PEN-DOR team wanted to avoid the "recreating the wheel" syndrome that can easily take place when a thorough investigation is not conducted before embarking on this type of project. Team members did not want to put time and effort into developing a scheme, only to find out during the implementation stage that a suitable scheme had already been developed. PEN-DOR team members considered the probability that a number of the existing schemes had benefited from input from experts in the field of resource description and discovery, and that some of these existing schemes were implemented in top-level educational-digital library projects and recognized as a standard within a defined community. These steps allowed the PEN-DOR team to benefit from work executed in projects with a similar or related scope.

In undertaking this part of the investigation, the following three well-documented metadata schemes were identified and examined on an in-depth level:

1. Gateway to Educational Resources (GEM) metadata scheme;[18]
2. EDUCAUSE Instructional Management Systems (IMS) metadata specification;[19]
3. Courseware Description Language (CDL) metadata dictionary for K-12 educational resources.[20]

The GEM and IMS metadata schemes, already mentioned above, were selected because they have enjoyed fairly widespread deployment and acceptance within the educational non-profit sector. The CDL educational-based metadata scheme was selected for evaluation because of its depth and thoroughness. Authors of this paper have not been able to document the exact impetus for the CDL metadata scheme, but it appears to have had a connection with activities focusing on networked access electronic educational resources that involved Apple Computer®. CDL is currently under the auspices of Intelligent Automation Inc., an artificial intelligence research and development company that sponsors activities ranging from robotics and manufacturing technology to education and training. The CDL scheme is composed of four segments: (1) resource, (2) curriculum, (3) instruction, and (4) user of resource. Each segment is comprised of a series of metadata element groupings, which include elements and sub-elements, and most of which map to the GEM and IMS schemes.

A crosswalk was designed to facilitate a closer comparison of the GEM, IMS, and CDL metadata schemes as part of PEN-DOR's in-depth study of existing metadata schemes for educational resources. The crosswalk not only permitted a mapping of the data elements that each scheme considered essential, but also allowed for a comparison of the following data element aspects: maximum occurrence (repeatable or non-repeatable), obligation (mandatory or optional), and source of generation (creator or system generated). A sample of element comparisons from the crosswalk is given in Table 1.

Metadata Design

The crosswalk served as a basis for the second step–designing the PEN-DOR metadata scheme. Three PEN-DOR team members formed a metadata task force. Task force members had expertise in the areas of metadata, educational-technology, abstracting and indexing, information retrieval, and digital library development. Through a series of meetings, task force members analyzed each of the individual metadata elements in the GEM, IMS, and CDL crosswalk, and considered each element's placement in the PEN-DOR scheme. During these discussions, task force members made decisions about the maximum occurrence, obligation, and source of generation for each element incorporated into the PEN-DOR scheme. The metadata task force also made decisions about the metadata content value for various elements. That is, they identified which metadata elements required the use of a controlled list of terminology or values. Specified lists of terms were developed for the "subject," "topic," "grade range," and "format" metadata elements. The most current version of the PEN-DOR metadata scheme contains 28 elements, which are user supplied or automatically generated. A synopsis of the PEN-DOR scheme is presented in Table 2. The full PEN-DOR Metadata Scheme is found in Appendix A.

In devising the metadata scheme, the task force needed to consider the project's goal to automate as much of the metadata creation as possible. The

TABLE 1. GEM, IMS, and CDL: A Comparative Crosswalk

Gateway to Educational Materials (http://www.geminfo.org/Workbench/Metadata/GEM Element List.html)	IMS Meta-data Specification (http://www.imsproject.org/metadata/index.html)	CDL Descriptors Key Index (http://www.i-a-i.com/services/cdl/allkey.html)
Grade Level Grade, grade span, or educational level of the entity's audience.	**Learning Level** Difficulty of the materials . . . Age and skill . . . prerequisites. Course and/or capabilities required to use the material.	**CDL Curriculum Descriptor** Describes materials' domain knowledge, prerequisite experience, suitable age range, suitable grade range, reading level, language, and suitability for users with limited English proficiency.
Identifier String or number to uniquely identify the resource, e.g., URL.	**Resource Identifier** String or number to uniquely identify the resource, e.g., URL.	**CDL Resource Descriptor** Location of the resource, e.g., URL.
Subject The topic of the resource, or keywords or phrases that describe the subject matter.	**Subject** The topic of the resource, or keywords or phrases that describe the subject matter.	**CDL Curriculum Descriptor** Describes materials domain in the curriculum, course subject.

TABLE 2. Synopsis of PEN-DOR's Metadata Scheme (Current: September 4,1998)

MANDATORY METADATA ELEMENTS: USER SUPPLIED	MANDATORY METADATA ELEMENTS: SYSTEM GENERATED	OPTIONAL METADATA ELEMENTS: USER SUPPLIED
Object Title	Submitted by	Standards
Grade level	Author/Creator	Teaching Method (Pedagogy)\
Object Type	Publisher	Audience
Subject	Date • Date deposited in repository • Date object was created • Revision date	Other contributor
Topic	Object Format	Description
Keywords	Identifier	Time Period
Copyright	Size	Location
	Version (IMS)	Relation
		Language
		Source
		Date • Date of source material(s).
		Duration
		Equipment Requirements

networked environment offers a host of advanced options for metadata creation, especially compared to more traditional metadata environments. The distributed networked environment permits subject experts, in PEN-DOR's case teachers, to participate in metadata creation activities by submitting metadata records to a central host through electronic means.

Perhaps the most significant development in the design and implementation in the networked environment is the ability to automatically generate metadata elements. Through communication paths, such as a creator's identification code, or the resource format, certain object or lesson plan aspects can be automatically captured for a metadata record. PEN-DOR supports the automatic generation of the following eight metadata elements: submitted by, author/creator, date deposited, object format, identifier, size, version, and repository location.

A final and primary consideration with the design of PEN-DOR's metadata scheme was the desire to adhere to the GEM metadata scheme. PEN-DOR and GEM project leaders plan to explore resource sharing as PEN-DOR progresses, and working with a compatible metadata scheme is essential for this activity. The wide-spread deployment of the GEM metadata scheme and the fact that its development has benefited from the input and expertise of leaders in resource discovery and computer-based educational technology is another reason that PEN-DOR elected to work with this scheme.

When the PEN-DOR metadata task force was relatively comfortable with their metadata scheme, they shared it with other team members. The PEN-DOR database designer, with the assistance of other PEN-DOR team members, implemented the metadata specifications. Work began on a module that would support the automatic generation of specified metadata elements and a template was designed for encoding of user-supplied mandatory and optional metadata elements. The metadata template included pull-down menus for the metadata elements that required selection of terminology from a controlled content value list. With this step complete, PEN-DOR team members made plans to obtain feedback from the advisory board, which included librarians and teachers who had a chance to work with the preliminary metadata scheme, and experts in the field of educational technology in the state of Pennsylvania.

Advisory Board Feedback

Once the preliminary PEN-DOR metadata scheme was implemented, the PEN-DOR team organized a session in which they could solicit feedback from the librarians, teachers, and other individuals who would eventually be working with the metadata scheme while contributing objects to, or constructing or modifying lesson plans in, the PEN-DOR database. In August 1998, members of PEN-DOR's advisory board gathered at the University of Pittsburgh for a meeting on PEN-DOR's development status. A segment of the meeting was devoted to discussing the PEN-DOR metadata scheme.

Participants were given the latest draft of the metadata scheme and a draft of the "Contributing Objects to the PEN-DOR Database: Object Uploading Process,"[21] which was to be used in conjunction with the metadata templates. During this session, participants were introduced to the concept of metadata, and presented with scenarios describing why a metadata scheme designed specifically for educational resources was required for the PEN-DOR database. A discussion session followed during which participants provided the metadata task force with feedback on the metadata scheme and the cataloging metadata template. Among the main issues discussed during this session was the option of breaking down the grade level element by ranges (e.g., grades 1-3, 4-6, etc.) as suggested by teachers in the state of Pennsylvania, or by providing individual grades (1st grade, 2nd grade, 3rd grade, etc.) as used in the GEM profile. Participants voted unanimously to follow the grade level range that was suggested by Pennsylvania state teachers. Attention was also given to clarification of the subject metadata element, which had initially been identified as "major" and "minor" subjects. Participants decided that "subject" and topic" were more appropriate labels for these elements. A final suggestion made was the creation of separate template fields for repeatable elements. The original metadata template required multiple "keywords" to be recorded in a single field and separated by commas. Participants indicated that it if the metadata template repeated the "keyword" field several times, metadata creators would not have to be concerned about syntactical punctuation. Overall, the August 1998 meeting was successful. A number of changes were incorporated into the overall metadata scheme that ultimately helped PEN-DOR to build a better and more serviceable project.

While the August 1998 meeting was significant in terms of unveiling the metadata a schema and soliciting feedback, the evaluation of and utility of the PEN-DOR scheme has a been an ongoing process. During the initial database seeding stages, two doctoral students, both of whom had experience as professional librarians and had backgrounds in the area of cataloging and information retrieval, worked with the PEN-DOR metadata scheme. The doctoral students communicated observations and concerns about the metadata scheme's utility and flexibility with PEN-DOR team members. In addition to this work, PEN-DOR team members participated in a series of overall database evaluations that addressed aspects of the metadata scheme. In particular, they focused on interface design, label clarity, accuracy of element terminology, labels, and pull-down menus of controlled lists. The use of metadata elements in the database's searching template was also evaluated. The evaluation activities highlighted above along with the general ongoing development of PEN-DOR have resulted in a robust and flexible metadata scheme.

THE PEN-DOR METADATA SCHEME

The current PEN-DOR metadata scheme consists of 28 elements (see Appendix A). PEN-DOR metadata elements fall into three categories: (1) mandatory metadata elements: user supplied, (2) mandatory metadata elements: system generated, (3) optional metadata elements: user supplied. The division of elements assists with creation of quality metadata records. Librarians and teachers who contribute objects or build or modify lesson plans are required to fill out the template for the mandatory elements, and can enhance the metadata records with the optional elements. The system-generated metadata elements are mandatory, and are automatically created by extracting data from the creator's PEN-DOR login identification code and the actual object or lesson plan that is being contributed or modified in the PEN-DOR database.

The PEN-DOR metadata scheme incorporates the GEM metadata scheme. As indicated above, PEN-DOR elected to use GEM because its development benefited from input of experts in the fields of education in general and educational technology, text encoding, and resource discovery and description. PEN-DOR also elected to use GEM because of the desire to be compatible with other educational-based digital library projects and a plan to share resources with the GEM project. The relationship between the PEN-DOR and GEM metadata scheme is discussed in Fullerton et al.[22]

An overall benefit of working with the GEM metadata scheme, which is not noted above, is that it is based on the Dublin Core.[23] The Dublin Core serves as a base for both the GEM and IMS schemes, but also for a host of other metadata schemes being developed in the networked world. The inclusion of Dublin Core element set supports interoperability and compatibility with other metadata schemes beyond the educational resource horizon. For example, metadata records for objects and lesson plans cataloged according to the PEN-DOR scheme can be easily transferred to a database using the another metadata scheme that is also based on the Dublin Core, such as the Visual Resource Association (VRA) Core Categories.[24] Exporting PEN-DOR records, with their base Dublin Core elements, to a visual image database, can make the latter more serviceable to the learning environment. This is because both resources (PEN-DOR and visual image resources) can be collocated during retrieval activities. The same interoperability and collocation would be supported if PEN-DOR metadata records were exported into a geo-spatial, humanities-oriented, or other network-based collection that is based on the Dublin Core metadata standard. And perhaps even more significant is the exchange of data in the reverse direction. That is, metadata records for objects and other lesson plans encoded according to the Dublin Core scheme can be imported into the PEN-DOR database. PEN-DOR's ability to import metadata records from Dublin Core-based databases will not only save time and money directed towards cataloging, but will also greatly assist PEN-DOR's becoming an even richer educational tool.

FUTURE PEN-DOR METADATA CHALLENGES

Developing and implementing the PEN-DOR metadata scheme has been a joint activity of the PEN-DOR metadata task force and PEN-DOR team members. Librarians, teachers, and other members of PEN-DOR's advisory board also contributed a great deal to PEN-DOR's metadata scheme development.

The next phase of PEN-DOR development plans to address several metadata-related challenges that have emerged throughout the project development process. These challenges deal with issues of metadata effectiveness, metadata preservation and transfer, and metadata flexibility and are discussed below.

Metadata Effectiveness

The PEN-DOR metadata scheme has been operational for a little over two years, and despite minor changes, it has remained relatively stable. The PEN-DOR team plans to evaluate the effectiveness of the metadata scheme through both content and transaction log analyses. A content analysis will involve sampling and examining the application and consistency of metadata elements in PEN-DOR object and lesson plan metadata records. Through transaction log analyses, the use and popularity of various metadata elements for search and retrieval activities will be documented. Together, both of these examination methods will provide empirical evidence about the metadata content and overall effectiveness of the PEN-DOR metadata scheme, and revision activities.

Metadata Preservation and Transfer

One of the central aims of PEN-DOR is to use atomic objects to create or modify existing lesson plans. This activity requires either the creation of a new metadata record, or revision of an existing metadata record. Creating a new metadata record is repetitive in that the atomic objects residing in PEN-DOR already have metadata records. One of the challenges for the PEN-DOR team is to develop a way in which the object level metadata can be preserved and transferred to the lesson plan metadata record, in order to avoid duplication of effort. Metadata literature often discusses this activity as metadata *inheritance*. A corresponding challenge is to develop a way in which metadata can be deleted or *divorced* from a lesson plan metadata records when an atomic object is removed.

Metadata Flexibility

The final PEN-DOR metadata challenge to note in this article deals with testing the metadata scheme's flexibility. The current metadata scheme has been applied to both objects and lesson plans. The PEN-DOR database also contains access to curriculum standards for the state of Pennsylvania and plans to build a community memory store to document the use of and opinions and experiences of working with lesson plans. Studies need to be conducted to see if and how well PEN-DOR's metadata scheme can support the description of these two additional classes of resources.

CONCLUSION

This article documents the PEN-DOR team's experience in developing and implementing a metadata scheme for objects and lesson plans. Issue of data creation, interoperability, and compatibility have been discussed. The current PEN-DOR metadata scheme was presented, and future PEN-DOR metadata-related challenges were highlighted.

The discussion of PEN-DOR's metadata-related challenges and the evolving nature of the overall PEN-DOR project clearly indicate that metadata monitoring, maintenance, and revision are necessary and critical components of educational-based digital library projects. In summing up PEN-DOR's current metadata activities, the existing scheme has been sufficient for current project needs, proven robust during the database transfer process, and remains intact as the central means of support for object and lesson plan discovery and use in the PEN-DOR database.

REFERENCES

1. American Memory: Historical Collection for the Digital Library at the Library of Congress. (1999). Available [on-line] at: *http://lcweb2.loc.gov/ammem/ammemhome. html*

2. University of Michigan Digital Library. (1999). Available [on-line] at: *http://www.si.umich.edu/UMDL/*

3. Informedia Digital Video Library. (1999). Available [on-line] at: *http://informedia. cs.cmu.edu/*

4. PEN-DOR, Pennsylvania Educational Network Digital Object Repository. (1999). Available [on-line] at: *http://cumorah.sis.pitt.edu/pen_dor/start.htm*

5. Marchionini, G., Niolet, V., Williams, H., Wei Ding, Beale Jr., J., Rose A., Garden A., Enomoto, E. and Harbinson, L. (1997). Content + connectivity => community: digital resources for a learning community. Proceedings of the 2nd ACM International Conference on Digital Libraries, Philadelphia, PA, 23- 26 July 1997. New York, NY: ACM, pp. 212-220.

6. The World Factbook 1999. Available from the CIA [on-line] at: *http://www. odci.gov/cia/publications/factbook/index.html*

7. Link 2 Learn Professional Development Classroom Activities. (1999). Available [on-line] at: *http://l2l.org/pd/success/*

8. Weibel, S. (1997). The Evolving Metadata Architecture for the World Wide Web: Bringing Together, Semantics, Structure, and Syntax of Resource Description. International Symposium on Research, Development, & Practice in Digital Libraries: ISDL97. November 18-21, 1997.

9. Roszkowski, M. and Lukas, C. (1998). A Distributed Architecture for Resource Discovery. D-Lib Magazine, July, 1998. Available [on-line] at: *http:// www.dlib.org/dlib/july98/*

10. Dublin Core Metadata Initiative. (1999). Available [on-line] at: *http:// purl.oclc.org/metadata/dublin_core*

11. Weibel, S. (1995). Metadata: The Foundation of Resource Description. D-Lib Magazine, July, 1995. Available [on-line] at: *http://www.dlib.org/dlib/july98/*

12. Encoded Archival Description. (1999). Available [on-line] at: *http:// lcweb.loc.gov/ead*

13. Government Information Locator Service. (1999). Available [on-line] at: *http:// www.oseda.missouri.edu/mogils/stategils.html*

14. NWOET Resources. (1999). Available [on-line] at: *http://nwoet.bgsu.edu/Services/ edserv/marc_records.html*

15. Gateway to Educational Materials. (1999). Available [on-line] at: *http:// www.geminfo.org/Workbench/Metadata/GEM_Element_List.html*

16. IMS Meta-data Specification. (1999). Available [on-line] at: *http://www.imsproject. org/metadata/index.html*

17. IMS/GEM Mapping. (April, 1999). Available [on-line] at: *http://www.geminfo. org/ Workbench/Metadata/IMS_Mapping.html*

18. Gateway to Educational Materials. (1999). Ibid.

19. IMS Meta-data Specification. (1999). Ibid.

20. CDL Descriptors Key Index. Available [on-line] at: *http://www.i-a-i.com/services/ cdl/allkey.html*

21. Greenberg, J. (Ed.) (1998). Contributing Objects to the PEN-DOR Database: Object Uploading Process. Draft.

22. Fullerton, K., Greenberg, J., Rasmussen, E., & Stewart, D. (1999). A Digital Library for Education: The PEN-DOR Project. The Electronic Library, 17 (2), 75-82.

23. Dublin Core Metadata Initiative. (1999). Ibid.

24. VRA Core Categories. (1999). Available [on-line] at: *http://www.oberlin.edu/~ art/vra/wc1.html*

APPENDIX A
Pennsylvania Educational Network Digital Object Repository (PEN-DOR)
METADATA ELEMENT SET
Current: September 4, 1998

Key:
I.   MANDATORY METADATA ELEMENTS: USER SUPPLIED
II. MANDATORY METADATA ELEMENTS: SYSTEM GENERATED
III. OPTIONAL METADATA ELEMENTS: USER SUPPLIED

*Note: Many of the examples are taken from the GEM Metadata Standard for Educational Resources at: http://www.geminfo.org/

I.   **MANDATORY METADATA ELEMENTS: USER SUPPLIED**

ELEMENT NAME	DESCRIPTION	EXAMPLE(s)
Object Title • Mandatory	The title of the work as provided by the author or by the cataloger in the absence of an author-provided title.	Title: Who Was William Penn
Grade Level • Mandatory	Grade, grade span, or educational level of the entity's audience. These include Elementary School - K; Elementary School - 1, 2, 3; Elementary School - 4, 5, 6; Middle School; and High School.	Grade level: Middle school
Object Type • Mandatory	Description of the genre of the object being described. The selection of object types include: Image, Video, Audio, JAVA, PDF, Text, and HTML.	Object type: HTML
Subject • Mandatory	The major subject of instruction. Major subjects include Art, English, Foreign Languages, Health and Physical Education, Mathematics, Life Sciences, Physical Sciences, Social Studies, Technology, Vocational Education, Multi-disciplinary & Integrated Subjects, Special Education, and Other.	Subject: Art
Topic • Mandatory	The topic of the object that is associated with the subject. A separate topic list exists for each subject (the above element). For example, the subject area "Art" has the following topics: Appreciation, History, Film/TV, Foundations, General Art, Performing Arts (Music, Dance, and Theatre).	Topic: Appreciation
Keywords • Mandatory	One or more words exemplifying the meaning or value of the object, that are also useful for retrieving the object.	Keywords: Mona Lisa, Leonardo DaVinci, Renaissance, Painting
Copyright • Mandatory	This includes copyright ownership information plus the copyright notice including the word "Copyright," year, and owner name. For public domain materials, the user will provide author/creator information such as "NASA Educational Division." User produced objects will have the user's name and school district automatically generated from the registration information. For external copyright owners, their name, address, and other contact information will be inserted here after permission has been obtained to store their material in PEN-DOR.	Right management: http://myserver.org/rights_statement.html

II.   MANDATORY METADATA ELEMENTS: SYSTEM GENERATED

ELEMENT NAME	DESCRIPTION	EXAMPLE(s)
Submitted by • Mandatory	The person or agency that created the catalog record. Includes elements, such as school district name, e-mail, etc.	Cataloging agency: Jane Doe, Acme School District
Author/Creator • Mandatory	The person(s) or organization(s) primarily responsible for the intellectual content of the object. For example, authors in the case of written documents, artists, photographers, or illustrators in the case of visual objects.	Creator: Charles Little
Publisher • Mandatory	The entity responsible for making the object available in its present form, such as a publisher, a university department, a corporate entity, or an individual.	Publisher: Pennsbury School District
Date • Mandatory • Date deposited in repository • Date object was created • Revision date	Date the object was deposited in the repository, date the object was created, and a revision date, if the object is revised.	Date deposited: 1997-01-13 Revision date: 1998-05-20
Object Format • Mandatory	The data representation of the object, such as text/HTML, ASCII, Postscript file, executable application, or JPEG image. This element is to provide information to allow people or machines to make decisions about the usability of the encoded data (what hardware and software might required to display or execute it).	Format: text/HTML Format: JPEG
Identifier • Mandatory	The object handle or the uniform resource name (URN) or uniform resource characteristics (URC).	
Size • Mandatory	Size of container in bytes.	Size: 30 KB
Version • Mandatory	Numeric indicator of the version or edition for framework lesson plans.	Version: 2nd edition

III. OPTIONAL METADATA ELEMENTS: USER SUPPLIED

ELEMENT NAME	DESCRIPTION	EXAMPLE(s)
Standards • Optional	State and/or national academic standards mapped to the entity being described.	Standards: Pennsylvania (English Language Arts)
Teaching Method (Pedagogy) • Optional	Pedagogy (teaching method) field allows a learner and/or teacher to select the style of pedagogythat is appropriate to the learner's needs or the teacher's purpose (GEM list will help).	Teaching Method: Integrated instructions Teaching Method: Cross Age Teaching
Audience • Optional	Describes the nature of the target audience for the object.	Audience: Teaching Professionals
Other Contributor • Optional	Person(s) or organization(s) in addition to those specified in the creator element who have made significant intellectual contributions to the object but whose contribution is secondary to the individuals or entities specified in the [author] element (for example, editors, transcribers, illustrators, etc.).	(see author/creator above examples for mandatory Creator element)
Description • Optional	A textual description of the object.	Description: This lesson plan includes multiple strategies for teaching the Pythagorean Theorem using common objects found in the students' immediate surroundings. Knowledge is reinforced by exploring the theorem from multiple vantage points.
Time Period • Optional	Free text description of time information relevant to the entity's topic.	Time period: Civil War
Location • Optional	Free text description of spatial information relevant to the object's topic.	Coverage: France
Relation • Optional	Relationship to other objects. This element specifies relationships among objects that have formal relationships to others, but exist as discrete objects themselves. For example, images in a document, chapters in a book, or items in a collection.	Relation: Item is Parent of http://server.com/lp_index.html
Language • Optional	Language(s) of the intellectual content of the object. Where practical, the content of this field should coincide with the 239.53 three character codes for written languages.	Language: English
Source • Optional	The work, either print or electronic, from which the object is derived, if applicable. For example, an HTML encoding of a Shakespearean sonnet might identify the paper version of the sonnet from which the electronic version was transcribed.	Source: James Smith's The Universal Compilation of Lesson Plans in Mathematics
Date • Optional Date of source material(s).	Date of the source material for the object. This can include a single date or a range of dates.	Date of source materials: 1889-1920
Duration • Optional	The recommended time or number of sessions needed to do the activity/lesson as stated in the entity being described.	Duration: Two one-hour sessions
Equipment Requirements • Optional	Objects essential to the effective use of the entity by the teacher (e.g., Plug-in browser, etc.).	Requires video display capabilities

Managing Digital Educational Resources with the ARIADNE Metadata System

E. Duval
E. Vervaet
B. Verhoeven
K. Hendrikx
K. Cardinaels
H. Olivié
E. Forte
F. Haenni
K. Warkentyne
M. Wentland Forte
F. Simillion

Erik Duval is a Post-Doctoral Fellow, Belgian National Fund for Scientific Research, and Part-Time Professor, K.U.Leuven. Erwin Vervaet is Database and Java Technology Researcher and Developer, K.U.Leuven. B. Verhoeven is Researcher, K.U.Leuven, specialising in user interfaces for database insertion and query tools. K. Hendrikx is XML and Java Expert, Hypermedia and Databases Group, K.U.Leuven. Kris Cardinaels is Research Assistant, Hypermedia and Databases Group, K.U.Leuven. Henk Olivié is Professor, K.U. Leuven, and heads the Research Group on Hypermedia and Databases. Dr. Eddy N. Forte is Coordinator, ARIADNE Project, Chairman, PROMETEUS Initiative, and Head, R&D Division, EPFL's Computer Aided Learning Lab (LEAO), founded in 1987. Mrs. Florence Haenni is a former graduate student at LEAO, and wrote the first specifications of the ARIADNE Metadata, the Indexation Tool and the Course Editor. Dr. Ken Warkentyne, a former post-graduate researcher at LEAO, is Senior Informatician at a Canadian Bank, and developed the first prototypes of the ARIADNE Indexation Tool, the Course Editor and the Learner/Manager Interfaces. M. Wentland Forte is Professor, Business School, University of Lausanne, working in the fields of Business Knowledge Management and Open and Distance Learning. Fabian Simillion is about to finish his PhD dissertation on a business model to integrate Information and Training.

[Haworth co-indexing entry note]: "Managing Digital Educational Resources with the ARIADNE Metadata System." Duval et al. Co-published simultaneously in *Journal of Internet Cataloging* (The Haworth Information Press, an imprint of The Haworth Press, Inc.) Vol. 3, No. 2/3, 2000, pp. 145-171; and: *Metadata and Organizing Educational Resources on the Internet* (ed: Jane Greenberg) The Haworth Information Press, an imprint of The Haworth Press, Inc., 2000, pp. 145-171. Single or multiple copies of this article are available for a fee from The Haworth Document Delivery Service [1-800-342-9678, 9:00 a.m. - 5:00 p.m. (EST). E-mail address: getinfo@haworthpressinc.com].

© 2000 by The Haworth Press, Inc. All rights reserved.

SUMMARY. The primary goal of the ARIADNE project, supported by the European Commission, is to foster share and reuse of digital pedagogical material. For this purpose, a Europe-wide repository of reusable pedagogical documents, called the Knowledge Pool System (KPS), has been set up. One of the key features of the KPS is the underlying metadata specification, which has been used in extensive experiments. The ARIADNE metadata scheme includes both mandatory and optional elements, and is at the basis of the emerging Learning Objects Metadata standard, developed by the IEEE Learning Technology Standards Committee. This article presents the ARIADNE metadata scheme and discusses ARIADNE tools developed to support metadata authoring and indexing, database querying, and course development activities. A discussion of the ARIADNE community's experience is also presented. *[Article copies available for a fee from The Haworth Document Delivery Service: 1-800-342-9678. E-mail address: <getinfo@haworthpressinc.com> Website: <http://www.HaworthPress.com>]*

KEYWORDS. ARIADNE project, metadata, Learning Objects Metadata (IEEE), metadata authoring tools

1. THE ARIADNE PROJECT: AN OVERVIEW

ARIADNE's primary goal is to foster the share and reuse of electronic pedagogical material, both by universities and corporations.[1,2] The project is supported by the European Commission, in the Telematics Applications Program *<http://ariadne.unil.ch/>*. The basic premise is that *it is difficult and time consuming to author good quality digital learning material*, not in the least because of the multidisciplinary expertise involved. It therefore makes sense to reuse existing material. However, it is difficult to find appropriate existing material, and to integrate into a course material collected from various sources.

In order to facilitate this process of share and reuse, we have set up an infrastructure for the:

- *production* of reusable learning content components,
- their *description* and *storage*,
- their *discovery* through the Knowledge Pool System (KPS),[3] and the
- development of well-structured *courses*.

This infrastructure is illustrated in Figure 1. The upper left boxes represent the production of digital learning material. In fact, our infrastructure makes no assumption about the nature of the authoring tools. So, pedagogical docu-

FIGURE 1. The ARIADNE Infrastructure

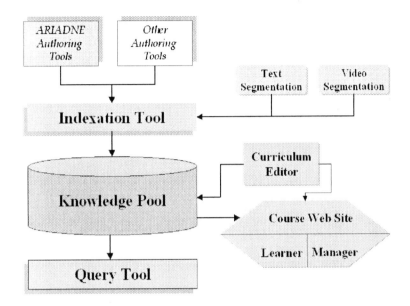

ments produced with any non-ARIADNE authoring tool (ToolBook, Director, IconAuthor, Powerpoint, etc.) can be accommodated just as well. However, ARIADNE's authoring tools support partial generation of metadata at authoring time. In fact, some of these metadata are generated automatically, and the author is prompted to provide other metadata when the document is saved.

The upper right boxes represent so-called *segmentation tools*.[13] They are quite illustrative of one of the basic tenets of ARIADNE: *reuse requires small granular components of multimedia content.* Indeed, earlier experience showed that larger components (a course, or a module) are almost never reused as such. This is probably due to the fact that large units of material are almost never suited for the specific circumstances of the learners that the authors try to serve. Therefore, we have developed tools that assist with breaking up larger bodies of text or video material into smaller, more homogeneous and hopefully more reusable components.

The boxes in the central left represent the ARIADNE *metadata tools.* They will be covered in more detail in section 3. In brief, the indexation tool enables an end user to describe any kind of pedagogical document, i.e., to create metadata for it. The Knowledge Pool System holds both the metadata and the documents themselves. Search criteria can be expressed through the query tool that enables an end user to identify and retrieve relevant material.

Finally, the right part of the figure represents the ARIADNE *course tools* that enable a 'pedagogical engineer' to set up well-structured courses, using the material from the KPS.[14] For this purpose, (s)he uses the curriculum editor to describe the structure of the course and to assign documents from the KPS to that structure. From the structural information in the so-called Curriculum Description File and the content in the KPS, we automatically generate a course Web site with different access and administration facilities for students and course managers.

One of the key features of the KPS is the underlying metadata specification, which has been used in extensive experimentations. The following section presents the conceptual structure of the ARIADNE metadata structure. Section 3 deals with the ARIADNE metadata tools.

2. THE ARIADNE METADATA SCHEME

2.1. Requirements for Usable Educational Metadata

The recommendations in this section are derived from work and experiments during the last two years by 10 European universities and 5 international corporations, using a simplified version of these specifications, as implemented in the ARIADNE prototype indexation tools and Knowledge Pool System.

We want to solve two practical problems that will arise in the case of the widespread use of any metadata system:

1. *indexation* work (i.e., the creation of the metadata itself by human persons) should be as easy as possible;
2. the *exploitation* of the metadata by users looking for relevant pedagogical material should be as easy and efficient as possible.

In the context of Europe, but also more generally of wide international cooperation, it is mandatory that the metadata system works in a multilingual and multicultural environment, and thus be neutral with regards to both the language of the original document being indexed and the language used to describe the document, i.e., to create the metadata. Mechanisms that ensure such a multilingual interoperability are not easy to design and implement.[5] We will not describe them here as they are really implementation issues. However, the metadata set must capture the necessary information to render such mechanisms feasible.

Metadata elements can naturally be regrouped into families that will make them easier to provide. This translates into a set of groups of metadata descriptors. In ARIADNE, most of the groups are mandatory, to ensure the stability of the scheme (even though those mandatory groups may contain optional fields).

ARIADNE does not intend to develop metadata about the learners involved in a process of education or training, e.g., to characterize or to record their educational performances. Neither is the intention of the present document to define the representation format for the metadata sets. For the latter purpose, use could be made of SGML (Standard Generalized Markup Language), XML (Extensible Markup Language), RDF (Resource Description Framework), a DBMS (Database Management System), etc. (The current Knowledge Pool System relies on a combination of SGML and a DBMS.)

2.2 ARIADNE Educational Metadata Recommendations

The following recommendations hold for material to be used in the context of education (as provided in universities, secondary schools, etc.). A very similar but not identical scheme can be produced for the purpose of training (in the sense of training in skills rather than in knowledge fields).

It is recommended that the following categories of descriptors, which are presented in a logical order, be mandatory for any educational resource being indexed.

1. general information on the resource itself,
2. semantics of the resource,
3. pedagogical attributes,
4. technical characteristics,
5. conditions for use,
6. meta-metadata information.

Examples of optional categories are as follows:

1. annotations.
2. physical data of the represented educational resource.

2.3. Review of the ARIADNE Metadata Set

2.3.1. General

This first group of ARIADNE metadata elements deals with general information on the resource itself. As is apparent from Table 1 that lists all

TABLE 1. List of Elements in the *General* Category

Name	Comment	Mandatory/ Optional	Dublin
1.0 identifier	A unique alphanumeric identifier for the resource.	M	Identifier
1.1 title	This is the title of the educational resource in an ordinary sense.	M	Title
1.2 authors	The authors or creators of the electronic resource, whether it is an original work or based on previous work, hereafter designated as the source	M	Creator
1.3 date	The release or publication date (if known) or, by default, the indexation date.	M	Date
1.4 language	The language of the document or the interface of the application.	M	Language
1.5 publisher	The publisher or university or corporation under whose responsibility the educational resource was released or published.	M	Publisher
1.6 sources	The source document (if any) on which the current pedagogical resource is based.	O	Source

elements in this group, there is a one-to-one mapping from each single element in this group to a single element in the Dublin Core metadata structure.[6] This is to be expected, as the Dublin Core scheme deals primarily with the general characteristics of a resource.

Most of the entries in Table 1 should be self explanatory. A few comments though:

- The *identifier* is typically transparent to the metadata creator and is generated by the system. This is relatively easy in the ARIADNE context: basically, each local site generates a unique identifier for that site. The global identifier is composed of an identifier for the site and the identifier generated for that site. To generate unique identifiers in a truly open environment, where, for instance, name clashes between sites can (at least theoretically) occur, is a far more difficult problem. That is the reason why, for instance, the IEEE LTSC LOM (Learning Technology Standard Committee/Learning Object Metadata)[4] has reserved the element identifier, but is currently refraining from actually using it. Initiatives such as the Digital Object Identifier[7] try to address this specific issue.

- A hypertext could be based on a book written by some other person. In that case, the *authors* element is used to indicate the authors of the derivative work, i.e., the hypertext. However, the source document will be indicated by the *sources* element, so that proper citation can be provided.
- If the resource is non-verbal (e.g., images, non-speech sounds), then the value of the *language* element is 'None'.
- As not all resources are based on previous works, the *sources* element is optional. If a pedagogical document is based on previous material, then it is recommended strongly to indicate the latter material through the *sources* element.
- All other elements in this category are mandatory. This means that all valid ARIADNE metadata carry values for these elements. Such values can be automatically generated (as in the case of the *identifier* element), generated by the indexing tool (that could for instance identify the value for the *title* element when it processes an HTML document, as illustrated by the DC-dot tool for Dublin Core metadata <*http://www. ukoln.ac.uk/metadata/dcdot/*>), or provided by the human indexer, through the ARIADNE indexation tool (section 3.2).
- A typical example, actually taken from the ARIADNE Knowledge Pool System content, is illustrated below (this example is referred to throughout the rest of this paper):

  - 1.0 identifier: BLKLKP560
  - 1.1 title: Capita Selecta van de Programmatuur: Ontwikkeling van Gebruikersinterfaces
  - 1.2 authors: Erik Duval
  - 1.3 date: 22 December 1998
  - 1.4 language: Dutch
  - 1.5 publisher: Katholieke Universiteit Leuven
  - 1.6 sources: Ben Shneiderman. Designing the User Interface.

This document actually is a set of slides, in HTML format, based on the textbook by Ben Shneiderman.

2.3.2. Semantics of the Resource

This group, defined in Table 2, is used to describe the semantic contents of the pedagogical document. Originally, we had intended to rely on general-purpose classification schemes, like the Dewey or Universal Decimal Classification, to model the semantics of the resource. It turned out that these schemes were not very useful for our purposes, because of a number of reasons:[5]

- these schemes were either not sufficiently detailed for some knowledge domain, or not well developed for others;
- compatible versions in more than one language are not generally available.

Especially the latter observation is extremely relevant in the multi-cultural and multi-lingual context of ARIADNE. We therefore developed our own approach, that relies on a hierarchical structure, with a *discipline* as the most general indication of the semantics. (In fact, the next generation of ARIADNE tools will rely on the combination of a discipline and a sub-discipline for this purpose.)

Within a discipline, the semantics is described by the *main concept*. Whereas we have restricted the set of terms for the discipline to an established vocabulary, we were unable to do so for the concepts. We do advocate the use of a restricted vocabulary when available for a specific discipline, such as the ACM (Association for Computing Machinery) Computing Reviews classification for computer science, and the Medical Subject Headings for medicine. However, those discipline-specific thesauri of terms suffer from the same problem as the more general classification schemes with respect to availability in more than one language.

When indexers enter their terms, they can also indicate main *concept synonyms*. This feature enables us to support multi-linguality in the descriptions, as synonyms can be used to express equivalent terms in different languages. It is our hope that, as the amount of information that enables us to cross language boundaries in document retrieval increases, the Knowledge Pool System will serve as an example to the metadata community, that all too often takes a too simplistic view on this issue of multi-lingualism.

Finally, the *other concept* list enables an indexer to indicate other important concepts that are treated in the document, but that do not describe the general content of the document.

Some remarks with respect to Table 2:

- All these elements map into the single Dublin Core element DC.Subject. In this sense, the ARIADNE metadata scheme is more specific with respect to the semantics than the Dublin Core scheme.
- An indexer needs to provide at least the *discipline* and main *concept*. The other elements are optional.
- It is recommended that the disciplines be chosen among a restricted list that can be of about 20 values, with an option for adding additional disciplines when really needed. This operation should be supervised by a suitable authority. In ARIADNE, the following list of disciplines is currently in use:
  - chemistry/bio-chemistry
  - civil engineering/architecture

- economy/management
- electricity/electrotechnics
- electronics/microtechnics
- informatics/information processing
- life sciences, bio-engineering
- mathematics/operational research
- mechanics/automatics
- medicine/health sciences
- physics/bio-physics
- telecommunications/transportation

It is clear that the above list of disciplines reflects the actual interests of the ARIADNE consortium. This is also true of the number of documents per discipline: currently, informatics/information processing, electronics/microtechnics and economy/management are the most populated disciplines. The list of disciplines will be carefully extended as the number and diversity of ARIADNE users increases.

- The same example document as before is described by the following metadata:
  - 2.1 discipline: informatics/information processing
  - 2.2 main concept: human-computer interaction
  - 2.3 main concept synonyms: -
  - 2.4 other concepts: -

TABLE 2. List of Elements in the *Semantics* Category

Name	Comment	Mandatory/ Optional
2.1 discipline	The knowledge field in the context of which the learning or teaching is to take place in the ordinary sense.	M
2.2 main concept	The main concept that is covered by the educational resource.	M
2.3 main concept synonyms	An equivalent term (if known) for designating the main concept.	O
2.4 other concepts	This is a list of important educational topics, other than the main concept, that are covered by the resource.	O

2.3.3. Pedagogical Attributes

This group certainly constitutes the more novel aspect of the ARIADNE metadata scheme: it tries to describe in some detail the educational characteristics of the document. This is extremely important in the ARIADNE context that deals with share and reuse of pedagogical documents.

The *end user type* element allows for an important distinction to be made between documents directly intended for learners, and those to be used by authors to produce new documents, that are meant in turn for learners. A multiple choice questionnaire is typically intended for learners; a questionnaire authoring tool is typically intended for authors.

The second element, *document type*, makes a distinction between documents according to their educational role:

- *Expositive* documents are typically used in learning by reading or by being told.
- *Active* documents require the production of semantically meaningful output by the learner, either in the form of text input or through the reasoned manipulation of the application interface.

Note that Navigation is not considered as a reasoned production. Hence, hypertext documents are *expositive* documents. What we refer to as *active* documents are often called interactive applications. However, in ARIADNE, we reserve the term *interactive* for synchronous human-to-human communication. We certainly do not advocate the removal of such an interactive component from education. However, because of their synchronous nature, interactive components cannot be stored, shared and reused: it is not possible to retrieve a conversation and then join it with the current state of technology. One can of course capture synchronous interactive exchanges and make the recording available as a document. Such a recording is an expositive document, like video footage, or the transcript of a discussion.

Depending on the document type, a document can be described as being of a particular *format*:

- Expositive document formats include: diagram, figure, graph, hypertext, image, index, slide, sound, table, text and video.
- Active document formats include: exam, exercise, experiment, multiple choice questionnaire, problem statement, self-assessment, simulation and quiz.

The *didactical context* is selected by the user from a controlled vocabulary that includes the values: primary education, secondary education, higher education, university first cycle, university second cycle, university post-

grade, technical school first cycle, technical school second cycle, professional formation, continuous formation, and other.

At this moment, the *course level* is expressed as a pair of nationally
dependent values, the first part being the designation of the country, and the
second part being a value taken from a nationally-dependent list of levels.
Examples are 'US, K-6' or 'FR, bac+3'. The intention is to be able to cross-
map from one national or regional educational system to another, so that an
end user looking for material appropriate for a '3de ingenieursjaar' in the
Flanders region of Belgium would also find 'bac+5' material for the French
educational system. Currently, this kind of search can be expressed with the
didactical context, though in a less precise way.

It is important to note that we call this group of elements the *pedagogical*
elements, because they capture information that can be used to set up peda-
gogically sound educational experiences for the learner. Typically, for
instance, the "pedagogical engineer" shall attempt to reach a balance between expositive and active material in a session: too much emphasis on the
former kind of material will lead to a passive, bored learner attitude; too
many active documents will exhaust students and put too-high demands on
their attention span. Similarly, the pedagogical duration can be used to make
sure that the learner can indeed cover the material within the time that he has
available, etc.

On the other hand, it is quite clear that these elements only cover the basic
information about the learning experience that can be triggered by the documents. This is the case because we believe it is very difficult to be more
precise regarding the pedagogical characteristics in a general way that is
neutral with respect to the pedagogical approach adopted by the teacher or
learner.

A few remarks with respect to Table 3:

- *Document type* and *document format* correspond with the Dublin Core
  element Type.
- For the document example given in section 2.3.1, the values are
  - 3.1 end user type: learner
  - 3.2 document type: expositive
  - 3.3 document format: slide
  - 3.4 usage remarks: -
  - 3.5 didactical context: university second cycle
  - 3.6 course level: -
  - 3.7 difficulty level: easy
  - 3.8 semantic density: -
  - 3.9 pedagogical duration: 45
- The *pedagogical* duration of a continuous resource can be quite different from the duration of that resource as such. One can for instance

imagine it takes a typical student 25 minutes to analyse a 4-minute video clip that illustrates President Kennedy's "Ich bin ein Berliner" speech. In that case, the duration of the document is 4 minutes, but the pedagogical duration is 25 minutes.

2.3.4. Technical Characteristics

This category of elements is probably the most simple and obvious one. First of all, it must be possible to retrieve the document. It is most important that the document is actually available through the *document handle*, as an end user may have spent a considerable effort to identify possibly relevant material. To be faced with the fact that documents have disappeared, or are at least no longer available at their original location, is a most frustrating experience that is all too common with ordinary Web searches.

TABLE 3. List of Elements in the *Pedagogical* Category

Name	Comment	Mandatory/ Optional
3.1 end user type	This field can take one of the following values: 'learner' or 'author'.	M
3.2 document type	This field can take one of two values: 'expositive' or 'active'.	M
3.3 document format	This field takes a value from a list whose content depends on the document type.	M
3.4 usage remarks	Comments by the metadata author on how the resource is to be used by the end user.	O
3.5 didactical context	A description of the kind of learners that are usually the targets of the resource. This field is only applicable if the user type is learner (as for all the following fields).	O
3.6 course level	A numerical evaluator, independent of any given national educational system, describing the level at which education is to be provided.	O
3.7 difficulty level	May take the value 'low', 'medium' or 'high', and is relative to the course level.	O
3.8 interaction quality or semantic density	A value taken from 'low', 'medium' or 'high' is attributed to either the semantic density of an expositive document, or to the interaction quality of an active resource.	O
3.9 pedagogical duration	An estimation in minutes of the time needed by an average learner of the stated category in the stated didactical context to work through the pedagogical resource.	M

Another simple, but most useful, element indicates the *file media types* that the document includes. For this purpose, we rely on the MIME type structure that is commonly used in Internet applications. It is important to include this descriptive information, because material will certainly not be relevant if the end user cannot access it, because of lack of appropriate viewers, helper applications, plug-ins, run-time environments, etc. For the same reason, the metadata include the *type* and *version* of the *operating system.*

In order to assess the requirements with respect to final distribution to the learners, the metadata also indicates the total uncompressed *package size:* clearly, it doesn't make sense to distribute a 54 MByte video clip over a 19Kbps modem line.

Finally, the metadata includes free text descriptions of *other platform requirements* and *installation remarks.* These elements are less useful for searching, because of their free text nature. However, they provide most useful information on the documents included in the result list of a search.

- In the ARIADNE Knowledge Pool System, the *document handle* equals the *identifier* from the *General* category. This is possible in our implementation, as we can retrieve the document based on the identifier. More generally, this need not always be the case. Hence the need for a separate element.
- In Dublin Core, there is an element *Format,* that maps into the element *file media types* of Table 4. The other elements are not present in Dublin Core.
- The same example document as before is described by the following metadata:
  - 4.1 document handle: BLKLKP560
  - 4.2 file media types: text/html
  - 4.3 package size: 15
  - 4.4 operating system type: multi-OS
  - 4.5 OS version: -
  - 4.6 other platform requirements: -
  - 4.7 installation remarks: -

2.3.5. Conditions for Use

In order to make sure that good quality educational material will be made available, we need to make sure that we can maintain intellectual property rights. First of all, the ARIADNE metadata set indicates whether or not the material is available for free. In the ARIADNE context, this means that no money transfer needs to take place in order to make use of the document. This is obviously quite important information, especially in an educational context where monetary resources are often very limited.

TABLE 4. List of Elements in the *Technical* Category

Name	Comment	Mandatory/ Optional
4.1 document handle	A string allowing to retrieve the resource. This is implementation dependent. It can be for instance a URL, a URN or a file name.	M
4.2 file media types	An ordered list of the MIME types used by the components of the resource.	M
4.3 package size	The size in kiloBytes of the electronic resource. *Note:* This refers to the real size of the resource and not to the size of the compressed resource that would often be used in a repository.	M
4.4 operating system type	May take a value from a fixed list that includes the 'other' value.	M
4.5 OS version	Lowest needed version of the required Operating System.	O
4.6 other platform requirements	Free text description of other hard- and software attributes necessary to run the educational resource. Examples are multimedia capability, decompression video cards, helper applications, etc.	O
4.7 installation marks	Free text describing any special procedure needed to correctly install and run the electronic resource.	O

If the material is not available for free, then the other fields of this category indicate how the document can be obtained, and at what cost. Obviously, this is not a complete provision for electronic commerce. In fact, within the context of the IEEE Learning Object Metadata Group, it has been agreed that, for that purpose, we would rely on the results of other projects that deal specifically and solely with e-commerce issues.[9] (See Table 5.)

This category maps into the *Rights* element of Dublin Core. The same example document as before is described by the following metadata:

- 5.1 rights of use: free
- 5.2 usage description: -
- 5.3 price code: -
- 5.4 pricing scheme: -

2.3.6. Meta-MetaData

Although the name of this category is somewhat intimidating, it simply refers to elements about the description, rather than about the document. This

TABLE 5. List of Elements in the *Condition_for_Use* Category

Name	Comment	Mandatory/ Optional
5.1 rights of use	May take the value 'free' or 'not free.'	M
5.2 usage description	Free text decription on how to acquire the right of using the resource when it is not free.	If the document is not free, as indicated in the rights-of-use field (5.1).
5.3 price code	Optional information concerning the price of a not free resource.	O
5.4 pricing scheme	An optional description of the pricing scheme that applies to the resource. Examples are 'flat fee,' 'price per hour,' 'price per page,' 'price per MByte.'	O

information is important, because it helps to maintain the quality of the metadata. First of all, the *author name* indicates who has contributed the metadata. ARIADNE metadata are not anonymous descriptions, as they can sometimes be found on the Web, newsgroups, etc.

We also include the *date of creation* and of the *last modification*. These dates refer to the production or modification of the metadata, not to any variation of the pedagogical document itself.

As end users may have difficulties understanding the meaning of metadata in a particular *language*, and as automatic translation only works satisfactorily for restricted vocabularies, which the tool can display in several languages, there is also a metadata element that indicates the language of the metadata. Note that this might be different from the language of the resource itself.

An optional *validation name* and *date* provide further information on the trustworthiness of the metadata. We believe that, as metadata become more widespread, there will arise communities with a certain prestige among the practitioners of a field. Existing professional associations could take on the responsibility of tagging certain material with their "seal of approval," so that end users would have a guarantee that the description and/or the document meet certain quality criteria. Section 4 presents the ARIADNE experience in this area.

The same example document as before is described by the following metadata:

- 6.1 author name: Erik Duval
- 6.2 creation date: 22 December 1998
- 6.3 last modified date: 22 December 1998
- 6.4 language: English

- 6.5 validator name: Erik Duval
- 6.6 validation date: 22 december 1998

Note that, in this example, the language of the metadata (6.4, English) is indeed different from the language of the document (1.4, Dutch). The example is not very representative in the sense that it has been validated on the day it was created, by the original indexer. This is very uncommon, as will be explained in section 4. (See Table 6.)

2.4. Optional Categories

2.4.1. Introduction

The categories already presented are all mandatory. This means that all metadata instances must carry these categories. In each of them, some fields

TABLE 6. List of Elements in the *Metametadata* Category

Name	Comment	Mandatory/ Optional
6.1 author name	The name of the creator of the metadata.	M
6.2 creation date	Date of the creation of the metadata.	M
6.3 last modified date	Date of the last modification of the metada.	M
6.4 language	Language in which the metadata is created.	M
6.5 validator name	The name of the supervisor that authorized the metadata.	O
6.6 validation date	Date of release by the supervisor of the metadata.	O

TABLE 7. List of Elements in *Annotation Entry*

	Annotations	
Name	Comment	Mandatory/ Optional
1. annotator name	The name of an authorized annotator that provides feedback on the actual use of the resource.	M
2. creation date	Date of the creation of the annotation.	M
3. content	Free text of the annotation.	M

are mandatory, some optional, and some may be conditional. Whether or not values for the latter kind of elements must be provided depends on the value of some other element. If, for instance, 5.1 ConditionsOfUse.RightsOfUse is 'not free,' then 5.2 ConditionsOfUse.UsageDescription must also be specified.

In contrast, the categories presented below are all optional. This means that a metadata instance need not include these categories. However, if it does, then the mandatory elements in the category must be included. As an example, if a metadata instance includes the Annotation category, which is not required, then it must include all three elements, as specified in section 2.4.2.

2.4.2. Annotation

An annotation comprises three entries, which define the *name* of the annotator, the *date* that the annotation was created, and the actual text of the annotation itself (see Table 7). There may be more than one annotation created at different times by different annotators. Once inserted, annotations cannot be removed by their authors.

2.4.3. Physical Characteristics of the Physical Resource

If a physical resource is described, then this optional category can be used to describe its physical characteristics. The general idea is to support an object type dependent set of numerical or qualitative attributes, like for instance the dimensions and quality of painting used in certain art objects whose image is being described.

As this category is not currently supported by the ARIADNE toolset, we will not further elaborate on it here.

3. THE ARIADNE METADATA TOOLS

3.1. Introduction

The ARIADNE metadata scheme, presented in the previous section, is not just a conceptual proposal. It is based on more than three years of experience gained during the development of our metadata infrastructure, and during its actual use by authors and developers, indexers, professors and students, trainers and trainees, 'pedagogical engineers,' etc.

Our metadata infrastructure will be presented briefly in this section. The interested reader is referred to notes 1,2,3,6,8 for more details. Section 3.2

covers the Knowledge Pool System (KPS) that holds all metadata, as well as the pedagogical documents themselves. Material enters the KPS through the indexation tool, which is presented in section 3.3. In order to support searches over the metadata, we have developed a rather generic query tool that will be presented in section 3.4. Finally, as the ARIADNE Management Interface, used to perform administration tasks on a course image, also relies on the metadata infrastructure, we cover that component in section 3.5.

3.2. Knowledge Pool System

The ARIADNE *Knowledge Pool System* (KPS) is in essence a distributed database of multimedia pedagogical documents (the data) and their descriptions (the metadata). In this respect, the term Knowledge Pool refers not to a system based on Artificial Intelligence techniques, but rather to an infrastructure that tries to capture and make available human knowledge, as it is captured in multimedia documents. In that respect, there certainly is a relationship with so-called Knowledge Management,[10] but we will not elaborate on that subject here.

The KPS is currently based on a star-shaped topology, with the *Central Knowledge Pool* (CKP) based in Leuven, Belgium. The central node stores all metadata, as well as all free documents. From the CKP, documents and metadata are replicated to *Local Knowledge Pools* throughout Europe. As alphanumerical data are relatively small, and as memory is becoming more and more cheap and bandwidth more and more available, all metadata are replicated at all sites, so that all users can always query the full set of ARIADNE documents.

With respect to *documents,* however, local sites can be configured to receive only those free documents that are relevant to them. We have chosen this approach, because there may be quite voluminous transfers involved (e.g., in the case of medical images) that may be quite irrelevant for local purposes (e.g., in the case of a business school that doesn't teach medicine). Moreover, local users can declare documents as local, which means that they will not be replicated to the central site, and hence not to the other local sites. This obviously limits the availability of these documents, but may be appropriate if the document is very specific to local circumstances, or if the author first wants to gain some experience from learners using his document locally before releasing it to the general public.

Not free documents (section 2.3.5) are only stored at the site where they have been introduced. We have adopted this policy because right holders feel comfortable about making their documents available locally, either because they have produced them for local use, or because a site license has been procured by that site, or because the licensing conditions are enforced locally. Interested parties at other sites can find out about the document, because its metadata are replicated. If they actually want to make use of the document, then the metadata carries the information on what needs to be done for them to acquire the necessary rights clearance.

Figure 2 illustrates the current topology of the KPS: the CKP is indicated as IND7, and is located in Leuven, Belgium. Some 15 Local Knowledge Pools are operational. It is expected that this number will increase by a factor of 2 to 4 within the next 18 months. During the night, all new metadata and free non-local documents are replicated from all the local sites to the CKP, and from there on to all the other local sites.

One may wonder why we care about storing the documents at all in the KPS. Couldn't we just store a Universal Resource Locator (URL), and retrieve the documents from the Web when needed? The answer is that the *Web* currently is *too volatile* a publishing medium to rely upon it for our purposes. One of the important reasons that documents cannot always be found with a URL reference is that, on the Web, URLs need to change when documents are moved to another server or within a server. Maybe, initiatives that aim to make Web resources more permanently available, such as the Digital Object Identifier,[7] will alleviate this problem. Even in that case, however, having the

FIGURE 2. The ARIADNE Knowledge Pool System in Early 1999

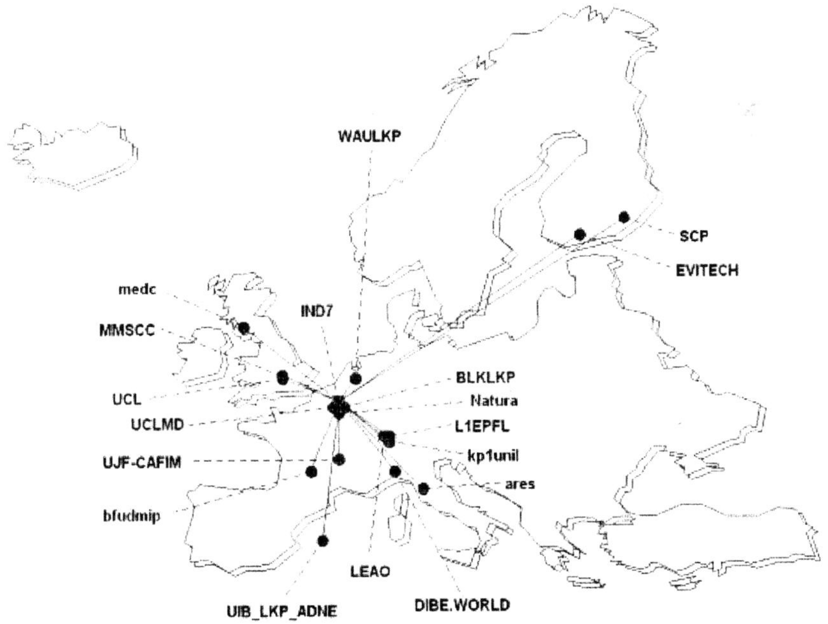

KPS act as a store of reference copies (much like national libraries in many countries do with printed publications) has great appeal.

Finally, we could also just keep the documents at the central site and retrieve them from there when needed. However, adopting such an approach would lead to longer response times, and would make the global infrastructure too vulnerable for failures, as nothing would remain operational when the CKP experiences problems. In the current set-up, only the replication suffers from CKP problems, as all end user tools interact with Local Knowledge Pools.

The *implementation* of our KPS relies on the Oracle Relational DataBase Management System for management of all alphanumerical data involved. These include all metadata. Within the database, we store a reference to the actual document, which is stored through the server file system. On top of the database, we have developed our own middleware component that shields client tools from the implementation details of the server. In essence, this middleware component is a Java application that uses the JDBC protocol to interact with the database. Client tools interact with our middleware through an XML based protocol.

3.3. Indexation Tool

In order to describe documents, i.e., to generate metadata for them, we have developed an indexation tool that interacts with a Local Knowledge Pool. This tool basically prompts the indexer to provide values for all the elements in the ARIADNE educational metadata set (section 2). Some of the values are generated automatically. In fact, one of the most interesting features of the ARIADNE authoring and segmentation tools (Figure 1) is that these tools can automatically fill in a larger portion of the metadata set. The video segmenter tool, for instance, will always produce MPEG clips, so that it can fill in automatically most of the technical metadata elements (section 2.3.4).

Figure 3 shows a typical screenshot of the indexation tool: on the figure, the panel with the pedagogical data elements is presented. This roughly corresponds with the pedagogical elements of section 2.3.3. The upper banner displays some management information, like the status of the connection with the KPS, the identity of the end user, etc. User can choose to either hide or display the optional elements. (On the figure, they are displayed.) For many fields, a list of values is displayed from which the user can either choose or is obliged to select one.

The indexation tool has been implemented as a Java application. As mentioned in section 3.2, it interacts with the KPS through middleware layer, using an XML based protocol.

FIGURE 3. The Pedagogical Panel of the Indexation Tool

3.4. Query Tool

The rich set of metadata that we generate and store in the KPS only becomes really useful to an end user through the *query tool* that we have developed to support searches. Figure 4 illustrates the basic user interface for this tool. The upper row of buttons provides access to the main functionality. In the upper left quadrant, end users define their search criteria over the ARIADNE metadata elements. Because the metadata elements are presented in 5 different panels, the search criteria are also summarized in the upper right quadrant.

In the down right quadrant, the number of 'hits,' i.e., the number of documents in the KPS that satisfy the search criteria, is displayed. Each document in the result set is represented by its title in a scrollable list. Finally, the down left quadrant can be used to display the full description of one of the documents in the result list. If the user wants to download the corresponding document, then he will be prompted for his user identification, so that permission to access the document can be verified.

Most users looking for material to include in a course start by specifying

FIGURE 4. The ARIADNE Query Tool

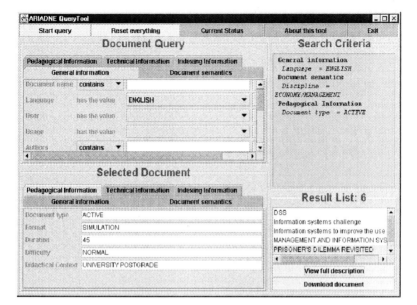

some search criteria until the number of hits gets relatively small–say, smaller than ten. Then, they review the full description for each remaining document and download the one or two that seem most relevant. This is a much more *effective and efficient* way of searching than the typical experience with Web search engines that deliver up to tens of thousands of mostly irrelevant hits.

The query tool has also been implemented as a Java application. In fact, its design has been quite carefully set up, so that it is quite *generic* and can be configured to query any relational database.[8] In order to make it easier to support this kind of flexibility, it interacts directly with the relational database that is at the core of the KPS, through the JDBC protocol, and the query tool thus bypasses the middleware XML based component.

3.5. Building Courses in ARIADNE

The end goal of ARIADNE is to promote share and reuse of educational material. So-called 'pedagogical engineers' build ARIADNE courses with the *Curriculum Editor* (Figure 1). That tool is based on a structured approach to learning: activities are structured in sessions that can either be fixed (i.e., taking place at a particular moment in time) or fuzzy (i.e., with a begin and end date, but without any obligation as to the precise moment that the activity is to take place).

FIGURE 5. Language Distribution of Documents in the Knowledge Pool (as per Early 1999)

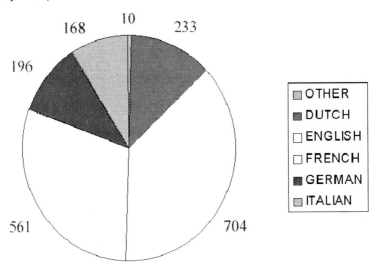

The typical scenario is that the course team first defines the so-called *pedagogical scenario* that outlines the general characteristics and goals of the course. Then, using the *Curriculum Editor*, the course is actually instantiated in digital format. Documents are discovered and retrieved from the KPS with the Query Tool (section 3.4). These documents are then allocated to particular sessions. From the structural information in the curriculum, and the content in the KPS, a course Website is generated automatically. This Website has separate facilities for managers and learners, as illustrated in Figure 1.

By generating a course Website, copying documents out of the KPS, the course can be distributed completely independently. In fact, the course can even be stored on a CD-ROM and distributed off-line. This helps to avoid the Local Knowledge Pool becoming a bottleneck, when students all start accessing course material if they have a synchronous session.

The implementation of the ARIADNE course relies on the Apache Web server *<http://www.apache.org/>* and the servlet mechanism to access Java programs we have developed for authoring and management of courses.

4. THE ARIADNE COMMUNITY AND EXPERIENCE

Over the years, we have learned a great deal from the practical experience by our user community. Some of the lessons we learned are listed below:

- We have had rather lengthy discussions within the consortium about standards for *validation* of the pedagogical documents. It turned out that it was extremely difficult to identify a set of quality guidelines that would be applicable across disciplines and cultures. What has been well accepted, though, is validation of the metadata, i.e., quality control of the descriptions rather than the documents (section 2.3.6). For this purpose, we have set up an organisation with individuals that can validate documents within their field of expertise. The latter is defined by the same metadata set presented above, so that user profiles can be matched against newly arrived documents and their metadata. Validators typically verify that the description is indeed consistent and that the document can actually be retrieved from the KPS and 'viewed' or 'launched' as per the instructions in the metadata (section 2.3.4). Only when a description has been validated, does the document become visible to other end users.
- In section 2.3.2, the current breakdown of pedagogical documents over disciplines was presented. Likewise, it is interesting to note the breakdown of that material over languages. From this distribution, it is very clear that the ARIADNE community is indeed a *multilingual* community. This characteristic presents particular problems (e.g., user interfaces in several languages need to be supported and developed for the toolset presented above), but, on the other hand, we consider this as an integral part of the European cultural heritage, that we want to support rather than ignore. Hence our emphasis on the importance of metadata elements that deal with language issues, both with respect to the document being described, as well as with respect to the language of the metadata.
- It is interesting to note that, despite the focus on market-oriented approaches even in the field of education, about 70% to 80% of all ARIADNE documents are available for free. This has been the choice of the authors, who seem to feel comfortable with this notion of share and reuse on a voluntary basis, much in the way that academic research is supposed to be freely available (if we ignore the commercial pressures from scientific publishers, the publish-or-perish phenomenon, etc.). Most authors do seem to appreciate that, in an ARIADNE context, reuse does not mean that anyone can take your material and publish it as if it were his own, but that it remains properly attributed (as the author is included in the metadata). In fact, there are many parallels between this notion of free share and reuse on the one hand and the open source software movement on the other hand.[11]
- Prospective users associated with a not-for-profit organisation become members of the ARIADNE User Group by signing a confidentiality agreement in which they basically confirm that they will not sell any of

our tools or any of the content in the KPS to third parties. As a member of the User Group, they receive a periodical newsletter and can participate in meetings where hands-on training sessions are organized for individual tools. There are now about 100 academic institutions that have indeed signed this agreement and have thus become a member of the User Group.

5. RELATED WORK

5.1. Introduction

In this section, we compare our work briefly with related efforts elsewhere. First of all, it is interesting to note that, at the time when the ARIADNE work started, there was very little attention for metadata in general, and almost none with a specific educational focus.

5.2. Dublin Core

Most of the general metadata work is, either formally or not, part of the *Dublin Core* initiative.[6] That work is less ambitious in scope, in that it only tries to deal with discovery of resources. The current status is that 15 elements have been defined and published in an RFC Internet-type standard. (This is sometimes referred to as DC1.0.) Work is ongoing on improving the definitions of the elements (DC1.1), and, more importantly, on defining mechanisms to qualify the elements (as in DC.Date.Creation) and the values (as in DC.Subject with Scheme=Library Of Congress Subject Headings), so as to increase the flexibility and precision of the metadata.

Roughly speaking, the ARIADNE metadata set includes all Dublin Core elements. In that sense, we have extended Dublin Core. However, we have also added an additional level of detail to the Dublin Core elements, and added a large number of elements that have no obvious counterpart in Dublin Core. As an example of the former, our semantic category (section 2.3.2) corresponds with the single field DC.Subject. As an example of an ARIADNE category with no counterpart in Dublin Core, the whole pedagogical category (2.3.3) has no direct equivalent in Dublin Core. This is to be expected as Dublin Core deals with general metadata for general documents, whereas the focus of ARIADNE work is on *educational* documents.

5.3. International Standardization

If share and reuse is to be realised on a large scale, then a critical mass of pedagogical documents is required. In order to achieve such critical mass, ARIADNE has become involved in international standardization efforts on educational metadata. More specifically, we are participating in the Learning Object Metadata (LOM) Working Group of the IEEE Learning Technology Standards Committee (LTSC, P1484).[4] In fact, the LOM proposed standard is based on the work presented above, as well as on similar work by the IMS project *<http://www.imsproject.org/>*. It is planned that the same LOM group will also define a standardized XML representation for educational metadata.

As mentioned above, the more specific European requirements with respect to multiculturalism are of crucial importance in our context. That is why ARIADNE has been involved also in the setting up of a CEN/CENE-LEC ISSS Workshop on Learning Technologies *<http://www.cenorm.be/isss/workshop/lt/>*. In a first phase, this standardisation body will set up a workplan for further work in this field. In the meantime, it will also work on localisation of the LOM metadata standard. This involves translation of the metadata structure, of the closed and open vocabularies involved, and an investigation into the applicability of the proposed metadata standard across cultures and disciplines.

Basically, the intention is that common standards for educational technology should realise the goal of interoperability between systems and services. This is the more important, as this is the only way that the current "vendor lock-in" can be remedied. Moreover, if such standards are truly adopted, then a global platform for learning can become reality and that is a requirement to make sure that technological innovations can have a real impact on education and training.[12]

CONCLUSION

In this paper, we have presented the ARIADNE educational metadata set, as well as a technological infrastructure that supports the indexation of pedagogical documents, their management and storage in the so-called Knowledge Pool System, query-based access and the incorporation of the documents in courses.

It is our hope that this work may contribute to the promotion of methodologies based on free and fair share and reuse, so that, in the end, we can realise higher quality learning experiences.

ACKNOWLEDGMENTS

ARIADNE is supported by the Telematics for Education and Training Program of the European Commission and by the Swiss Fund for Scientific Research. Erik Duval is supported as a post-doctoral fellow by Belgian National Fund for Scientific Research-Flanders. Hewlett-Packard and Oracle have sponsored the ARIADNE project.

REFERENCES

1. E. Forte, M. Wentland-Forte & E. Duval, *The ARIADNE project (Part 1): Knowledge Pools for Computer-based and Telematics-supported Classical, Open and Distance Education*, European Journal of Engineering Education. Vol. 22, nr. 2, pp. 61-74. 1997.

2. E. Forte, M. Wentland-Forte & E. Duval, *The ARIADNE project (Part 2): Knowledge Pools for Computer-based and Telematics-supported Classical, Open and Distance Education*, European Journal of Engineering Education. Vol. 22, nr. 2, pp. 153-166. 1997.

3. K. Cardinaels, K. Hendrikx, E. Vervaet, E. Duval, H. Olivié, F. Haenni, K. Warkentyne, M. Wentland-Forte & E. Forte, *A Knowledge Pool System of Reusable Pedagogical Elements*, Proceedings of CALISCE98: 4th International Conference on Computer Aided Learning and Instruction in Science and Engineering. pp. 54-62, June 1998.

4. *Learning Objects Metadata Base Scheme*, version 3.5, July 1999. *<http:// grouper.ieee.org/groups/ltsc/wg12/index.html>*.

5. E. Forte, F. Haenni, K. Warkentyne, E. Duval, K. Cardinaels, E. Vervaet, K. Hendrikx, M. Wentland Forte & F. Simillion. *Semantic and pedagogic Interoperability Mechanisms in the Ariadne Educational Repository*. SIGMOD Record, Vol. 28, No. 1, pp. 20-25, March 1999.

6. S. Weibel. *The State of the Dublin Core Metadata Initiative*. D-Lib Magazine, April 1999. *<http://www.dlib.org/dlib/apri199/04weibel.html>*.

7. D. Berman, E. Miller, G. Rust, J. Trant & S. Weibel. *A Common Model to Support Interoperable Metadata: A progress report on reconciling metadata requirements from the Dublin Core and INDECS/DOI Communities*. D-Lib Magazine, Vol. 5, No. 1, Jan. 1999. *<http://www.dlib.org/dlib/january99/bearman/01bearman.html>*.

8. B. Verhoeven, E. Duval & H. Olivié. *A Generic Metadata Query Tool*. Proceedings of WebNet99, November 1999. Accepted. *<http://www.aace.org/conf/webnet>*.

9. G. Rust & M. Bide. *The <indecs> metadata model*. July 1999. *<http://www. indecs.org/pdf/mode13.pdf>*.

10. H. Maurer. The Heart of the Problem: Knowledge Management and Knowledge Transfer, Proceedings of ENABLE99: Enabling Network-Based Learning, pp. 8-17, 2-5 June 1999. *<http://www.enable.evitech.fi/enable99>*.

11. T. O'Reilly. *Lessons from Open-Source Software Development*. Communications of the ACM, Vol. 42., No. 4, pp. 32-37, April 1999.

12. E. Duval. *An Open Infrastructure for Learning–the ARIADNE project–Share and reuse without boundaries*, Proceedings of ENABLE99: Enabling Network-Based Learning, pp. 144-151, 2-5 June 1999. *<http://www.enable.evitech.fi/enable99>*.

13. S. Hill & M. Wentland-Forte. *OPHELIA, Object-oriented Pedagogical Hypertext Editor for Learning, Instruction and Authoring*, Proceedings of Hypermedia et Apprentissage, 15-17 Oct. 1998.

14. E. Forte. *Building Targeted Curricula for the Learning Citizen within a European Knowledge Pooling System*, Proceedings of EITC'97, European IT Conference, pp. 48-49, 24-26 Nov. 1997.

Disiecta Membra:
Construction and Reconstruction
in a Digital Catalog of Greek Sculpture

Amy C. Smith

SUMMARY. Ancient sculpture is fragmentary. Some sculptures exist only in pieces; others have been split up; and many of the ancient world's most famous statues now survive only in multiple copies created later than the originals. This paper discusses the evolution of a Greek sculpture catalog on the Perseus Project and its recent redesign that brings the visitor's attention to these complexities of ancient art. A data field in our 4th Dimension database categorizes artworks according to their degree of entirety and automatically generates links to related objects. More than one relation for each object is permitted, which encourages users to investigate the whole range of possible connections. This multirelational database enables our next phase of catalog development, which will include the construction of series of copies, the contextualization of groups of sculptures, and the reconstruction of lost originals. *[Article copies available for a fee from The Haworth Document Delivery Service: 1-800-342-9678. E-mail address: <getinfo@haworthpressinc. com> Website: <http://www.HaworthPress.com>]*

KEYWORDS. Ancient art, Greece, sculpture, Classics, reconstruction, contextualization, instructional technology, digital library, multimedia catalog

Amy C. Smith is Art and Archaeology Editor, Perseus Project, Department of Classics, Tufts University, Medford, MA 02155 (e-mail: acsmith@perseus.tufts. edu). Dr. Smith received her PhD from Yale University, where she studied in the Program in Classical Art and Archaeology.

The author wishes to thank Jeffrey A. Rydberg-Cox (Assistant Editor for Greek Language and Lexicography, Perseus Project) for his interest in this paper and for his helpful comments on several drafts of it.

[Haworth co-indexing entry note]: "*Disiecta Membra:* Construction and Resconstruction in a Digital Catalog of Greek Sculpture." Smith, Amy C. Co-published simultaneously in *Journal of Internet Cataloging* (The Haworth Information Press, an imprint of The Haworth Press, Inc.) Vol. 3, No. 2/3, 2000, pp. 173-189; and: *Metadata and Organizing Educational Resources on the Internet* (ed: Jane Greenberg) The Haworth Information Press, an imprint of The Haworth Press, Inc., 2000, pp. 173-189. Single or multiple copies of this article are available for a fee from The Haworth Document Delivery Service [1-800-342-9678, 9:00 a.m. - 5:00 p.m. (EST). E-mail address: getinfo@haworthpressinc.com].

© 2000 by The Haworth Press, Inc. All rights reserved. *173*

As with most multimedia projects–and perhaps all digital libraries–the development of the Perseus Project has been evolutionary rather than pre-planned, and the addition of a catalog of Greek sculpture–which itself has followed an evolutionary course–came relatively late in Perseus' coverage of the Archaic and Classical Greek world (ca. 700-330 B.C.). Developing of a catalog of ancient Greek sculpture for the Perseus Project has provided new solutions to old problems that are not easily tackled in print media. In this paper I discuss the evolution of a catalog of Greek Sculpture on the Perseus Project, and the ways in which it may introduce Internet visitors–now and in the future–to a comprehensive and realistic vision of ancient Greek sculpture. To highlight the evolutionary nature of this work, three distinct phases in the development of the Perseus Project's Greek sculpture catalog are discussed: the initial HyperCard catalog that was incorporated into *Perseus 1.0: Interactive Sources and Studies on Ancient Greek Culture* and *Perseus 2.0* on CD-ROMs;[1] the enlarged and redesigned catalog that is now available on the Perseus Project's Website (http://www.perseus.tufts.edu); and the future changes envisioned by the developers of the Perseus Project.

A HYPERCARD CATALOG ON CD-ROM

The Perseus Project, a digital library for the humanities, contains an interactive encyclopedia of Archaic and Classical Greek civilization–comprised of texts, lexica, plans, maps, images, and archaeological catalogs–and is considered the flagship of digital tools for the study of Classics.[2] The brainchild of Gregory Crane, it originated in 1985 as a linguistic tool to facilitate the learning of the ancient Greek language.[3] After a morphological tool was combined with texts (in ancient Greek) and translations of Greek literature, Crane quickly realized the multimedia promise of such digital educational tools; that this project could also combine literary sources with history, art, and archaeology, as a means of exposing the student/scholar to the full range of remnants of ancient Greece, including primary materials beyond his/her specific focus. Perseus has been published subsequently in two Mac-platform CD-ROMs and is available on the Internet at http://www.perseus.tufts.edu.

The archaeological materials added to the Perseus Project in its earliest phases (up to 1996) included a selection of objects (coins and painted vases as well as sculpture), buildings, and sites from the world of Archaic and Classical Greece–279 buildings, 522 coins, 134 sculptures, 137 sites, and 137 vases in *Perseus 1.0* and 381 buildings, 522 coins, 366 sculptures, 179 sites, and 1415 vases in *Perseus 2.0*. Over 70 museums generously shared images of their art objects, which were included in *Perseus 2.0*. The atomic objects, i.e., those that constitute discrete movable entities–coins, vases, sculptures, and even entire buildings–were each given their own catalog entries, which followed traditional lines (noting specific dates and locations, fabric, subject, and form descriptions, etc.).[4] Some more flexible information was added for the archaeological sites, which in most cases spanned several occupation periods. Relevant images were linked to each entry. These catalog entries were designed for and perfectly suited the HyperCard environment in which the Perseus Project was published.[5] With the Perseus Project at her/his fingertips the student of ancient Greece could now shuffle through the relevant stacks, applying morphological tools to ancient texts, as needed, investigating discrete catalog entries, or sorting through lists of various archaeological materials–organized in whichever order he/she selected. Thus a student of Homer's *Iliad* could search for ancient representations of the hero Achilles with which to envision a main character of this epic.

The growth of the sculpture catalog after the release of *Perseus 1.0* in 1992 has been largely supported by a generous grant from the Getty Grant Program.[6] The work plan, submitted in 1992, was to photograph and document 400 Archaic and Classical sculptures in Greek Museums,[7] and to add them to the catalog in progress, which itself included objects in museums worldwide–Berlin, Boston, London, Munich, New York, and Paris. The reluctance of Greek Museums to share images on CD-ROMs, and of most museums to share images of their art works freely on the Web, however, slowed development of this and indeed most art and archaeology portions of the Perseus Project.

At this primary stage the sculpture catalog, like each of Perseus' archaeological materials, consisted of a stand-alone relational database, with files for documentation, available images, relevant bibliography, and keywords (to assist in searching for objects by subject matter). Except for the bibliography, which exists as an EndNote® database, the databases were constructed and maintained in a 4th Dimension environment.[8] The 4th Dimension application allows for some interrelations as well as great flexibility at the input level, so that a researcher/catalog writer without advanced programming knowledge may use it. The format of the actual database was adapted from that of Perseus' other archaeology databases, with 33 separate fields–indexed fields and (descriptive) text fields. The 10 indexed fields contained simple information that might be searched and sorted–about the collection (current location of the object), catalog number, type (by which a rudimentary classification of the type of object was meant), scale, style, sculptor, context (an unsatisfying amalgam of original context and findspot), associated building, material summary, and period. Descriptive text fields (19) included another title by which the sculpture might be known (besides the catalog number), subject summary and description, dimensions, preservation summary and description, material, stylistic, and technique descriptions, associated inscriptions, dates and date discussion, collection history, parallels (comparanda), primary texts, other objects associated with the sculpture, replicas, (bibliographic) sources used, and other bibliography. Four additional fields were created to accommodate simple text modifiers for indexed and descriptive fields–sculptor, context, dates, and placement on an associated building.

While 4th Dimension provides the front-end database at present, the back end is more complicated. The data is transferred through a multi-step process of exporting from 4th Dimension, transferring data to a UNIX system, performing some text transformations, and importing the data into Postgres.[9] All Perseus texts, including the sculpture catalog, are archived in SGML (Standard Generalized Markup Language), which allows the text to be parsed, validated, and otherwise manipulated (e.g., all bibliographic references could be extracted from the catalog).[10] This feature is particularly important in the case of the descriptive text fields that otherwise would not be easily searched or sorted. SGML has also allowed for relatively simple translation of the catalog databases from their input environment to virtually any other database or output environment. Thus the data created for the HyperCard stacks used for the CD-ROMs were easily converted to a useful database for Perseus' inaugural manifestation on the Web in 1995.

Despite its immediate usefulness, the catalog described above was hampered by some limitations inherent in the HyperCard and the laborious nature of early multimedia. In a 1997 review Marek Kohn ironically remarked that *Perseus* required "the patience that studying classics is supposed to inculcate."[11] The Perseus Project developers chose HyperCard because of its adaptability. In 1988, Elli Mylonas, then Managing Editor of the Perseus Project, remarked, "HyperCard has given us the most democratic and flexible system so far. It has its limitations–for example, it can only support one font style in a window, so you can't have English and Greek in the same window."[12] In 1996 the HyperCard presentation seemed less flexible than it had seemed in 1992; as Nick Eiteljorg justifiably complained, "the complete separation of text and graphics elements in *Perseus 2.0* seems more than dated; it projects a bias toward words and against images."[13]

Hindsight has allowed us to discover other problems that cropped up at the input level, such as awkward handling of alternate names. Variations in spelling and nomenclature are standard in ancient studies. The Greek hero Achilles, for example, is correctly referred to by transliterations of his Greek name (Akhilleus or Akhilles), by Latinized versions of that name (Achilleus or Achilles), and by at least one other name, Ligyron. While a database of alternate names was built in anticipation of variation in spellings and names that the users would wish to employ, it was built into the CD-ROMs and the earlier Website as a didactic tool. That is, the user would be presented with the variety of names by which an object, site, or person might be known, but would then have to search individually each alternate name.[14] Even synonyms and alternate spellings (e.g., pottery v. ceramic or terracotta v. terra cotta) were not sufficiently standardized in either descriptive or indexed fields to enable the program to infer all necessary cross-references. A system of keywords was established to allow for searching across multiple catalogs and lists of catalog entries: a keyword search for "barley" would generate a list of 17 coins with images of this food item. Yet the keywords were limited to iconographic terms (scenes shown, individuals pictured, and attributes worn/held by those characters). And although the developers went to great lengths to include the vast majority of iconographic types–to the point at which keyword searches were inconveniently tedious and slow–the original database of keywords was limited to subject matter included in the original group of archaeological materials; additional keywords for novel subjects shown on newer materials had to be generated by hand, rather than inferentially in the program. Thus the uninitiated user could not find the "Kritios Boy" (a famous sculpture in Athens, known generally by this popular name) except by typing in its inventory number–Athens, Acropolis 698–or by sorting through lists from within the sculpture catalog.

ADAPTING CATALOGS TO THE INTERNET

Perseus' art and archaeology databases, initially published, as described above, in a HyperCard user environment, were imported with relative ease to a Postgres database for Perseus' debut on the Web in September 1995. On the Perseus Web site, as on the CD-ROMs, art and archaeology databases are presented as discrete catalogs that are interlinked with other materials in this ever-expanding digital library. The databases also have undergone constant expansion. As museums have become more comfortable with the existence of the Web, and in some cases are especially eager to find a Web presence, progress has been made on the breadth of images in the Perseus Project. Now over 20,000 images of art works in museums, as well as illustrations of sites and buildings, are freely available on the Perseus Website.[15] And the revised Greek sculpture catalog, which on the latest CD-ROM comprised 366 discrete objects, included 588 objects when it was released on 19 May 1998,[16] now includes over 1000 objects.

Despite the multitude of images, the hypertext environment, and multiple search options, however, Perseus' early art and archaeology Web catalogs fell far short of the promise of the Internet, in that they barely allowed for interrelation between atomic objects. In his 1997 review of *Perseus 2.0*,[17] Nick Eiteljorg provided the most substantial and useful criticism of the sculpture catalog–that the catalog information was overly simplified so that, for example, no explanations or reasons were given for the existence of multiple copies of the same original statue and some Roman copies of sculptures were misleadingly and incorrectly dated to the Classical Greek period in which the original artworks that they copied would have been dated. In sum, little allowance had been made for the existence of copies of famous original statues and their relation to each other. Indeed a complex challenge is posed by the fragmentary nature of extant Greek sculpture: some sculptures are comprised of fragments located in a variety of museums; many more (particularly architectural sculptures) once belonged to a group that may have been separated through time; and the most famous statues from Greek antiquity are lost, yet recognized in multiple copies of the originals that proliferated in Roman society.

Repetition of material and limited opportunities for comparison are age-old dilemmas among catalogers. Indeed print catalogs compiled by museums throughout the world have always had to treat each art work as a separate piece, regardless of its relation to a larger monument, with at best a cross-reference to or citation of a relevant work in another museum. The addition of multiple images and artificial links to comparable or related objects on a Web catalog greatly surpasses the illustrative material traditionally available in print catalogs. Ease of access to disparate resources and usability of primary resources are further benefits to the basic Web catalog, such as that launched on the Perseus Project's Website in 1995. Yet this basic Web catalog does not reach the potential of today's digital world, let alone tomorrow's metadigital universe. In the case of ancient art–particularly sculpture–it obscures the most complex and intriguing aspects of the artworks and fails to present an accurate impression of these monuments as they were in antiquity.

During 1997-1998, the Perseus Project's Greek sculpture catalogue was entirely rethought so that the presentation could bring each visitor's attention to the three features that distinguish the study of Greek sculpture from that of more completely preserved artworks: works comprised of more than one sculpture, such as statuary groups and architectural sculptures; multiple copies; and separated fragments. A preeminent example of all of these relationships is the Parthenon, or Temple of Athena Parthenos in Athens (Figure 1). This building was decorated with three different types of sculptural forms, metopes–square (relief) plaques–on the outer frieze, a continuous relief zone on the interior (Ionic) frieze, and two sets of pedimental sculptures, one on the East façade and one on the West. Each of these sculptural forms relates to one another and to the building as a whole. But each of these forms also represents a separate group (or multiple groups) of sculptures, e.g., the discrete metopes originally numbered 92, but may be divided into four thematically distinct groups depending on which of the four faces of the building they decorated. Through the ravages of time, many of these sculptures have been separated from each other, and some reliefs and figures have been broken, yet these fragments should still be studied in relation to each other.

FIGURE 1. Top plan of the Parthenon on the Acropolis, Athens (447-432 B.C.), indicating the themes of its sculptural decoration. After Susan Woodford, *The Parthenon* (Cambridge 1981): fig. 4.9. Reprinted with permission of Cambridge University Press.

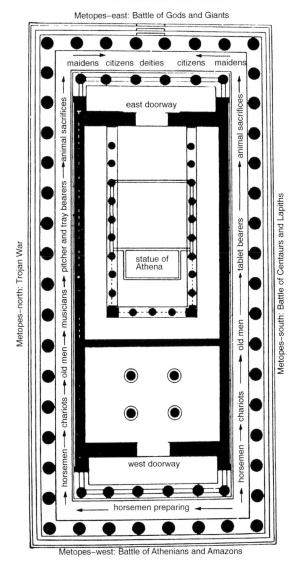

Pediment: east (front)
Contest of Athena and Poseidon

Metopes–east: Battle of Gods and Giants

maidens citizens deities citizens maidens

east doorway

animal sacrifices

animal sacrifices

pitcher and tray bearers

tablet bearers

statue of Athena

Metopes–north: Trojan War

Metopes–south: Battle of Centaurs and Lapiths

musicians

old men

old men

chariots

chariots

west doorway

horsemen

horsemen

horsemen preparing

Metopes–west: Battle of Athenians and Amazons

Pediment: west (back)
Contest of Athena and Poseidon

The issue of multiple copies is somewhat less well known. Whereas painted Greek vases share many iconographic and stylistic features with each other, only on the rare occasion may any two vases be identified as duplicates, or as a matched set. Many Greek sculptures, however, are known only through almost identical copies produced in Roman times, rather than the original art work, and such is the case with the chryselephantine (gold and ivory) cult statue of Athena Parthenos that originally stood within that Temple, but had been lost by late antiquity. Yet multiple copies of the original statue of Athena Parthenos were subsequently created–most during the Roman period (first-third centuries A.C.). These copies help us to visualize the original; see, e.g., a copy in the National Museum, Athens, the so-called Lenormant Statuette (Figure 2). It is also instructive to the scholar to compare sculptures that seem to have copied the same original, as an indirect means of perceiving the original, or as a means for understanding the copying industry and/or the methods of Roman sculptors; compare the Lenormant Athena, for example, to a contemporary but larger-scale Roman copy of Athena Parthenos, now in the Museum of Fine Arts, Boston (Figure 3).

The Perseus Project's sculpture catalog was redesigned in the preexisting 4th Dimension format with almost no changes to the existing data and relatively few strategic changes to the database itself.[18] The most important change was the creation of a new data field, named "category," that was used to specify the particular relation by which a sculpture might be connected to another. One of a discrete number of possible relations would be indicated for each piece: "single monument," "statuary group," "original/copies," or "separated fragments." The pertinent relation thus residing in the database would then indicate the way in which that monument should be linked to related monuments. In the case of single monument, no relation would be necessary. "Statuary group" would generate a link to a specified "group" to which the sculpture belonged. "Original/copies" would generate a link to a specified "original" that this sculpture copied. And "separated fragments" would likewise generate a link to a specified "whole" to which the sculpture originally belonged. Thus, for example, the entry for the "Rampin Rider" (Figure 4) links to separate entries for the body in Athens (Athens, Acropolis Museum 590) and the head in Paris (Louvre Ma 3104), both of which, in turn, provide links to the main entry. Additional fields provide for such implicit links between additional relations. If the "class" of the object (formerly called "type") is "architectural," then an "associated building" may be specified and the "placement" of the sculpture of the building may be indicated.

The database also permits the existence of more than one such relation for each sculpture. Thus the complexity of the sculptural program of the Parthenon, for example, may be fully appreciated with a few clicks of the mouse:

FIGURE 2. The Lenormant Statuette of Athena Parthenos. From Athens (2nd century A.C.). Athens, National Museum 128. Photo author.

FIGURE 3. Roman copy of Athena Parthenos (2nd century A.C.). Museum of Fine Arts, Boston 1980.196. Photo author.

FIGURE 4. Composite figure of the Rampin Rider in the Louvre, Paris. Original head (Louvre Ma 3104) with a plaster cast of the body in Athens (Athens, Acropolis Museum 590). Photo author.

from a catalog entry on the Parthenon in our architecture catalog one may access catalog entries on groups of sculptures that adorned the building, e.g., the east pediment or the frieze. Within each group entry one may then access separate entries on single metopes, individual figures in each pediment, or separate blocks in the frieze. And joining fragments of frieze blocks in separate museums are interlinked and may be compared. We are fortunate, in the case of the Parthenon, that so much of the original sculpture remains; yet the lost Athena Parthenos may also be accessed on the Perseus Project through several extant and illustrated Roman copies of the statue that are linked to the main catalog entry on this lost masterpiece.

A second way in which the 4th Dimension environment was adapted to speed data entry as well as ensure the coherence of the database was the addition of restricted vocabulary for indexed fields. Pop-up menus now provide for one of two basic answers (or modifications thereof) in specifying whether the sculpture is an original or a copy (made in Hellenistic or Roman times, but based on a famous original work of art). A greater variety of choices (often including indeterminate answers such as "unknown") is provided for the following categories: museum name, scale, material summary, sculptor, class (a general classification of the type of monument), function, (architectural) placement, period, style, author, condition summary, technique summary, original context, and region.[19] Some of these categories–functions and known findspots[20]–were added to the range of information provided for individual objects.

We have now begun the process of transporting our 4th Dimension database to FileMaker in order to eliminate the front end-back end disconnect currently inherent in our system.[21] FileMaker will provide an easy-to-use graphical environment to serve as the front end for our Postgres back end. Several years ago we transported part of our 4th Dimension database to FileMaker to facilitate our collaborative work with the Museum of Fine Arts, Boston, which already possessed an in-house FileMaker database. By entering our data on MFA, Boston objects into FileMaker we could then generate a catalog that would serve our purposes as well as those of the Museum. At the present time FileMaker provides a flexible system as adaptable as that on 4th Dimension but which is easier to learn and to share among multiple users. Its compatibility with Postgres should also eliminate the tedious intermediary programming that is required with our current system.

FUTURE WORK

The next stage in the evolution of the Perseus Project's catalog of Greek sculpture is the contextualization of the individual sculptures, alone and in groups. More work is needed–on the part of scholars as well as cataloguers–

in establishing the variety of relations between individual sculptures, and representing them intelligibly to the widest possible audience. We hope to improve the user interface on the Perseus Project's Website to contextualize and otherwise enhance the educational experience of visitors to our catalog. Already our comprehensive text browser facilitates access between our sculpture catalog and other Perseus materials.[22] To this tool we expect to add a thumbnail browser that will allow users to visually compare a selection of images of the same or different objects and the reconstruction of spatial and architectural complexes in which many of the sculptures in our catalog were originally found. Full advantage of the multimedia digital environment may be employed to enable us to present students with an overview of the relationships between particular sculptures and of their relationship to sites and buildings. 3-D visualization of these relationships–particularly of broken fragments, sculptural groups, and architectural placement–is more easily accomplished with the multimedia tools available today. Rapid advances in the accuracy of 3-D digital representations are now allowing us to accomplish faithful digital reconstructions not only of architectural spaces, but also of actual objects–first to digitally rebuild those that exist today, and then to extrapolate in an attempt to visualize those that are lost to us.

Work has already begun on establishing a related database of sculpture types–the art works on which copies were based. Scholars have begun to realize that Hellenistic and Roman copies of Greek originals should not only be studied in their own right (with regard to issues of production, collections, taste, and architectural placement/decoration), but that there is not necessarily a one-to-one relationship of copies to originals.[23] That is, copies seem to have copied intermediate types or copies of copies of originals. An appropriate treatment of these copies–as copies of copies, not necessarily copies of originals–may be easily tackled in a relational database, so that an infinite genealogy of original types, variations, copy types, and subsequent copies thereof, may be built into the database. In the case of complicated examples–such as that of Praxiteles' Aphrodite of Knidos[24]–a program might even generate a genealogical table that would provide the interested viewer with a quick overview of the relation of several related sculptures in the nexus of originals and copies.

Access to multiple views of individual objects, at a wider range of resolutions, is demanded by today's Internet user. At present each image on the Perseus Project is represented in the form of a 72-dpi jpeg image that is scaled to fit onto the smallest of monitors (at 480 x 640 dpi resolution). While such low resolution images (in the range of a few hundred K) are loaded with relative ease by most institutional users, speed of access might be facilitated by the use of thumbnail images, for browsing purposes. While the CD-ROM editions of the Perseus Project included a thumbnail browser with which students could glance at multiple images of the same object, no such browser has been implemented, as yet, on our Website. We hope soon to provide a more complex thumbnail browser that will allow for the comparison of all (or a selection of) views of the same sculpture, of two or more sculptures, of one or more sculptures with comparable coins or vases, or of sculptures alongside the architectural monuments or spaces that they adorned.

Beyond a visualization of the relation of multiple sculptures to each other, accurate visualizations of the original context and form of the sculptures, whether lost originals or broken copies, are also warranted. An exciting multimedia means of visualization is 3-D reconstruction of the original place-ment of the sculptures, which would show each sculpture in relation to one another and to the architectural complex of which it played an integral part. Although several ambitious projects have attempted to provide accurate scholarly reconstructions of some important monuments from classical antiq-uity, none, to our knowledge, have attempted to provide accurate renderings of the sculptural decoration of these monuments, but have rather aimed to provide architecturally precise spaces. While we appreciate that this problem arises from the fact that the nascent technology to provide accurate 3-D renderings of 3-D art is expensive, whereas the tools through which one may render 3-D architectural spaces (Auto-CAD and VRML, to name a few) are relatively commonplace, rudimentary architectural reconstructions may at least provide contexts in which images of sculptures–both architectural and those in the round–may be visualized. We thus propose to provide architec-tural contexts–sanctuaries as well as buildings–as backdrops for the contextu-alization or placement of a variety of sculptures in the Perseus database.[25] We have proposed initially to provide reconstructions of three buildings–the Parthenon at Athens, the Temple of Aphaia at Aigina, and the Siphnian Treasury at Delphi–as well as reconstructions of two of the sanctuary sites that house these buildings–the Acropolis at Athens and the Sanctuary of Apollo at Delphi.

A more ambitious future project that involves the relation of copies to originals, and of separated fragments to each other, is the implementation of 3-D scanning technology to create digital images of existing copies or frag-ments and subsequent reconstructions of the original sculptural works on which they were based or to which they belonged. A detailed measurement and analysis of the copies/fragments would enable one to usefully superim-pose missing parts of some copies on others, to scale each copy to the same "actual size," to adjust for copyists' additions or changes (e.g., to account for dimensions that may have been foreshortened in a relief representation), and finally to arrive at a clearer picture of the original statue(s) on which copies were based. The technology to enable an accurate digital rendering of the originals is already available, and is now being employed by its inventor,

Marc Levoy of the Stanford University Computer Graphics Lab, in the study of the sculptures of Michelangelo.[26] While this laser scanning technology has proved successful in the digital recreation of known sculptures, the data acquired through such a process has not yet been used as a basis for comparison of similar copies and extrapolation that might render the most faithful recreations of long-lost ancient masterpieces. Such an adaptation of this scanning technology might also enable students at all levels to digitally create their own reconstructions.

CONCLUSION

One of the biggest challenges faced by students of ancient art–namely, how to tackle fragmentary sculptures–is no older than the printed catalog. Severed arms, heads, and torsos are scattered throughout the world's museums and several thousand pages of printed catalogs. The process of connection and comparison required to reconstruct the separated parts or to visualize the originals is thus daunting and laborious. In taking advantage of the hypertext medium of the Internet our newly configured database now allows students to bring together these *disiecta membra* or "disjoined limbs" of Greek sculpture for a range of comparison impracticable in print media. It is our sincere hope that the Perseus Project will soon provide its visitors with a means for visual comparison and reconstruction of these original fragments, multifigured groups, multiple copies, and lost originals. When visually exciting and historically accurate 3-D renderings and reconstructions of fragmentary ancient sculptures have been provided, it should be relatively simple to apply similar database structures and visual tools to more streamlined corpora of ancient art, such as coins and painted vases, and to thus present a comprehensive view of the ancient world that is recognized now only through the fragmentary evidence that has survived from antiquity.

REFERENCES

1. Gregory R. Crane ed., *Perseus 1.0: Interactive Sources and Studies on Ancient Greek Culture* (New Haven 1992); Gregory R. Crane ed., *Perseus 2.0* (New Haven 1996). A platform independent CD-ROM is now available through Yale University Press.

2. Or so it was termed by Mary Beard, "Go Greece enlightening," *The Guardian* (February 6, 1997): 12. The Perseus Project is named for the Greek hero Perseus–a cipher for the mastery of knowledge over ignorance–who travelled to the corners of the civilized world to behead the monster Medusa.

3. For a discussion of the evolution of the Perseus Project from the Thesaurus Linguae Graecae via the Harvard Classics Computer Project see Linda W. Helgerson,

"CD-ROM and Scholarly Research in the Humanities," *Computers and the Humanities* 22 (1988): 111-16.

4. Now the Getty Information Institute has established a controlled vocabulary for art, architecture, and material culture: "The Art & Architecture Thesaurus" (AAT), available on the Web at http://shiva.pub.getty.edu/aat_browser.

5. For an overview of the evaluation of the Perseus Project 1.0, see Delia Neuman, "Evaluating Evolution: Naturalistic Inquiry and the Perseus Project," *Computers and the Humanities* 25 (1991): 239-46. For descriptions of the Perseus Project in its early years see Gregory Crane, "Challenging the Individual: The Tradition of Hypermedia Databases," *Academic Computing* 4 (1990): 22-38; Gregory Crane, "Redefining the Book: Some Preliminary Problems," *Academic Computing* 2 (1988): 6-11, 36-41; Gregory Crane and Elli Mylonas, "The Perseus Project: An Interactive Curriculum on Classical Greek Civilization," *Educational Technology* 28 (1988): 25-32; V. Judson Harward, "From Museum to Monitor: The Visual Exploration of the Ancient World," *Academic Computing* 3 (1988): 16-19, 69-71; and John J. Hughes, "Studying Ancient Greek Civilization Interactively–the Perseus Project," *Bits & Bytes Review* 2 (1988): 1-12.

6. "A Visual Database of Archaic and Classical Greek Sculpture." Information on the Getty Grant Program is available at http://www.getty.edu/grant.

7. The list includes museums in Athens (Acropolis Museum, Epigraphic Museum, Kerameikos Museum, and National Museum), as well as the Delos, Delphi, Samos, Sparta, Thasos, and Thebes Archaeological Museums.

8. ACI's 4th Dimension, of which version 6.5 is currently available, is distributed in the US through ACI US, Inc. (http://www.acius.com). EndNote®, now available in version 4.0, is available through Niles Software Inc. (http://www.niles.com).

9. Postgres is available on the Web at http://www.postgresql.org.

10. Members of the Perseus Project has been associated with the TEI (Text Encoding Initiative), and all SGML texts on the Perseus Project are TEI-conformant.

11. Marek Kohn, "Technofile" review section, *Independent on Sunday* (February 9, 1997): 32.

12. Janice Bultmann, "Perseus: Heroic Explorations. HyperCard on a Tour of Ancient Greece," *Macintosh Horizons* (September 1988): 42.

13. Harrison Eiteljorg, II, "*Perseus 2.0*–A Review," *CSA Newsletter* 10.1 (Spring 1997): 6.

14. A new "Lookup Tool," released on 11 May 1999 (http://www.perseus.tufts.edu/PR/sor.ann.html), which searches each entity and its alternate names (unless the user deselects this option), is now available on the Perseus Website.

15. Museums that to date have permitted Perseus Project site visitors free access to images of their works are the Berlin Museums, Berlin, Germany; Museum of Fine Arts, Boston, Masachusetts; Indiana University Art Museum, Bloomington, Indiana; Harvard University Art Museums, Cambridge, Massachusetts; J. Paul Getty Museum, Malibu, California; Musée du Louvre, Paris, France; University of Mississippi, Oxford, Mississippi; University Museum, University of Pennsylvania, Philadelphia, Pennsylvania; Rhode Island School of Design, Providence, Rhode Island; Smith College Museum of Art, Northampton, Massachusetts; Tampa Museum of Art,

Tampa, Florida; Toledo, Ohio; Williams College Museum of Art, Williamstown, Massachusetts; and the Martin von Wagner-Museum, Würzburg, Germany.

16. Http://www.perseus.tufts.edu/sculpture.ann.html.

17. Supra n. 13.

18. I gratefully acknowledge here the help and advice of David A. Smith (Programmer, Perseus Project) and Professor D. Neel Smith (Associate Professor of Classics, College of the Holy Cross) in revising the Greek Sculpture database. I am also grateful to David A. Smith for his constant help in implementing these changes, and facilitating the subsequent changes in the user interface.

19. Answers in some of these categories–period and style–in particular, are now automatically linked to explanations in the Perseus Project Encyclopedia. E.g., "High Archaic," as a designated period, is highlighted in the user interface to indicate a link to the Perseus Project Encyclopedia entry on "Art Period," which itself includes a definition of "High Archaic."

20. Note that known findspots are now distinct from "context," because the original context is not always the same as the modern findspot, particularly in the case of famous monuments that were removed in antiquity as war booty to distant locations.

21. FileMaker is available at http://www.filemakerpro.com.

22. The first stage in improving our browser has already been accomplished–with the recent release of our "Lookup Tool" (see n. 14), whereby visitors may find sculptures and other materials by typing in keywords or any other descriptive terms or questions in which they are interested. Further work must be done in the sculpture catalog, however, to provide easy access from the sculptures to related objects, comparable objects, and primary texts, as well as to improve the usability of our bibliography of secondary sources.

23. See Miranda Marvin, "Copying in Roman Sculpture: The Replica Series," in Kathleen Preciado ed., *Retaining the Original, Multiple Originals, Copies, and Reproductions. Studies in the History of Art* 20 (Washington, D.C. 1989): 29-45 for a general discussion of these issues, and Christine M. Havelock, *The Aphrodite of Knidos and Her Successors. A Historical Review of the Female Nude in Greek Art* (Ann Arbor 1995) for an important case study.

24. See Havelock, *ibid.*

25. We anticipate that the specific placement of objects within these contexts might be dictated both by default choices (according to scholarly consensus, as it is recorded in our catalog entries) and, in some cases, by user preference. In this manner a student might compare, for example, how the placement of different pedimental sculptures within the West Pediment of the Parthenon might have affected its overall appearance.

26. Marc Levoy, "Digital Michelangelo Project," http://graphics.stanford.EDU/projects/mich.

The National Engineering Education Delivery System (NEEDS) Project: Reinventing Undergraduate Engineering Education Through Remote Cataloging of Digital Resources

Brad Eden

SUMMARY. The Synthesis Coalition has developed computer courseware modules that can be readily transferred and adapted to different student and campus needs via the Internet using the National Engineering Education Delivery System, or NEEDS. This article provides an overview of the Synthesis Coalition and documents the NEEDS cataloging effort. The article examines both the application of library standards to Internet-accessible and retrievable information, and an experiment in remote cataloging that involved materials developed by the Synthesis Coalition. The article also comments on the future of telecommuting and remote cataloging of digital resources. *[Article copies available for a fee from The Haworth Document Delivery Service: 1-800-342-9678. E-mail address: <getinfo@ haworthpressinc. com> Website: <http://www.HaworthPress. com>]*

KEYWORDS. NEEDS project, Synthesis Coalition, remote cataloging, telecataloging, engineering education (higher), databases

---

Dr. Brad Eden is Head of Cataloging, University of Nevada-Las Vegas, Las Vegas, NV (e-mail: beden@ccmail.nevada.edu).

[Haworth co-indexing entry note]: "The National Engineering Education Delivery System (NEEDS) Project: Reinventing Undergraduate Engineering Education Through Remote Cataloging of Digital Resources." Eden, Brad. Co-published simultaneously in *Journal of Internet Cataloging* (The Haworth Information Press, an imprint of The Haworth Press, Inc.) Vol. 3, No. 2/3, 2000, pp. 191-202; and: *Metadata and Organizing Educational Resources on the Internet* (ed: Jane Greenberg) The Haworth Information Press, an imprint of The Haworth Press, Inc., 2000, pp. 191-202. Single or multiple copies of this article are available for a fee from The Haworth Document Delivery Service [1-800-342-9678, 9:00 a.m. - 5:00 p.m. (EST). E-mail address: getinfo@haworthpressinc.com].

© 2000 by The Haworth Press, Inc. All rights reserved.

SYNTHESIS COALITION

The Synthesis Coalition is a National Science Foundation (NSF) grant project whose mission is to reform undergraduate engineering education by developing new curricular and pedagogical models that emphasize multidisciplinary content, teamwork, communication, hands-on and laboratory experiences, and open-ended problem formulation and solving. In meeting this objective, the Synthesis Coalition has been involved the development of computer-based instructional material, or courseware, which integrates the diverse analytic, design, experimental and intuitive skills that are required by a practicing engineer. The Synthesis Coalition has found that digital courseware greatly enhances experiential and constructivist learning approaches. The Kolb model of experiential learning has been adopted by Synthesis as its model for integrative learning, which cycles students through four cognitive/experiential modes: reflective observation through active discussion; abstract conceptualization through theory, modeling, and analysis; active experimentation through design labs, experiments, and simulation; and concrete experience through case studies and dissection.[1] The strategy for curriculum reform and courseware development by Synthesis members is directed towards five key goals:

1. Synthesis Interdisciplinary Content: Curricula needs to expose students to open-ended problem solving experiences and use creative synthesis to teach process as well as content. Inter- and multidisciplinary areas within engineering are emphasized that are considered critical to national competitiveness.
2. Concurrent Engineering and Industry Practice: Life-cycle design and concurrent engineering practices, taught through team design experience, group experiences, and team building, are focused upon along with industry "best practices" and multimedia case studies of engineering design.
3. Laboratory/Hands-On Experience: Computer laboratory courses offer students the opportunity for real-life experience in experimental design and using teamwork to solve open-ended engineering problems.
4. Communication and Social Context: Opportunities for students to develop their verbal, written, and graphical communication skills are provided by Synthesis curricula. Teamwork in solving problems with people of diverse backgrounds and different levels of experience is fundamental in courseware design.
5. Advanced Delivery Systems and Learning Environments: Digital courseware models must be designed for a wide range of environments and for easy update. Active learning and different learning styles must be

taken into consideration. Rapid transfer of new technologies must be facilitated through a shared resource of information retrieval.

The objective of the Synthesis Coalition is to improve engineering education by bringing more process- and team-oriented experiences into the classroom. Diverse resources, therefore, must be available to instructors through a national database that can retrieve and assemble computer courseware items into a unified course. The cornerstone of Synthesis, therefore, is the National Engineering Education Delivery System (NEEDS), a distributed database comprised of computer courseware modules designed by academic engineering professors for use in undergraduate education, and available worldwide via the Internet. Types of courseware elements available are:

- Elements: These are the basic building blocks of courseware, such as video clips, photos, interviews, textual data, or scanned images.
- Modules: These are self-contained, unique assemblies of courseware elements. Their scope can range from material for a single class meeting that addresses one engineering concept to a full semester case study.
- Applications software: These are large-scale utilities such as finite-element programs or simulation systems.
- Hardware links: These are either digital records, such as drawings and components lists, that will permit construction of hardware portions of a course; or pointers to the location of actual hardware available for distribution.
- Complete courseware: This is an assembly in digital form of all material needed to instruct a complete course.

Due to the high number of media elements in NEEDS courseware, a separate database that supports visual searches of these elements as thumbnail sketches was also adopted. The NEEDS Idea Navigator (NINa) is a browsing and retrieval tool to obtain the individual multimedia elements within the courseware using SQL. The user can download the courseware element to their local computer, and either display the image or launch the needed courseware.

More of the technical and historical information on the Synthesis Coalition and the NEEDS database, as well as access to recent articles and presentations, are available at http://www.synthesis.org and http://www.needs.org.

AN EXPERIMENT IN REMOTE CATALOGING OF DIGITAL RESOURCES

In December 1994, while I was checking e-mail, a job advertisement for a NEEDS Cataloger appeared on AUTOCAT. The position required skills not usually developed by catalogers, including the chance to work with digital media, which sounded particularly exciting to me. After reading about the Synthesis Coalition and the NEEDS database, I was motivated to apply for the position. I had recently obtained my MLS degree after ten years as a support staff cataloger in the academic and government arenas, and was looking for my first professional position.

In early 1995 I was invited to Iowa State University for an interview. While the project was of intense interest to me, the NEEDS project was at the end of their five-year NSF grant. The U.S. government, at this time, was intensely examining government grants due to public concerns regarding accountability and waste. My concern for non-renewal of the grant would mean I might not be employed with NEEDS for an extended period of time, moving to Iowa only to lose the position due to depleted funds. At this point, the engineering faculty member on the search committee, who was also one of the major initiators of the NEEDS database, made the point that the computer courseware could be accessed via the Internet internationally, so why couldn't the computer courseware also be cataloged from any location? The thought intrigued the search committee, as well as myself. Before I was offered the position, I was invited to attend a meeting in Berkeley, California, of the NEEDS team members, in order to meet the people involved in the project, and to obtain some idea of the direction and history of the database itself. When I was finally offered the position, my concerns about the grant renewal situation were addressed, and it was decided that I would be cataloging remotely, or telecataloging, from my home in Houston, Texas. The opportunity to work with digital media in this type of situation made the job doubly interesting, and the status of Assistant Professor provided the same benefits and professional stature as the rest of the technical services catalogers, despite my distance from ISU itself.

A number of concerns, both from ISU/NEEDS and from myself, needed to be answered. Library administration was concerned about supervision, training, communication, and accountability, while I was concerned about similar topics as well as computer equipment needs and home office working space. A three-week training and orientation period at ISU was agreed upon once employment was accepted. Airline and housing costs for the training period were reimbursed by the NEEDS project. A temporary office space in Technical Services was provided by the library, and NEEDS provided me with an IBM laptop, printer/fax machine, and modem to use for e-mail communication and cataloging functions, which I brought back with me to Houston after the training period. The ISU Library's Technical Services Department also provided copies of the appropriate cataloging reference sources to take back to Houston. These included AACR2R, the LCSH manuals, Bibliographic

Standards and Formats manual, Nancy Olson's Computer Files book/manual, and the OCLC computer files template instructions.

During my training period I worked with the ISU library's technical services staff and the engineering faculty NEEDS members to acquaint myself with both the NOTIS system and the NEEDS project protocols, as well as the NEEDS interface. I was able to peruse the catalog records of the previous NEEDS cataloger, in order to examine the computer files format in depth, both through example and through LC manuals and OCLC documentation. At the same time, I was working with NEEDS faculty on a crosswalk between MARC and the NEEDS interface, providing an HTML structure with embedded MARC tags.

At this time, NEEDS cataloging was a two-fold process. Master catalog records were created through ISU's NOTIS system using the computer files format. These records were then sent to the University of California at Berkeley's NEEDS system staff, who mounted the records in HTML format. The catalog records could then be accessed and viewed via the Internet, with computer modules and files directly downloaded from the record via hypertext links.

Once the three-week training at ISU was completed, I returned to Houston to set up an office space in my home. Working with the ISU library systems staff, I was able to obtain an Internet provider and configure the laptop to communicate with the ISU NOTIS system. It was agreed before I left Iowa that communication with my ISU library supervisor would be continuous, and that I would return to ISU in two months for another two-week period, as well as for another two-week period three months after that.

Between the initial training at ISU and my second visit, NEEDS arranged for me to attend a staff meeting of all major program participants at California Polytechnic State University at San Luis Obispo. At this meeting I was able to meet many of the faculty involved in creating the computer courseware I would be cataloging, as well as the major NEEDS administrators. I was also able to hear updates on funding, work on problem-solving situations regarding NEEDS, and receive goals and objectives to work towards as NEEDS cataloger.

THE CATALOGING PROCESS

To examine the NEEDS cataloger position during my tenure, some explanation must be given regarding the history of the job itself, and its long-term objective in NEEDS. The NEEDS cataloger position in the project was meant to be eventually phased out in the final version. The ultimate goal of the NEEDS database was to be entirely user-driven and user-cataloged, with perhaps minimal examination and adjustments to computer courseware submissions by a NEEDS staff member or a team of professional catalogers. Since the NEEDS project was at the end of its initial five-year NSF grant, and still in the process of renewal applications and negotiations, it was important that the database itself was actively moving towards this goal. The NEEDS cataloger prior to myself, centered in the Technical Services Department at Cornell University for three years, had accomplished the initial work of building the database, communicating with NEEDS faculty on a regular basis, and working towards the totally user/faculty-driven cataloging interface. When I took the position in Year 5 of the project, the focus was not only on maintaining the database, communicating with NEEDS contributors, and promoting use of the database, but also on the eventual elimination of the NEEDS Cataloger position as it currently existed, and redirecting the focus. The ultimate goal, from the project's inception, was for courseware creators to become the initial catalogers of their own courseware.

The cataloging procedure involved the following:

1. NEEDS engineering faculty, located in the eight universities participating in the project, created computer courseware following the objectives and goals indicated in the NSF grant.
2. Faculty would then contact me, and provide me with computer files or Internet addresses where these courseware modules were stored.
3. I would then view the computer courseware and all of its elements for both cataloging and operability, and create a MARC catalog record in ISU's NOTIS system.
4. A copy of the record would be ftp'd to the Berkeley computer staff, who would then translate the file into HTML and mount both the catalog record and the courseware into the NEEDS database.
5. Any future changes to the catalog record, such as Internet address changes or courseware module version updates, would be written on the ISU master catalog record first, in order to maintain accuracy and quality control of the database.

The current version of NEEDS allows for searching both the courseware catalog and the NINa multimedia elements database concurrently. A courseware search on the keyword "mechanical engineering" produces a ranked query list (Figure 1).

The HTML manifestation of the MARC document type definition (DTD) can be seen by calling up one of the catalog records from the ranked list, seen in the multiple screens of Figure 2. The goal was for subject headings to be clickable, in order to search for related courseware items. Access to the courseware itself is provided directly through a click of the mouse (Figure 3), and reviews and comments on the courseware are also available.

FIGURE 1

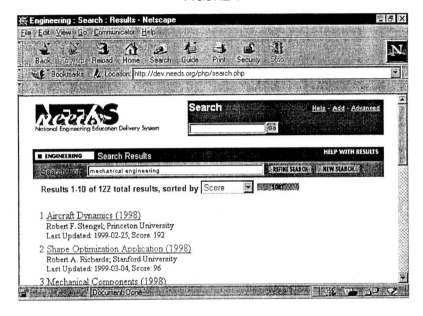

FIGURE 2a

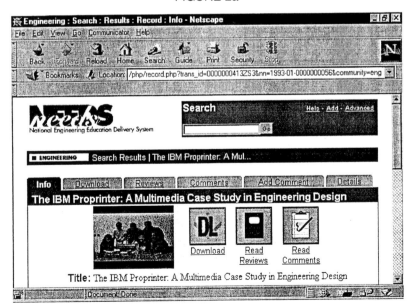

FIGURE 2b

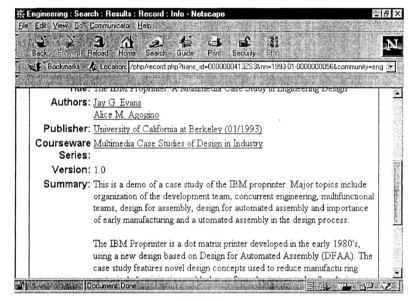

Title: The IBM Proprinter: A Multimedia Case Study in Engineering Design

Authors: Jay G. Evans
Alice M. Agogino

Publisher: University of California at Berkeley (01/1993)

Courseware Series: Multimedia Case Studies of Design in Industry

Version: 1.0

Summary: This is a demo of a case study of the IBM proprinter. Major topics include organization of the development team, concurrent engineering, multifunctional teams, design for assembly, design for automated assembly and importance of early manufacturing and a utomated assembly in the design process.

The IBM Proprinter is a dot matrix printer developed in the early 1980's, using a new design based on Design for Automated Assembly (DFAA). The case study features novel design concepts used to reduce manufactu ring

FIGURE 2c

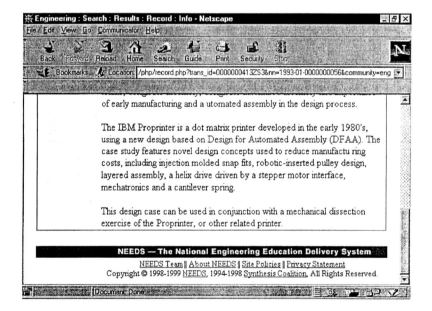

of early manufacturing and a utomated assembly in the design process.

The IBM Proprinter is a dot matrix printer developed in the early 1980's, using a new design based on Design for Automated Assembly (DFAA). The case study features novel design concepts used to reduce manufactu ring costs, including injection molded snap fits, robotic-inserted pulley design, layered assembly, a helix drive driven by a stepper motor interface, mechatronics and a cantilever spring.

This design case can be used in conjunction with a mechanical dissection exercise of the Proprinter, or other related printer.

NEEDS — The National Engineering Education Delivery System

NEEDS Team || About NEEDS || Site Policies || Privacy Statement
Copyright © 1998-1999 NEEDS, 1994-1998 Synthesis Coalition, All Rights Reserved.

FIGURE 3

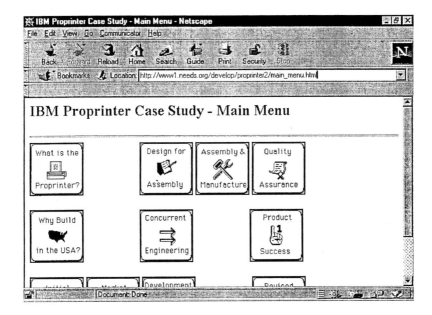

PROJECT CONTINUATION

During the summer of 1995, two additional trips were made to ISU. They were two weeks in length and approximately three months apart. During these stays, work would ensue with NEEDS faculty on the cataloging interface, participation and association with ISU technical services staff members would develop, and questions and concerns regarding cataloging and communication would be addressed. While working from home during this summer, a minimal number of problems were encountered. Computer setup and Internet connections were quickly enabled and solved by the ISU Library's computer personnel. Regular phone meetings between myself and NEEDS administration were fairly frequent. Another trip to Berkeley was taken during this time, again to meet with NEEDS administration, receive updates on the grant renewal process, and work towards the refinements needed to make the NEEDS cataloging database user-enabled. Another part of the job was to actively work with and encourage NEEDS faculty at the eight participating universities not only to produce courseware, but also to involve them in the cataloging process through subject classification consultation in both LCSH and Engineering Information (EI) thesaurus[2] headings, through personal information included in the catalog record (such as homepage or resume locations of authors), and through current server and computer file connections.

SUBJECT CLASSIFICATION OF NEEDS DIGITAL RESOURCES

One of the most important and exciting aspects of the project was decisions regarding subject classification. Early on in the project, LC classification of computer courseware was agreed upon in the ISU master record. The use of call numbers was approved for the ISU master catalog record, but would not be viewable in the Internet NEEDS catalog. This would allow NEEDS administration the opportunity to inventory the NEEDS catalog records for collection development purposes, but would also not hinder NEEDS users with unnecessary information in the Internet version of the catalog.

Subject heading designations were taken from LCSH, but the EI thesaurus as well as cataloger-derived local subject headings were also assigned. Most of the NEEDS catalog records were assigned a combination of two or more of the above subject designations. While most of the engineering NEEDS faculty were and are familiar with the EI subject headings, more library and Internet users are familiar with LCSH subject headings. Local subject headings fill in for any courseware-specific subjects not covered by LCSH or EI.

FUTURE OF THE NEEDS PROJECT

Two recent Internet articles on NEEDS summarize and succinctly report on the future of the project. *D-Lib Magazine*, in the April 1999 issue (Volume 5, Issue 4), has an article on the future of NEEDS, which includes the adoption of the Educause Instructional Management Systems (IMS) metadata descriptors in its current and future cataloging interface, as well as a description of the NEEDS courseware quality review process, including the Premier Award for Excellence in Engineering Education Courseware.[3]

The second article is a Powerpoint slide show, presented at the 1997 International Conference on Engineering Education (ICEE), titled "The National Engineering Education Delivery System (NEEDS): Supporting the Transformation of Engineering Education."[4] In this article, the future of NEEDS focuses on its long-term vision of serving as a model for the Digital National Library (DNL) currently under development through government initiatives. Obviously, the future for NEEDS is bright indeed.

CONCLUSIONS

There were many lessons learned through this experience, regarding both the cataloging of digital resources and the viability of remote cataloging. The most important lesson learned was that remote cataloging of computer files and Internet resources can be successful, if communication issues and computer hardware setup and maintenance are addressed early in the process. Given that library cataloging reference materials are now readily available in digital form, the problem of access to these documents remotely can also be solved.

The challenges associated with cataloging digital formats and working with real-time solutions to the current situations in engineering education and team training were especially exciting. The cataloging operation was a priority to the NEEDS project, so that the focus and importance of the cataloger's work was constantly scrutinized and focused upon. Being able to work with the creators of the digital courseware during the cataloging process, as well as the frequent contact with both NEEDS administration and the ISU Technical Services professionals, meant that the "remote" aspect of the work only meant walking from the bedroom to the office area of my home every day, rather than an extended commute time via automobile.

The opportunity to learn about telecommuting (and remote cataloging, and telecataloging) also meant discovering resources about this type of work environment. There are numerous Internet sites devoted to this subject, including a special issue of *LIBRES,* an electronic peer-reviewed library journal, on telecommuting.[5]

An added "perk" of this position was the fact that all expenses associated with the job were paid for by NEEDS. Not only was the computer hardware (an IBM laptop and a Macintosh, since courseware was constructed in both formats), Internet connection, printer/fax, and library reference materials taken care of, but all travel and training expenses incurred on the project were reimbursed. This included plane fares, room, and board for seven weeks of training and onsite work at the ISU library, as well as all the associated expenses from two trips to Berkeley, California, and one trip to California Polytechnic State University at San Luis Obispo. As a temporary Assistant Professor, I accrued all the same benefits as other ISU librarians, even though I was physically located on campus only part of the time.

FUTURE OF TELECATALOGING/REMOTE CATALOGING OF DIGITAL RESOURCES

One of the reasons why I was interested in and eventually decided to accept this position was not only the experimental (at that time) cataloging and classification of digital education resources, but also the opportunity to experience and experiment in a career option which I feel should and will become more of a possibility in the future–the ability to work either part of one's schedule from home, or even to work remotely. Digital resources, in their many and varied manifestations and formats, will only proliferate in the coming years, and the options required to provide quality access to and description of these resources will also require creativity and innovation in the work environment. Obviously, a number of issues have to be decided and agreed upon by both employee and employer, but I think that telecommuting and telecataloging lend themselves well to the library situation in the description of and access to digital resources.

Those librarians involved in digital library projects, Web page design and maintenance, and special projects such as faculty grants involving database design or extensive scanning/imaging projects, should be able to accomplish required tasks from virtually anywhere–virtually. Hopefully, my experience will promote and encourage more experimentation in this area.[6]

NOTES

1. Kolb, D.A. *Experiential learning: Experience as the source of learning and development*. Englewood Cliffs, N.J.: Prentice-Hall, 1984.

2. *EI thesaurus*. Hoboken, N.J.: Engineering Information Inc., 1992-

3. See *http://www.d-lib.org/dlib/april99/muramatsu/04muramatsu.html* to view this paper.

4. See *http://www.needs.org/needsinfo/presentations/ICEE97/ICEE97-slides/* for this presentation.

5. See *http://bubl.ac.uk/journals/lis/kn/libres/v06n0102.htm* to view this special issue, which I edited.

6. Telecommuting and remote cataloging in the library environment has only recently entered the literature. The work of Leah Black and Colleen Hyslop has been crucial in this area. See their articles in the July 1995 issue of *College & Research Libraries* (p. 319-23), and the April/June 1996 issue of *International Cataloguing and Bibliographic Control* (p. 37-39). Besides the special issue on telecommuting in *LIBRES* already mentioned, an interesting article with resources by Wendy S. Klepfer was published by *Library Mosaics* on this topic in its July/August 1997 issue (p. 21).

Providing Access to Course Material
at Deakin University

Cate Richmond
Ebe Kartus

SUMMARY. Deakin University Library was requested by Deakin Australia, the corporate arm of Deakin University, to suggest ways to provide access to their course material. The project looked at how metadata could be incorporated retrospectively and into new print and electronic course material. Although the material is produced in two formats, the archival format would be electronic. Even though access to the Deakin Australia material would be by instructional designers only, the project was seen as the first steps in the exploration of issues the Library would need to consider in providing public access to the University's general course material. This article outlines the recommendations made to Deakin Australia and the reasons behind them. *[Article copies available for a fee from The Haworth Document Delivery Service: 1-800-342-9678. E-mail address: <getinfo@haworthpressinc.com> Website: <http://www.HaworthPress.com>]*

KEYWORDS. Metadata, Deakin University Library, Deakin Australia, course material

DEAKIN UNIVERSITY

Deakin University is located in the State of Victoria, Australia. Deakin University offers on-campus and off-campus studies to more than 62,000

Cate Richmond, GradDipLib, is Strategic Planning Manager, Deakin University Library, Geelong Waterfront Campus, 1 Gheringhap Street, Geelong, Victoria, Australia, 3217 (e-mail: cate@deakin.edu.au).

Ebe Kartus, GradDipLib, MIM, is Project Cataloguer, Deakin University Library, Geelong Waterfront Campus, 1 Gheringhap Street, Geelong, Victoria, Australia, 3217 (e-mail: kartus@deakin.edu.au).

[Haworth co-indexing entry note]: "Providing Access to Course Material at Deakin University." Richmond, Cate, and Ebe Kartus. Co-published simultaneously in *Journal of Internet Cataloging* (The Haworth Information Press, an imprint of The Haworth Press, Inc.) Vol. 3, No. 2/3, 2000, pp. 203-216; and: *Metadata and Organizing Educational Resources on the Internet* (ed: Jane Greenberg) The Haworth Information Press, an imprint of The Haworth Press, Inc., 2000, pp. 203-216. Single or multiple copies of this article are available for a fee from The Haworth Document Delivery Service [1-800-342-9678, 9:00 a.m. - 5:00 p.m. (EST). E-mail address: getinfo@haworthpressinc.com].

© 2000 by The Haworth Press, Inc. All rights reserved.

students and professional clients in Australia and overseas. A significant component of the University's courses are offered via distance education. Five Faculties–Arts, Education, Health and Behavioural Sciences, Business and Law, Science and Technology–deliver a range of undergraduate, post-graduate and professional training courses. Schools within each Faculty concentrate on specialist areas of study. The University has six campuses: Burwood, Rusden and Toorak in Melbourne; Geelong and Geelong Waterfront in Geelong; and Warrnambool in Western Victoria.

DEAKIN UNIVERSITY LIBRARY

Deakin University Library provides a complete range of services to meet the information needs of the University in support of its teaching, learning and research. There are campus libraries at all six of the University's campuses, that provide an inter-campus lending service for all University students and staff. The Library's off campus service is internationally recognised for the timely and excellent service it provides to off campus students, who may be located within Australia or anywhere overseas. Electronic delivery of resources to both on and off campus students is a major focus of the Library's activities. A well developed Faculty Liaison Program ensures that the Library is responsive to the needs of academic staff. The Library also works closely with the other academic support areas of the University to ensure the provision of complementary and integrated support services for students and academic staff.

DEAKIN AUSTRALIA

Deakin Australia provides professional education, training and employee development services with more than 35,000 participants enrolled in its programs both in Australia and internationally. As the corporate arm of Deakin University, it also provides corporations, industry, government, unions and professional associations with accessible modes of training for their workplaces. Deakin Australia also customizes training packages for corporate clients. Deakin Australia's education and training professionals work with a large network of industry specialists, consultants and practitioners within the University, and in the corporate and government sectors.

OPPORTUNITIES FOR THE LIBRARY
FROM THE DEAKIN AUSTRALIA PROJECT

The Deakin Australia project was seen by Deakin University Library as a way to explore the various issues that the Library would need to consider in moving to provide access to the University's course material in not only print and audio-visual but also electronic format. Deakin University Library provides an archival function for the University's publications and is responsible for preserving at least one copy of all course material. Currently the material is mainly in printed format but also includes audio-visual materials and CD-ROMS as well as interactive Websites. The Library has undertaken to provide timely cataloguing, and thus access, to the University's course material via the National Bibliographic Network. This access is not only Library wide but Australia wide. Catalogue records for the print and common audio-visual materials (cassettes and videos) are to AACR2R level three standard with a searchable note field containing the course code. While the majority of this course material is still being produced in print and audio-visual formats the University is moving rapidly to production, and most importantly storage, in electronic format for an increasing proportion of its course material. The electronic format consists of both electronic versions of pre-existing print materials and materials only available online.

The exploration of various metadata issues for Deakin Australia was seen as the preliminary step in considerations of how to provide access to electronic course material for both staff and students at all six campuses. This access would in preference be via the Library catalogue rather than via a separate database.

The WebPAC catalogue provides access to the Library's print and non-print collections. It also provides electronic links to past exam papers and descriptive lists to the Library's special manuscript collections. Recently Deakin University Library has provided access to the individual full-text journals carried by large databases like Expanded Academic, Lexis-Nexis and ScienceDirect by cataloguing each title, as well as providing the electronic link for the host database. Preference is given to the practice of format integration with holdings being added to pre-existing records for the print or microform equivalents. Access to the current range of material is constantly being improved with the emphasis being to provide users with one entrance, the Library catalogue, to all the different information sources. Providing access to course material in another format can be seen as an incremental development.

BACKGROUND TO THE DEAKIN AUSTRALIA PROJECT

Deakin Australia's Intellectual Property Taskforce went through a process of mapping Deakin Australia's intellectual property and hierarchy of course contents. This process was completed before Deakin Australia asked the Library to develop a model to facilitate improved access to Deakin Australia's bank of existing online course material, and to recommend a process for the creation of indexing and retrieval capabilities for newly created course material.

Deakin Australia staff create and store course material in PageMaker, Illustrator and MSWord. The material consists of:

- Courseware
- Participant manuals
- Facilitator's guides
- Distance materials
- Study guides
- Self directed materials

Most of the materials consist of the following main elements:

- Topic
- Learning objectives
- Assessment statements
- Activities

The types of course material listed above are currently disseminated in paper format in the majority of cases. Deakin Australia's instructional designers need to have the ability to search and access components of data like the elements listed above, so that when new course materials are being prepared, they can draw on existing material rather than create the entire course anew each time. The instructional designers need to access course material via unit titles, topic titles and learning objectives and in some cases down to the level of previously written concept definitions.

Access to the electronic versions of the course materials is by Deakin Australia staff only. There is no student access, so the solution had to fulfil the needs of only one stakeholder. After initial discussion it appeared that the best solution to Deakin Australia's needs might be provided by metadata. Therefore, the project proceeded on the assumptions that Deakin Australia would require a solution that would:

1. Use metadata to create a searchable repository of their existing course materials, and
2. Develop a process for the creation of metadata for all newly created course materials.

GENERAL ISSUES

The repository of course material should be able to provide the following functionality:

- Documents stored in a format that facilitates exchange of data between systems, and migration to future systems (i.e., a recognised international standard format)
- Flexible data structure
- Easily accessed by a metadata search engine
- Fast retrieval and display of search results
- Allows data to be retrieved by searching on all metadata elements
- Permits the use of templates to create metadata
- Has reporting functionality (to answer queries such as how many unique courses were delivered in 1998, etc.)

MAIN ISSUES CONSIDERED

The main issues considered were the format of the archival documents to be stored in the repository, the type of metadata to use and the repository search engine. As stated earlier the pre-existing documents were in three different formats. The project needed to recommend an archival format that would allow easy manipulation of the data currently, but one that was also flexible enough for future transportability.

Archival Format

Two other developments in the area of archival formats in Australia were investigated by the authors. The National Library of Australia (NLA) captures electronic items in HTML, PDF, XML and MSWord. Their preferred archival formats are XML and SGML. The NLA is experimenting with this work, but will not have any implementations until at least mid-1999. They are currently testing two software packages–*SGML Author for Word* and a native SGML editor called *Author/Editor*.

The University of New South Wales (UNSW) is hosting the Australian Digital Theses Project. The aim of the project is to establish a distributed database of digital versions of theses produced by the postgraduate research students at the participating institutions. The theses will be available via the Web. The documents will be held in two different formats: SGML due to its platform independence and PDF to ensure high quality printouts.

The NLA currently stores some documents in PDF format. The UNSW project has opted to store documents in both PDF and SGML formats because high quality printed versions of theses are required as an output. Concerns have been raised that there are possible problems in using proprietary software including compatibility, and upward and downward convertibility.

Bearing the above concern in mind and as quality of printing is not currently a requirement for the material in the Deakin Australia repository, the project recommended XML as the preferred storage format. XML is a descriptive markup 'language' (in that it states what the text is rather than how to format it), and is simpler than SGML, therefore the XML format had greater applicability. The language also allows the construction of DTD's (document type definitions) which define various types of documents and their structures by listing what elements (tags) are needed for each type. (This could also have applications in the initial preparation of course material.) The use of DTD's would allow greater uniformity in document construction which in turn would allow a greater ability to manipulate various parts of a document to generate machine constructed metadata. In using this format Deakin Australia would be well placed to exploit future development in this area.

One drawback with XML is that it is a relatively new development and is still being implemented. Thus it was also recognized that it was important to choose a format that would provide a short-term solution, but one that would also allow migration to the preferred longer-term solution, so that resources invested now would not be wasted. As an immediate solution it was recommended that existing documents be converted to HTML, until suitable XML tools were readily available. HTML conversion to XML should be straightforward should Deakin Australia decide to use this format in the future. It was also borne in mind that any current material on the Web would already most likely be in HTML and if any current material needed to be mounted onto the Web this then would be a simple exercise. The added advantage with using HTML would be that there are various tools in the public domain that can construct metadata records from Webpages. A tool such as *Reggie Metadata Editor* provided on the MetaWeb site could be tested for this purpose.

Metadata and Element Sets

Metadata has been described as 'structured data about data' or cataloguing 'for dummies.' There are now many different element sets of metadata available in the public domain. Some organisations have developed and defined their own element sets, while others have adopted existing sets *per se*, or extended those sets to provide greater flexibility and applicability.

One of the most accepted element sets is Dublin Core, a 15-element metadata set intended to facilitate discovery of electronic resources. Originally conceived for author-generated description of Web resources, it has also attracted the attention of formal resource description communities such as museums and libraries. The Dublin Core is intended to be useable by non-cataloguers as well as by those with experience with formal resource description models.

Extensive development work has already been done with Dublin Core. This element set also formed the base for the AGLS (Australian Government

Locator Service) metadata format which is being actively developed. It was recommended that the metadata standard for Deakin Australia's course material repository be based on the Dublin Core element set. It was also suggested that the Dublin Core set be extended to include additional elements which would specifically meet Deakin Australia's needs for document storage and retrieval.

Appendix 1 illustrates how the Dublin Core elements could be mapped across to course material elements. Appendix 2 is an example of a possible metadata record. Both of these examples are first level efforts, and further testing is required. One thing that did become evident in constructing the sample record was that levels of depth would have to be very clearly delineated. For example, if the metadata record was for the whole of a 300 page folder made up of 12 topics, then only a very broad description can be given. To get to some of the level of specificity required, each topic would need a record of its own with a link back to the main item. Even sections of each topic might need their own records. These questions would need further exploration as would the currently suggested metadata elements to see that these provided the proper linking up the 'hierarchy tree.'

Searching the Course Material Repository

Staff at Deakin Australia have suggested the method by which they could currently access the course material repository:

1. Instructional designer searches the repository
2. A list of results is displayed
3. Instructional designer locates the documents in a separate directory or application where these are stored in their original format (e.g., MSWord, PageMaker, etc.)
4. Having located the required document in its original format, a copy is printed and the hard copy is used to mark up the text to create new course material documents. (Later this could also be done online.)

In the future it may be desirable to access and print the document from the repository itself, without having to search and retrieve it from another directory or application. Initially, it was suggested that it would be helpful if the instructional designers were at least able to view the documents from the list retrieved at Step 2 so they could assess whether the documents contained the required content.

There are a number of metadata search engines available. Several of these are in the public domain. For example, the NLA as part of its MetaWeb Project has made search engine software available to download for both the Unix and Windows NT platforms. The authors' investigations have indicated that software for metadata search engines may require some modification to suit the local environment, especially if extended element sets are used.

CONVERSION OF EXISTING COURSE MATERIAL
TO A METADATA REPOSITORY

The Project suggested two options for the conversion of existing material. Part of both options presupposed some type of automatic conversion of sections of data to metadata elements, with Deakin Australia's Information Technology staff providing some programming support. The reason full manual retrospective conversion was not considered was the stated need, at that time, for speed of implementation. An assumption made by the authors was also that large components of like material were in a similar format. The authors did have access to a very small selection of material at the time the options were proposed. The basic assumption of uniformity would have to have been further tested. Thus the options given below have that as the unstated assumption.

The first option was that if it was not possible to generate a basic metadata record at the point of conversion, then a separate program would need to be written and run once the documents were in the repository format. If the material was in a standard or even a semi-standard format, then it should be possible to generate a basic metadata record for each document. Subject descriptors could initially be taken from the various headings which appear in the document. This solution would give Deakin Australia staff some access to the material, but there would inevitably be a number of inaccuracies and mapping errors, and only some of the metadata elements would be searchable. The constructed metadata would still need to be upgraded and reviewed at a later stage.

Alternatively, more time could be devoted initially to creating a more complete metadata record. While it may still be possible to use some level of machine conversion, a Library Cataloguer could review the machine-generated metadata and add subject terms and other required elements. This option would take more time but the data would be accurate from the beginning. This scenario would also provide Deakin Australia and Deakin University Library with a good training and testing opportunity.

NEW MATERIAL

As new course material documents were completed, these would be converted to the repository format on a nightly basis. Part of this conversion process could entail the creation of a basic set of metadata elements. These basic elements would need to be reviewed and enhanced. When the converted document was re-opened the following day this would generate a template that contained the machine-generated metadata. The design and content of the template could be developed by Deakin Australia Information Technology staff with input from the Library as to the elements and validation required. The intention was to include drop down lists where elements have a limited number of input options.

Two options suggested for the review and upgrading of the machine-generated metadata were:

Option 1

The original creator could access the converted version of the document the following day, check the machine-generated metadata, and add additional elements. Elements such as the subject field which require the use of terms from a controlled vocabulary could be added by the creator under the guidance of a Library cataloguer, or left for the cataloguer to supply later. If the Dublin Core descriptor element is used, the creator could 'leave notes' on subjects for the cataloguer. Either the creator or the cataloguer could have responsibility for the final quality check of the metadata.

Option 2

The cataloguer could access the documents on the following day, undertake the review of the machine-generated metadata, complete the element set by adding additional information, including the controlled subject terms, and provide the final quality check.

The advantages of the second option are:

- The creator does not have to remember to re-open the document the following day
- The creator does not have to access, select, and maintain terms from controlled vocabulary lists
- The review and enhancing of the metadata elements can be performed in one step by the cataloguer
- Broad uniformity in the data is maintained because one person is basically responsible for the quality of the metadata creation, rather than a number of creators.

LOCATION OF AND ACCESS TO THE REPOSITORY

The repository would be stored on a Deakin Australia server and managed by Deakin Australia Information Technology staff.

The options described above assume that the cataloguer would have read/write access to the repository. An alternative may be to save the converted documents to a network drive accessible to both Deakin Australia and the cataloguer, although this method of providing indirect access to the repository would make overall quality control and maintenance of the metadata more difficult for the cataloguer.

CURRENT STATE OF DEAKIN AUSTRALIA'S PROJECT

Deakin Australia's requirement for a course material repository is one component of their overall requirement for an integrated online document management and stock control system. Deakin Australia's Information Technology Manager decided that the development of the infrastructure for the entire system must proceed before committing to a system solution for the course material component. That development work is currently under way.

While Deakin Australia recognises that access to specific elements within their course material products will require content creators and/or cataloguers to index individual documents, they are yet to decide on an appropriate and supportable level of specificity. Whether they use metadata to achieve the desired level of access may depend on the software solution adopted for their integrated online document management system. The Library will continue to liaise with Deakin Australia to provide support if required, and to test their chosen solution for possible application in the wider University context.

OTHER METADATA APPLICATIONS BEING EXPLORED AT DEAKIN UNIVERSITY

Deakin University is currently implementing an online instructional management system and a digital repository. This integrated online system will be available to all University staff, and will enable the storage and retrieval of electronic course materials in all formats. The system will interface with existing University Oracle databases, and will support XML and SGML. The Library has participated in the selection and testing of this system, and will advise on the development and implementation of indexing standards using metadata. The model for assigning metadata tags for electronic course material has yet to be finalised, but will probably involve a combination of some system-generated tags at the point of document creation, some author-generated tags, and additional controlled terms supplied by professional cataloguers.

The digital repository will also store copyright-cleared electronic images published in print and online versions of course materials. The repository will provide standard rights management information, and the images will be indexed by cataloguing staff using metadata to facilitate retrieval. This will enable course developers to gain easy online access to a wide variety of images that may be re-used if permitted under the terms of the copyright clearance.

Long-term, the digital repository will also fulfil the University's need for an archival store of all University material that has been published in either print or electronic formats. Printed publications will be scanned, and cataloguing staff will catalogue new printed and electronic publications. These publications will be searchable via the Library's Web catalogue and viewed via the user's Web browser by selecting a link within the catalogue record.

The Library is currently working with the University's Information Technology Services Division to develop some basic metadata standards to be applied to all Web pages stored on University servers. This will enable a basic level of document control and verification, facilitate retrieval, provide statistical information, and report on the currency of pages. A metadata creation tool that supports both automated and manual generation of metadata tags is being developed. The standards will be based on the Dublin Core element set. Metadata will be stored in a separate repository that will provide a high standard of XML functionality, and will be searchable via a Web browser.

The Library will extend this basic set of metadata elements to facilitate access to material on its own public Website and its staff Intranet, as well as to the collections of manuscript material.

METADATA STANDARDS FOR TEACHING AND LEARNING

Australian educational institutions, through the Australian Department of Education, Training and Youth Affairs (DETYA), are participating in the Instructional Management Systems (IMS) Project: a global collaborative project to define Internet architecture for learning. IMS is currently developing a set of standards, including specifications for metadata. The specifications will provide guidelines for software developers to ensure the interoperability of content and management systems. The standards developed by IMS will assist Deakin University and other educational institutions to develop instructional management systems and course repositories to enable international compatibility and resource-sharing.

AUSTRALIAN SITES OF INTEREST

Australian Digital Theses Project
http://www.library.unsw.edu.au/thesis/thesis.html

Australian Government Locator Service
http://www.naa.gov.au/govserv/agls/

Deakin University Library
http://www.deakin.edu.au/library

Distributed Systems Technology Centre, Resource Discovery Unit
http://www.dstc.edu.au/RDU/

MetaWeb Project
http://www.dstc.edu.au/RDU/MetaWeb/

National Library of Australia, Digital Services Project
RFQ–Metadata repository and search system
http://www.nla.gov.au/dsp/rfq/index.html

Recordkeeping Standard for Commonwealth Agencies
http://www.naa.gov.au/govserv/techpub/rkms/intro.htm

Records Continuum Research Group
http://www.sims.monash.edu.au/rcrg/index.html

State Library of Queensland Internet Services Unit
http://www.slq.qld.gov.au/meta/metaguid.htm

SELECT BIBLIOGRAPHY

Hillmann, Diane, ed. "A user guide for simple Dublin Core: Draft version 5.1."
    http://purl.org/DC/documents/working_drafts/wd-guide-current.htm (accessed 30.
    September 1998).
"Instructional Management Systems Project." http://www.imsproject.org (accessed
    23. June 1999).
McKemmish, Sue & Dagmar Parer. "Towards frameworks for standardising record-
    keeping metadata." http://www.sims.monash.edu.au/rcrg/publications/recordkeeping
    metadata/smckrmp1.html (accessed 26. November 1998).
Thornely, Jenny. "The road to meta: The implementation of Dublin Core metadata in
    the State Library of Queensland website." *The Australian Library Journal* 47, no.
    1 (1998): 74-82.
Xu, Amanda. "Metadata conversion and the library OPAC." http://web.mit.edu/
    waynej/www/xu.htm (accessed 23. September 1998).

APPENDIX 1. Map of Dublin Core elements to sample course material elements.

Dublin Core elements	Course material elements
Title	Unit title Module title Other titles
Creators	Contributors (main contributor first)
Keywords	Keywords
Description	Element
Date	Effective date Review date
Contributor	
Publisher	
Type	
Format	Record 'original' format
Resource Identifier	File name
Source	Type Course no.
Language	
Relation	Name of higher unit/course
Coverage	
Rights	Any limits to reuse of information Confidentiality, etc.

Element Extension

Outline	Part no. Accreditation level Currency
Client	Name of organization/course
Material	Product

APPENDIX 2. Sample record based on a sample course module.

Metadata elements	Metadata
Title	Team development and leadership Characteristics of an effective team Effective team leadership Team assembly and membership Team development Evaluating team performance
	Richmond, Cate Kartus, Ebe
Keywords	Leadership Crossfunctional teams Teams in the workplace Performance indicators Delegation
Description	This module addresses the issues of team development and leadership in a systematic and practical way. Define what is meant by a team approach and describe the characteristics of an effective team. Includes definition of team Assessment by 150 word tasks Readings included
Date	1995-01-01 1998-12-31
Format	MS Word
Resource Identifier	L:\DA\Teams\Module\ABC123
Source	Unit–Workshop
	ABC123
Relation	Timbuktoo Company Leadership Workshop
Rights	All company information confidential. Limited copyright clearance. Prefer not to reuse this material

Element Extension

Outline	Non Accredited Not Current
Client	Timbuktoo Company
Material	Workbook materials Assessment guide

Using the Online Catalog as a Publishing Source in an Academic Institution

Ana Torres
Cynthia Wolff

SUMMARY. This article reports on the Digital Library Project in 1995 at the Bern Dibner Library of Science and Technology at Polytechnic University in Brooklyn, New York. The project's goal was to deliver electronic information generated by faculty and/or university organizations through the online catalog, by providing a seamless link from a bibliographic record in the OPAC to the electronic item via the Internet. Catalysts for the project included the faculty's need to share and distribute electronic information and the library's need to reduce traffic at the Service Desk, where course materials were kept. Student can now access course-related material remotely, eliminating long lines at the Service Desk, and faculty can exchange electronic information on a secure network. *[Article copies available for a fee from The Haworth Document Delivery Service: 1-800-342-9678. E-mail address: <getinfo@haworthpressinc.com> Website: <http://www.HaworthPress.com>]*

KEYWORDS. Digital library, electronic content, courseware, course material, metadata, publishing

Ana Torres (e-mail: atorres@poly.edu) is Bibliographic Control Specialist, and Cynthia Wolff (e-mail: cwolff@poly.edu) is Coordinator of Digital Applications, Bern Dibner Library, Polytechnic University, Brooklyn, NY 11201.

The authors gratefully acknowledge the creativity and technical skill of the Library's LAN team and the support of their Director.

[Haworth co-indexing entry note]: "Using the Online Catalog as a Publishing Source in an Academic Institution." Torres, Ana, and Cynthia Wolff. Co-published simultaneously in *Journal of Internet Cataloging* (The Haworth Information Press, an imprint of The Haworth Press, Inc.) Vol. 3, No. 2/3, 2000, pp. 217-225; and: *Metadata and Organizing Educational Resources on the Internet* (ed: Jane Greenberg) The Haworth Information Press, an imprint of The Haworth Press, Inc., 2000, pp. 217-225. Single or multiple copies of this article are available for a fee from The Haworth Document Delivery Service [1-800-342-9678, 9:00 a.m. - 5:00 p.m. (EST). E-mail address: getinfo@haworthpressinc.com].

© 2000 by The Haworth Press, Inc. All rights reserved.

217

INTRODUCTION

The Bern Dibner Library services an academic community where the curriculum emphasizes engineering and the sciences. In the past, the library has provided traditional paper access to course material, such as professors' notes and practice exams. This method of disseminating information was no longer sufficient for our students' needs. Many disciplines taught at the university required the use of technology as an instructional tool. The nature of the material had changed from paper to electronic format. We needed to find a different way of disseminating this type of information. Moreover, drawbacks to traditional paper access were becoming more apparent. Course material was accessed from one location in the library; availability was limited to the number of paper copies held and to library hours. Our highly computer literate student body needed remote access to course-related materials. For these reasons the library initiated the Digital Library project that focused on facilitating the electronic exchange of learning material between faculty and students.

It was an opportune time for the library to develop new resources and utilize the talent of the Local Area Network (LAN) team members and other library departments. The recently purchased integrated library system had Windows and Web versions of its OPAC. The system provided the utilization of the MARC 856 field that allowed for hypertext links to the electronic content. The library's first objective was to assess staff and other resources that could be used to develop a system that would allow professors to disseminate information to their students through the library catalog. The following resources were already available:

1. The library's LAN team
2. An integrated library system that facilitated access to Web content via the 856 field
3. Coordinator of digital applications (hereafter referred to as the coordinator) who organized workflow and trained other staff in new technological developments implemented by the library.

The library determined they needed the following in order to carry out the Digital Library project:

1. Additional programmers working with the LAN team
2. A full-time cataloguer who would serve as a bibliographic control specialist
3. The coordinator to serve as an intermediary between the LAN team and the cataloguer
4. Additional funding made possible through a grant.

BETA PROJECT-PHASE I

Phase I had two objectives. The first objective was to solicit paper course material from faculty. The library director generated interest among the faculty along with the coordinator. The library sent out a mass mailing inviting faculty to submit class notes, syllabi, and practice exams (see Appendix 1). Library staff followed up by meeting with faculty department heads to encourage their colleagues to add material to the Digital Library. Library staff also worked with the ILC (Information Literacy Center) in creating workshops that introduced the Digital Library to faculty. The response was very favorable. Other members of the university, such as administrators from non-academic departments, were invited to utilize this service. However, this article will concern itself with faculty submitting course material for student access.

Once the library had faculty cooperation, the second objective was to disseminate their widely used paper course material through the online catalog. After staffing was in place, a simple workflow was established. When the library received a document for submission to the Digital Library, the bibliographic control specialist (hereafter referred to as the cataloguer) assigned LC call numbers to these documents. Work-study students were trained to scan documents and maintain image quality control before saving the files onto the network. The directory for storing files was based on LC call number hierarchy. The subfolders were labeled using Cutter numbers assigned to faculty names and the "publication" date, which referred to the semester. For example, a course taught by Professor Smith during the fall 1999 semester would have a folder labeled "S65_1999." This structure was first created by the LAN team and the coordinator and then maintained by the cataloguer. Once the files were uploaded onto the network, the cataloguer created a MARC record using metadata to describe the submitted course content. The call number assigned was used in the MARC 856 field as the address (URL) for the document. As a final process, the cataloguer activated the bibliographic record and assured functionality of the link to the electronic document.

PHASE II

During this phase of the project, the LAN team created software that allowed faculty to submit a greater variety of electronic formats to the Digital Library directly from their desktops and accommodated their request for controlled access. Some professors requested restricted access to their material, allowing viewing privileges to registered students only. The LAN team created another module to aid staff in processing a professor's submitted files. This component of Phase II streamlined procedures once material was submitted (see Appendix 2).

The basic steps to adding electronic content to the Digital Library were as follows:

1. *Submission of Course Material*–Faculty still had the option of submitting material electronically or in printed format. When faculty sent their material electronically, they first signed into a Web page maintained by the library. Here, they completed a form that served as a bibliographic template. This page also allowed for large groups of files to be compressed or "zipped" before submitting, and allowed faculty members to create an authorized user list along with passwords. If a professor hand-delivered a paper copy of the course material, student workers scanned the paper materials and the cataloguer submitted them to the Digital Library using the same procedure noted above.

2. *Receiving Electronic Submission*–Once a form was submitted, an e-mail automatically notified the cataloguer that a document was ready for processing. Processing was done using a staff module designed and programmed by the LAN team that reflected all workflow steps (see Appendix 2).

3. *Downloading Material*–The first step in processing involved the cataloguer downloading the submitted material to her desktop via the staff module.

4. *Attaching the User Group*–A list of users assigned by the professor was attached to the submitted material. Based on the list, the cataloguer created a user group via the staff module. If the professor wanted the material for general viewing, the cataloguer attached the content to a user group called "Public."

5. *Making Material "Web-Ready"*–The cataloguer unzipped the submitted files and made them "Web-ready." Content was not altered, but all files were converted to formats supported by Web browsers if they were not done so before submission.

6. *Creating the MARC Record*–The cataloguer created a minimal level open-entry MARC record based on the submitted form (see Appendix 3). Descriptive cataloguing was based on Nancy Olsen's *Cataloging Internet Resources: A Manual and Practical Guide*. The following MARC fields were used:
   a. *090*–the cataloguer assigned a LC call number and recorded it in the 090 field cuttered under the instructor's name. This call number also served as a unique URL address for the material.
   b. *100*–the professor's name as author

   c. *245, 246*–the course number and campus location as title. The 245 contained the course number and the 246 field reflected the official title of the course as it was listed in the university course catalog.

   d. *250*–the cataloguer noted the semester (e.g., Spring 1999) in the 250 field as a type of edition.

   e. *490*–it was decided that all material created by the professors would be considered part of the Digital Library series and thus, it was recorded in the 490 field. This made all electronic content available using one search query.

   f. *500*–a 500 field contained a local note that informed the user how to access the material.

   g. *505*–the name or title of the document submitted was included in the contents.

   h. *506*–this field included any special access restrictions.

   i. *516*–recorded a unique description of the item.

   j. *520*–summary of the course materials.

   k. *6XX*–subject headings were assigned based on a professor's description of the submitted material. The library believed that faculty, as creators of the course material, would be best suited to describe their own content.

   l. *740*–contained an added title entry reflecting the contents submitted, such as a lecture topic, for example.

   m. *856*–Depending on the content, the cataloguer created an 856 for each item submitted for the course (e.g., notes, practice exams, syllabus, etc.) unless the professor stipulated that all the files should be treated as an entire course package. The cataloguer then gave the entire course package a single 856 field.

7. *Saving to the Catalog and Uploading to the Network*–The cataloguer saved the MARC record to the database and uploaded the electronic course document for storage in the Digital Library. Any further editing of the MARC record was done through a Windows cataloging module and changes to user group access were made through the Digital Library module.

8. *Searching the OPAC*–The student searched the OPAC for course material by the instructor's name as the author, the course number/name, or by the document title. A bibliographic record was displayed containing hyperlinks to the electronic content. The student was allowed to view the material only after supplying a user name and password.

CONCLUSION–THE FUTURE

The library completed Phase II of the Project in the spring of 1999 and received positive feedback from students and faculty. The faculty are currently taking advantage of some of the features that are being offered in Phase III. Plans for this phase of the Digital Library include:

1. Library staff will aid professors in creating multimedia courseware, including audio and animation (began in the summer of 1999).
2. Multimedia course material will be available through the OPAC. This has been available since the spring of 1999.
3. The LAN Team designed an authoring module allowing professors to update files without having to resubmit the entire courseware package, while at the same time, alerting the cataloguer that its bibliographic record needs updating.
4. The LAN team designed a module that tracks usage for statistical purposes and will be available for the library and for faculty to monitor effectiveness of the course material created.
5. The process of tracking and deleting obsolete electronic items from the catalog is being further refined.
6. The LAN team designed a billing component that will be used to pass access charges to the patron when required. Any fees collected would then be passed on to the copyright owner.
7. The library will seek permission to incorporate copyrighted material as a part of courseware on behalf of the professor who wishes to utilize such materials. Currently, the library is accepting original material only.

The Digital Library Project at the Bern Dibner Library is an ongoing process with great potential for both the creators and users of its content. The in-house development requires close communication and cooperation among librarians, programmers, coordinators, and faculty. The library's current goal is to provide a means for faculty to publish course material to a source that would allow them full control over their content with the freedom to add and edit course material from anywhere at anytime while providing students with access. Response from students and faculty alike has been favorable.

BIBLIOGRAPHY

Atkinson, Ross. "Library Functions, Scholarly communication, and the Foundation of the Digital Library: Laying Claim to the Control Zone." *Library Quarterly* 66 (July 1996): 239-265.
Cataloging Internet Resources: A Manual and Practical Guide. 2nd ed. Nancy Olsen, ed. [book online] (Dublin, Ohio: OCLC Online Computer Library Center, Inc., 1997); available from http://www.purl.org/oclc/cataloging-internet; INTERNET.
Costers, L. "The Electronic Library and Its Organizational Management." *Libri* 44 (1994): 317-21.

Graham, Peter S. "Electronic Information and Research Library Technical Services." *College and Research Libraries* (May 1990): 241-50.

Levy, David M. and Catherine C. Marshall. "Going Digital: A Look at Assumptions Underlying Digital Libraries." *Communications of the ACM* 38 (April 1995): 77-84.

Payette, Sandra D. and Oya Y. Rieger. "Supporting Scholarly Inquiry: Incorporating Users in the Design of the Digital Library." *The Journal of Academic Librarianship* (March 1998): 121-9.

Schwarzwalder, Robert. "The Sci/Tech Invasion: Approaches to Managing the Digital Library." *Database* (August/September 1995): 81-4.

Zhang, Jun. "Digital Information Bank Network Retrieval System: A Digital Library." Bern Dibner Library, Polytechnic University.

APPENDIX 1. Invitation to Faculty

From: Polytechnic University Libraries

To: All faculty

Dear Faculty,

If you have documents available for circulation at the library, you can have them scanned and made available to your students through our online catalog. Students can search them in the catalog and print them out. Possible items to be scanned are exams, course notes, syllabi and assignments, including documents with images.

If you would like to send us course material for scanning, you can do so the following ways:

1. Send your documents to the library by fax (718/260-3756) or through interoffice mail to the attention of Cynthia Wolff. You can also send them to us on a diskette.
2. Email (cwolff@poly.edu) the documents as attachments if they are word-processed or in spreadsheet format.

Ideally, notes or exams should be word-processed, but in the event that they need to be hand-written, due to the use of formulas or equations, please use a medium-point pen. Fine point pens have a tendency to look very faded. A legibly written page will be easier to scan and easier for students to reproduce.

Please send us any documents at least two weeks prior to the date you want them available.

Please call us if you have any questions or problems. Contact Cynthia Wolff at ext. 3764, or email at cwolff@poly.edu

APPENDIX 2. Flow Chart for Processing Submitted Material

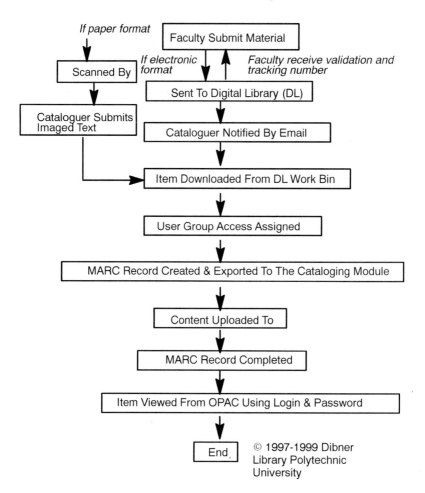

© 1997-1999 Dibner Library Polytechnic University

APPENDIX 3. Sample of MARC Record

090        $a LC call number $b Cutter of professor's name and submit date

100   1 $a Professor's last name, first name.

245   1   0 $a Course number and campus

246   3 $a Course number

246   3   3 $a Course title

250        $a Semester and year

256        $a Online service(s)

260        $a [Brooklyn, New York: $b Polytechnic University], $c1999

490   0   Polytechnic University Digital Library

500   Academic Department

500   ACCESS MATERIAL BY CLICKING ON THE VIEW IMAGE/VIEW
CONTENT TAB.

505   0 $a Lecture 1--Lecture 2

506        $a Available only to registered students (or other note describing access)

516        $a Online courseware

520        $a On-line course materials for EE100

650   0 $a Subject 1

650   0 $a Subject 2

700   1 $a Additional instructor

740   0 $a Added title entries for contents

856   4 $u URL where electronic content is stored $z Hyperlink describing content.

Cataloging Economics Preprints:
An Introduction to the RePEc Project

José Manuel Barrueco Cruz
Thomas Krichel

SUMMARY. Cataloging resources that assist in educating a domain specific community can require a finer level of granularity than objects that are to be accessed by a more general domain community, and can become a costly process. One possible approach towards cataloging such resources is to get a community of providers involved in cataloging the materials that they provide. This paper introduces RePEc (http://netec.wust.edu/RePEc) as an example for such an approach. RePEc is mainly a catalog of research papers in Economics. RePEc is based on set of over 80 archives, which all work independently but are interoperable. The key issue of the paper is to evaluate the success in providing data of reasonable quality a decentralized approach. *[Article copies available for a fee from The Haworth Document Delivery Service: 1-800-342-9678. E-mail address: <getinfo@haworthpressinc.com> Website: <http://www.HaworthPress.com>]*

José Manuel Barrueco Cruz is Librarian, Biblioteca de Ciències Socials "Gregori Maians," Universitat de València, València, Spain (e-mail: jose.barrueco@uv.es).

Thomas Krichel is Lecturer in Economics, Department of Economics, University of Surrey, United Kingdom (e-mail: T.Krichel@surrey. ac.uk).

Address correspondence concerning this paper to <wopec@netec.mcc.ac.uk>.

The authors are grateful to Christopher F. Baum, Robert P. Parks, Thorsten Wichmann and Christian Zimmermann for comments on the questionnaires. William L. Goffe and Christian Zimmermann made many helpful suggestions. Sophie C. Rigny kindly pointed out many stylistic and grammatical errors in an earlier version.

The work discussed here has received financial support by the Joint Information Systems Committee of the UK Higher Education Funding Councils through its Electronic Library Programme.

[Haworth co-indexing entry note]: "Cataloging Economics Preprints: An Introduction to the RePEc Project." Cruz, José Manuel Barrueco, and Thomas Krichel. Co-published simultaneously in *Journal of Internet Cataloging* (The Haworth Information Press, an imprint of The Haworth Press, Inc.) Vol. 3, No. 2/3, 2000, pp. 227-241; and: *Metadata and Organizing Educational Resources on the Internet* (ed: Jane Greenberg) The Haworth Information Press, an imprint of The Haworth Press, Inc., 2000, pp. 227-241. Single or multiple copies of this article are available for a fee from The Haworth Document Delivery Service [1-800-342-9678, 9:00 a.m. - 5:00 p.m. (EST). E-mail address: getinfo@haworthpressinc.com].

© 2000 by The Haworth Press, Inc. All rights reserved.

227

KEYWORDS. Metadata, cataloging, economics, educational resources in economics

1. INTRODUCTION

Some scientific disciplines have a preprint tradition. Essentially these are Mathematics, Physics, Computer Science and Economics. Preprints are not issued in the same ways across those disciplines. In Mathematics and Physics preprints are essentially issued by individual academics. In Computer Science and Economics, it is more the department that distributes the preprints. In this paper we deal with Economics preprints, usually called working papers.

Economics is the dismal science. Its bad reputation is founded on two conceptions. The first is that economists never agree on anything. Winston Churchill claimed, "If you put two economists in a room, you get two opinions, unless one of them is Lord Keynes, in which case you get three opinions." And on the other side of the pond, President Truman sought to hire a one-armed economist because he would not be able to say "on the other hand." The other conception is that Economics is very theoretical to the point of being totally useless. A popular tale is that of the two economists who sit down to play chess. They study the board for 24 hours and eventually declare a stale-mate. Fortunately both of these conceptions do not fully apply to all sections of Economics. There is a large mainstream literature that is based on a common set of principles. It is true that this literature is heavily mathematical but that does not follow that it is completely useless. There are counterexamples. For example, the calculation of option values is important for anybody who is dealing with financial options. Trade in such options has only taken off since a pricing formula has been found. Another example is studies relating to competition. These are used by government organizations who work on regulating industries and on anti-trust measures.

Economics research documents are therefore useful to a wide variety of people, not only to students. In the past years more and more Economics departments and research institutions have made their working papers available on the Internet. However in that form the papers can only be found by specialists who know who has been working in a certain area, where that researcher is based and whether there are any papers of that researcher available on the Web pages. This is the kind of knowledge that is circulated at scientific conferences–usually on the back of business cards and napkins–and therefore this data is not available to the people outside the research community. The normal mortals will only be able to benefit if a catalog of these papers is available.

In this paper we describe attempts to build a catalog of online and offline working papers in Economics called RePEc. We introduce the concepts behind RePEc and explain the underlying archives. The paper describes and reviews the RePEc dataset and considers user interfaces. The conclusion raises questions about the cost of providing access through a model such as that presented by RePEc.

2. RePEc

The electronic dissemination of Economics working papers can be traced back to the start of the Working Papers in Economics (WoPEc) project in April 1993. By May 1999 this single archive has grown into an interconnected network of over 80 archives holding over 14,000 downloadable working papers and over 50,000 descriptions of offline papers from close to 1,000 series. The network of archives is called RePEc. This term was initially conceived to stand for "Research Papers in Economics." Nowadays it is best understood as a literal, because the objectives of RePEc go way beyond a database of scientific papers.

RePEc data is freely available in the sense that the provider pays for the provision of the data–not the user. In order to make such a system viable without public subsidy, the cost of providing the data must be spread among many agents (understood here and in the rest of the paper as a person or institution). This requirement has been a feature of RePEc right from the start of the collection in May 1997. Each participating provider sets up an archive on a http or ftp server. The archive supports the storage of structural data about objects relevant to Economics, and possibly the storage of some of the objects themselves. All objects in RePEc are uniquely identified following by handles.

RePEc data can be accessed through a plethora of user services. Some are heavily used, for example the "IDEAS" (*http://ideas.uqam.ca/*) user service had one million hits in just over 2 months in 1999. The main interest of this paper is to examine the collection aspect of the data. It remains to be demonstrated if a coherent literature catalog that aims to educate a specific domain community can be put together by a large group of people who have a base discipline knowledge, are physically dispersed, have very little personal communication, and don't need extensive training nor intensive coordination.

At the time of writing this paper RePEc is two years old. We feel that this is a good time to review the operations of RePEc and the data that it has collected. Clearly the RePEc data is in a constant state of flux. To keep matters simple we took a dump of the data on 1 May 1999. In this paper we are only referring to the state of the data on that date.

The nature of RePEc is not precisely defined. Most people think about it as a collection of archives and services that provide data about Economics.

More precisely, RePEc is most commonly understood as referring to three things. First, it is a collection of archives that provide data about Economics. Second, it is the data that is found on these archives. Third, it is often also understood to represent the set of agents who build archives and channel the data from the archives to the users. In that latter sense RePEc has no formal management structure. RePEc has two aims. The "cataloging aim" is to provide a complete description of the Economics discipline that is available on the Internet. The "publishing aim" is to provide *free* access to Economics resources on the Internet.

The basic principle of RePEc can be summarized as follows:

Many archives --> One dataset --> Many services

Basic RePEc concepts are: archive, site and service.

- An "archive" is a space on a public access computer system which makes data available. It is a place where original data enters the system. There is no need to run any software other than an ftp or http daemon that makes the files in the archive available upon request. Each archive is identified by a three-letter code. Some elementary metadata about the archive like its name, its url and some basic contents information are polled by a special central archive with the handle RePEc:all, where "RePEc" is the naming authority and "all" is the archive code.
- A "site" is a collection of archives on the same computer system. It usually consists of a local archive augmented by frequently updated ("mirrored") copies of remote archives.
- A "service" is a rendering of RePEc data in a form that is available to the end user.

All archives hold papers and metadata about papers, as well as software that is useful to maintain archives. Everything contained in an archive may be mirrored. For example, if the full text of a paper is in the archive, it may be mirrored. If the archive does not wish the full text to be mirrored, it can store the papers outside the archive. The advantage of this "remote storage" is that the archive maintainer will get a complete set of access logs to the file. The disadvantage is that every request for the file will have to be served from the local archive rather than from the RePEc site that the user is accessing. Of course an archive may also contain data about documents that are exclusively available in print.

There is no need for every site to mirror the complete contents of every archive in the system. To conserve disk space and bandwidth some sites only mirror bibliographic information rather than the documents that an archive may contain. Others mirror all the files of an archive. Others may mirror only parts of a few archives. The software that is used to mirror the archive is provided at RePEc:all. It first mirrors the central archive. This software then reads a configuration file and then writes batch calls to the popular "mirror" program for ftp and the "w3mir" script for http archives.

An obvious way to organize the mirroring process would be to mirror the data of all archives to a central location. This central location would in turn be mirrored to the other RePEc sites. The founders of RePEc did not adopt that solution, because it would be quite vulnerable to mistakes at the central site. Instead each site installs the mirroring software and mirrors "on its own," so to speak. Not all of them adopt the same frequency of updating. Many update every night, but a minority only updates every week. It is therefore not known how long it takes for a new item to be propagated through the system.

Each service has its own name. A service that is based on mirrored scripts may run on many locations. Within reason, all services are free to use any part of the RePEc data as they see fit. For example, a service may only show papers that are available electronically, others may restrict the choice further to act as quality filters. In this way services implement constraints on the data, whether they be availability constraints or quality constraints. The user service infrastructure is quite well developed, we list the most important ones in *Section 5*. This distribution via several user services is an undisputedly successful feature of RePEc. It is therefore not given further attention here.

3. THE STRUCTURE OF AN ARCHIVE

RePEc stands on two pillars. First, an *attribute:value* template metadata format called ReDIF. This acronym stands for *R*esearch *D*ocumentation *In*formation *F*ormat but it is best understood as a literal. ReDIF defines a number of templates. Each template describes an object in RePEc. It has a set of allowable fields, mandatory, and some repeatable. The second pillar is the Guildford protocol. It fixes rules how to store ReDIF in an archive. It basically indicates which files may contain which templates. It is possible to deploy ReDIF without using the Guildford protocol. But in the following we will ignore this conceptual distinction, because it is easiest to understand the structure and contents of an archive through an example. This is done in *Subsection 3.1*. Therefore we will list files in the way required by the protocol as well as the contents of the file that is in fact written in ReDIF. This is done in *Subsection 3.1*. We return to technical aspects of ReDIF in *Subsection 3.2*.

3.1. The Guildford Protocol

RePEc identifies each archive by a simple identifier or handle. Here we look at the archive RePEc:sur which lives at *ftp://www.econ.surrey.ac.uk/*

pub/RePEc/sur. On the root directory of the archive, there are two mandatory files. The file *surarch.rdf* contains a single ReDIF archive template.

Template-type: ReDIF-Archive 1.0
Name: University of Surrey Economics Department
Maintainer-Email: T.Krichel@surrey.ac.uk
Description: This archive provides research papers from the
Department of Economics of the University of Surrey, in the U.K.
URL: ftp://www.econ.surrey.ac.uk/pub/RePEc/sur
Homepage: http://www.econ.surrey.ac.uk
Handle: RePEc:sur

In this file we find basic information about the archive. The other mandatory file is *surseri.rdf.* It must contain one or more series templates.

Template-Type: ReDIF-Series 1.0
Name: Surrey Economics Online Papers
Publisher-Name: University of Surrey, Department of Economics
Publisher-Homepage: http://www.econ.surrey.ac.uk
Maintainer-Name: Thomas Krichel
Maintainer-Email: T.Krichel@surrey.ac.uk
Handle: RePEc:sur:surrec

These two files are the only mandatory files in the Guildford protocol. If these are the only files present in the archive then all the archive is doing is to reserve the archive and the series codes. All documents have to be in a series. The papers for the series RePEc:sur:surrec are confined to a directory called *surrec.* It may contain files of any type. Any file ending in ".rdf" is considered to contain ReDIF templates. Let us consider one of them, *surrec/ surrec9601.rdf* (we suppress the Abstract: field to conserve space).

Template-Type: ReDIF-Paper 1.0
Title: Dynamic Aspect of Growth and Fiscal Policy
Author-Name: Thomas Krichel
Author-Email: T.Krichel@surrey.ac.uk
Author-Name: Paul Levine
Author-Email: P.Levine@surrey.ac.uk
Author-WorkPlace-Name: University of Surrey
Classification-JEL: C61; E21; E23; E62; O41
File-URL: ftp://www.econ.surrey.ac.uk/pub/
RePEc/sur/surrec/surrec9601.pdf
File-Format: application/pdf
Creation-Date: 199603

Revision-Date: 199711
Handle: RePEc:sur:surrec:9601

Note that we have two authors here. The "Author-WorkPlace-Name" attribute only applies to the second author. We will come discuss this point now.

3.2. The ReDIF Metadata

The ReDIF metadata is mainly an extension of the Karlsson and Krichel (1999)[1] commonly known as the IAFA templates. In particular it borrows the idea of clusters from the draft.

> There are certain classes of data elements, such as contact information, which occur every time an individual, group or organization needs to be described. Such data as names, telephone numbers, postal and email addresses, etc. fall into this category. To avoid repeating these common elements explicitly in every template below, we define "clusters" which can then be referred to in a shorthand manner in the actual template definitions.

ReDIF takes a slightly different approach to clusters. A cluster is a group of fields that jointly describe a repeatable attribute of the resource. This is best understood by an example. A paper may have several authors. For each author we may have several fields that we are interested in, the name, e-mail address, homepage, etc. If we have several authors then we have several such groups of attributes. In addition each author may be affiliated with several institutions. Here each institution may be described by several attributes for its name, homepage, etc. Thus a nested data structure is required. It is evident that this requirement is best served in a syntax that explicitly allows for it such as XML. However in 1997–when ReDIF was designed–XML was not available. We are still convinced that the template syntax is more human readable and easier understood. However, the computer cannot find which attributes correspond to the same cluster unless some ordering is introduced.

We proceed as follows. For each group of arguments that make up a cluster we specify one attribute as the "key" attribute. Whenever the key attribute appears a new cluster is supposed to begin. For example if the cluster describes a person then the name is the key. If an "author-email" appears without an "author-name" preceding it the parsing software aborts the processing of the template. Note that the designation of key attributes is not a feature of ReDIF. It is a feature of the template syntax of ReDIF. It is only the syntax that makes nesting more involved. We do not think that this is an important shortcoming. In fact we believe that the nested structure involving the persons and organizations should not be included in the document

templates. What should be done instead is to separate the personal information out of the document templates into separate person templates:

Template-Type: ReDIF-Person 1.0
Name: Thomas Krichel
Email: T.Krichel@surrey.ac.uk
Author-Paper: RePEc:sur:surrec:9404
Author-Paper: RePEc:sur:surrec:9601
Homepage: http://gretel.econ.surrey.ac.uk
Handle: RePEc:per:1965-06-05:thomas_krichel

We can then replace the author information for the first author in the paper
template for RePEc:sur:surrec:9601 by:

Author-Name: Thomas Krichel
Author-Person: RePEc:per:1965-06-05:thomas_krichel

The benefits of such a relational structure are clear. There is a much
reduced load on administration of the system. When one element of author
data–e.g., her phone number–changes, this change has to be registered at only
one point in the system. A pervasive use of these relational features will
allow the resolution of current author information through the current person
template of the author. The user of a RePEc service would therefore find the
author of the paper even though the contact information on the paper's title
page may no longer be current. We leave the implementation of such systems
for future work.

4. THE TOTAL DATASET

4.1. Aggregrate Contens

In Table 1, we examine the document data in RePEc. For each field we
give the total occurrences of the field in the "all" column and the maximum
of occurrences that the field has within a single template in the "max"
column. The document data appear in the ReDIF-paper and the ReDIF-article
templates. There are two characteristics that potentially set articles apart from
papers. First, the paper can be understood as a preprint. From that point of
view the article is a paper that has gone through some sort of peer review. In
that case the distinction between paper and article has to do with the contents
only. Secondly, the distinction between paper and articles could be through
their physical manifestation. From that point of view the article would be a

TABLE 1. The Total Dataset

	ReDIF-paper		ReDIF-article	
field	*all*	*max*	*all*	*max*
template-type	58254	1	10112	1
handle	58251	2	10110	1
title	58235	2	10110	1
author-name	98321	14	13855	6
creation-date	52730	1	8819	1
revision-date	536	8		
publication-date			510	1
abstract	22984	3	1896	1
classification-jel	20194	2	436	1
keywords	39219	3	9084	1
keywords-attent	457	1		
publication-status	6227	3	1568	1
note	9011	1	1479	2
series	4124	2		
number	16021	2	1501	1
price	4175	3		
file-url	17259	22	1853	2
order-url	2417	1		
contact-email	1141	1		
availability	7169	2		
length	33342	12		
pages			7920	1
month			489	1
issue			8705	1
volume			1293	1
year			1293	1
journal			488	1
paper-handle			19	1

document that is bound with others in a journal issue and it would therefore carry page numbers, issue numbers, etc. This is the official criterion according to the ReDIF documentation. But it is not neat since the pagination may become redundant if the journal becomes electronic. In the following we will use the term "document" when we wish to refer to papers and articles simultaneously.

Total numbers for documents are given by the "template-type" and "handle" fields. Since each template should have exactly one type and exactly one handle the tiny difference between the two numbers is made up of mistakes in the dataset. The title field is also required. It is encouraging to see that most documents have a creation date attached to them, because as the dataset grows it will become increasingly important to distinguish between recent and dated documents; only the former are likely to be of much interest. By contrast "revision-date" information is rare. Articles may also have a "publication-date." The difference of this field with the "creation-date" field is not clear. We consider this to be a design error in the template structure.

Let us consider the elements that refine the contents description. We encourage contributors to provide abstracts. The presence of abstracts for about one in three papers is very positive. The abstract field can be repeated. This is desirable when there are abstracts in different languages. A large number of the papers have a *Journal of Economic Literature* (JEL) classification code attached to them. However almost all papers in the offline papers only archive RePEc:fth have the codes and that explains a very large proportion of the classified material. Note that this data has been compiled by a librarian.

For the electronic papers there are only two in five papers that have a classification field. We agree that this is a serious limitation to the quality of the data. It would have been possible to require a classification number for each paper right from the start. This would have hampered the collection effort. In particular it would have made it impossible for the WoPEc team to "snarf" bibliographic data from sites where this JEL data was not available. There is also some concern among economists that their areas of work do not match with these codes. The use of more complete and sophisticated classification schemes would not be possible. The main argument against requiring JEL classification codes was, however, that there is considerable opposition against the scheme in the heterodox Economics community. They feel that the JEL classification scheme reflects the view of the orthodoxy. Requiring JEL classification codes would have meant excluding these contributors. Then and now only a tiny part of the collection could be grouped as heterodox. However our aim is that RePEc be a broad church. This was the decisive argument against requiring the use of JEL codes.

There is a large number of templates that have keywords. About 50% of these templates come from RePEc:fip where each paper has a keyword. ReDIF allows for both free and qualified controlled vocabulary. This facility is used by for the internal keyword scheme of the Attent: Research Memoranda[2] database. They are only used by the RePEc:dgr archive.

The "publication-status" field can be used to indicate where the paper has been submitted and where the paper has been formally published. This field appears in the data from large research bodies that have been issuing a series of papers for many years and that have data about the formal publication of the paper. The fields "series" and "number" are somewhat redundant since this information should also be available from the handle. The "price" field normally refers to the delivery of a printed copy. The mode of delivery is often just expressed in the "price" field. The "file-url" field refers to the "full text" locus of a part of the full text. Usually it is the complete full text.

The document may have several components in addition to the full text. These can be listed as several "file" clusters. Each may carry an uncontrolled field about its function within the paper. For example, the author may wish to supply a computer program that was used to produce the paper. In that case a whole series of files may be made available. However that is not the way the option of having many files is actually exercised. Most of the time it is used to include elements like graphics or tables that the author did not manage to include into the main document file.

The "order-url" field is used to point to an intermediate page that sits between our description and the files of the document. In that case we are not aware if the resource does actually exist online. "order-url" may be used in conjunction with the "file-url" attribute. Note that there is no "order-email" field in the document templates. Such a field figures in the series template, because the ordering of a paper should be the same for all papers in the series. The "contact-email" may otherwise be used to contact the somebody who has any connection with the paper. This field is only used by the contributors to the RePEc:wpa archive. The "availability" is used most of the time to signal that the paper is no longer in print.

Finally a "length" attribute can be used to indicate how many pages the reader has to go through to read the paper. This field is present in all templates provided by RePEc:fth and it seems to appear in a surprisingly large number of other templates. Articles have a number of specific attributes that are listed at the bottom of the table. Strictly speaking these are not descriptive elements of the articles themselves, they rather relate to the position the article has within the journal. Finally the "paper-handle" allows to point from the preprint version to the article template.

4.2. The Clustered Data

The data available in Table 1 is not the complete set of information available in the dataset. It only lists the individual attributes and the key attributes of clusters in the paper and article templates. In Table 2 we have the data that is contained in the clusters in this subset of the RePEc data. This data is therefore consistent with the data in Table 1. There are three types of clusters, "file," "organization" and "person." The numbers that are present suggest that there are significant possibilities for a relational structure in the dataset between persons and their organizations. An interesting consideration in the person cluster is the high number of workplace templates. Providers of the data seem to attribute more importance to the workplace of a person rather

TABLE 2. Clusters Subset of the RePEc Data

file			person			organization		
name	*all*	*max*	*name*	*all*	*max*	*name*	*all*	*max*
url	19112	1	name	112176	1	name	8598	1
format	19024	1	postal	8	1	postal	2118	2
size	2630	1	homepage	1557	2	homepage	596	2
function	1661	1	email	3166	2	email	1451	3
restriction	2548	1	phone	282	1	phone	164	1
			fax	259	1	fax	197	1
			workplace-name	8598	4			

than to her strictly personal data, e.g., her homepage. The only explanation that we can offer here is that most likely the data is provided by an agent of the workplace. The low number of homepages is an indicator which also suggests that in most cases the provider is not the author herself. Note also that the workplace information–when it is present–is much more complete than the corresponding data for the individuals.

5. USER SERVICES

There would be little point in collecting all that data if there were no users to use them. Note that there is no official user service for RePEc. The implicit ability and explicit intention to allow for many user services at one time is a key feature of RePEc. This provides an important selling point once a potential provider understands that submitting data to RePEc means submitting the data to all the user services at once. Here we list the most important user services in *Subsection 5.1*, before we critically discuss them in *Subsection 5.2*.

5.1. The Main User Services

By order of historical appearance, they are:
BibEc (http://netec.mcc.ac.uk/BibEc.html) and *WoPEc* (http://netec.mcc.ac.uk/WoPEc.html) provide static html pages for all working papers that are only available in print (BibEc) and all papers that are available electronically (WoPEc). Both datasets use the same search engines. There are three search engines, a full text WAIS engine, a fielded search engine based on the mySQL relational database and a ROADS fielded search engine. Note that the mySQL database is also used for the control of the relational components in the RePEc dataset. BibEc and WoPEc are mirrored in the United States and Japan as part of the NetEc project.

IDEAS (http://ideas.uqam.ca/) provides an Excite index of static html pages that represent all Paper, Article and Software templates. This is by far the most popular RePEc user interface.

NEP: New Economics Papers (http://netec.wustl.edu/NEP/) is set of reports on new additions of papers to RePEc. Each report is edited by subject specialists who receive information on all new additions and then filter out the papers that are relevant to the subject of the report. These subject specialists are PhD students and young researchers. They work as volunteers. On 27 June 1999 there were 1766 different e-mail addresses that subscribed to at least one list.

Tilburg University Working papers and research memoranda (http://kubaxc. kub.nl:2050/, follow link.) This site also operates a Z39.50 server for all downloadable papers in RePEc that is available at dbiref.kub.nl:9997. The database name is "repref." The attribute set is Bib-1, and the record syntax supported are Usmarc, SUTRS, GRS-1 (only string tags, tag type 3).

RuPEc (http://www.ieie.nsc.ru:8101/RuPEc/) is a server in Russian. It not only provides search facilities for Russian users but also archival facilities for Russian contributors.

INOMICS (http://www.inomics.com/query/search) not only provides an index of RePEc data but also allows simultaneous searches in indexes of other Web pages related to Economics. The "Tilburg University Working papers and research memoranda" service is operated by a library-based group that has received funding from the European Union. INOMICS is operated by the Economics consultancy *Berlecon*. All the other user services are operated by junior academics.

5.2. The Usage of User Services

Thomas Krichel founded both the WoPEc user service in 1993 and NEP in 1998. José Manuel Barrueco has been intensively involved in WoPEc user education. Our experience suggests that the average users from developed countries are at the postgraduate and doctoral level. There are many users in developing countries. In these countries the user community includes more senior levels, i.e., more junior academics and professional researchers rather than students. For them the RePEc user services are one of the very few means to get hold of research papers. We think that this is the most rewarding aspect of our work. The free provision of RePEc helps to reduce the gap between the informationally rich and the informationally poor.

The use of RePEc services among senior academics in the developed countries seems to be low. Perhaps this may be a result of these persons being too much set in their ways to use these modern facilities? We do not think so. We believe that the current user services do not meet the information needs of these people. Academics do not need large-scale information services that they can search. The larger the scale the more likely they are to find information they did not seek and the less likely they are to find information that they want. Since they are working within a very narrow field and only have little time to read a small amount of literature, small-scale information services are more tailored to their needs. In addition the contents of the service should be highly selective. Among the current user services that are built on the RePEc data, NEP comes closest to such services. Our anecdotal evidence suggests that this is the service that has the largest proportion of tenured academics.

RePEc as such cannot provide small-scale user services. It can only provide the basis for such user services to exist. We are aware of two approaches to build such services. Section 4 of Krichel, Lyapunov and Parinov (1999)[3] design features for a current awareness portal system where each researcher could register the subject and type of records that she is interested in. The portal would then be able to inform the researcher about new resources in her field. A second approach is outlined is Section 6 of Baum and Krichel (1999).[4] Here the idea is to build peer review Web ("SurWeb") services. These are supposed to extend NEP to full peer review. It is too early to speculate if such a system can be put into place.

6. CONCLUSIONS

The free provision of educational material can be implemented through a central institution. Such an institution needs to be subsidized by central funds. The alternative is to provide the resources by a large number of agents. Then the cost of providing access can be absorbed within each institution. In that case the question of a comprehensive catalog arises. Such a catalog is needed to provide access to the collection in a unified way.

In this paper we have dealt with the provision of a key resource, i.e., academic papers. We have presented a collection of metadata that is provided by decentralized archives. We have found that it is possible to build such a collection to a reasonable degree of accuracy if some archives where mistakes occur are aided by others. There needs to be a small group of people who actively support the collection. However, this support can be given in decentralized fashion without the need for much coordination between supporters.

The academic library community in the United Kingdom as a whole has made a important contribution to RePEc by donating funds to the work of the WoPEc project. This has allowed the WoPEc project to collect metadata about papers that are published by institutions that are not yet contributing to RePEc. This was a vital aspect of WoPEc project. The data collected by WoPEc constituted 90% of the RePEc data when RePEc was founded. However, nowadays that proportion is falling. The funding for WoPEc has run out but the WoPEc Website continues to expand because of the contributions made by RePEc archives. The software is maintained by volunteers.

Librarians should carefully consider the vision of this project. RePEc is an academic self-organization where academics publish and catalog their own work to assist in educating a domain-specific community. RePEc benefits from network externalities. The more academics join, the more others will consider joining. With freely available data, authors can communicate with their peers without the need of intermediaries. This project raises questions about the role of intermediary providers, such as publishers *and* librarians. In closing, these authors believe that intermediaries need to play a more active part by supporting developments like RePEc because, ultimately, it offers them a new role–one that ought to be seriously considered as traditional jobs are being automated by technological developments

NOTES

1. Deutsch, Peter, Emtage Alan, Martijn Koster, and Markus Stumpf (1994). Publishing Information on the Internet with Anonymous FTP. Internet draft, expired March 1, 1995.

2. Attent: Research Memoranda. Available [on-line] at: http://cwis.kub.nl/~dbi/english/info/attent.htm

3. Krichel, Lyapunov and Parinov (1999). Available [on-line] at: http://gretel.econ.surrey.ac.uk/papers/zhenya.pdf

4. Baum, C. F. and Krichel, T. (1999). EDEL: Economics Distributed Electronic Library. Available [on-line] at: http://netec.mcc.ac.uk/AcMeS/edel.html

Metadata Issues, Document Architecture, and Best Educational Practices

Richard Giordano

SUMMARY. This paper outlines metadata issues for documents created for a Web-based environment concerned with issues of best educational practices. Metadata describing the documents related to educational practice must be able to describe context of the practice. Moreover, document structure itself is problematic because, in a Web-based environment, a document that appears on a user's workstation as a single object may in fact be an assembly of linked, yet discrete, documents residing in distributed databases. The paper discusses in detail the problem of describing the context of practice, a distributed document architecture, and metadata based on the Dublin Core and GEM metadata standard. The paper ends with a discussion of weaknesses of the Dublin Core when documenting physically distributed documents. *[Article copies available for a fee from The Haworth Document Delivery Service: 1-800-342-9678. E-mail address: <getinfo@haworthpressinc.com> Website: <http:// www.HaworthPress.com>]*

KEYWORDS. Dublin Core, GEM, metadata, document architecture, best educational practices

BACKGROUND

From the articulation of the President Clinton's views on failing schools, to the standards movement in many states, to the changing roles of teachers'

Richard Giordano is Research and Development Specialist, Northeast and Islands Regional Educational Laboratory, Brown University, 222 Richmond Street, Providence, RI (e-mail: Richard_giordano@brown.edu).

[Haworth co-indexing entry note]: "Metadata Issues, Document Architecture, and Best Educational Practices." Giordano, Richard. Co-published simultaneously in *Journal of Internet Cataloging* (The Haworth Information Press, an imprint of The Haworth Press, Inc.) Vol. 3, No. 2/3, 2000, pp. 243-261; and: *Metadata and Organizing Educational Resources on the Internet* (ed: Jane Greenberg) The Haworth Information Press, an imprint of The Haworth Press, Inc., 2000, pp. 243-261. Single or multiple copies of this article are available for a fee from The Haworth Document Delivery Service [1-800-342-9678, 9:00 a.m. - 5:00 p.m. (EST). E-mail address: getinfo@haworthpressinc.com].

© 2000 by The Haworth Press, Inc. All rights reserved.

unions, to the explicit concerns of parents, there is a recognizable, broad-based view that public education in the United States is failing, and that only a clear political and public commitment to educational excellence can turn things around. A public commitment to excellence implies that action–on the part of the Federal government, the states and localities, school districts, teachers and parents–be taken with the single strategic goal of improving teaching and learning.

Uninformed action, however, not only wastes resources, but often results in outcomes that are worse than the problem. Action, such as the shaping of policy at all levels of government, changed teacher practices, community involvement, requires the provision of rich, reliable information and resources to assure its success. More than that, successful school reform efforts need to be guided by practical experience that is itself informed by current research, in real world settings. This is to say, reform is guided by both information and knowledge.

Networked information technologies are important large-scale resources that can inform educational reform from the shaping of policy to the shaping of practices by localized groups of teachers because these technologies allow access to information, resources and services. Most important, networked computer-mediated communications support the collaborative sharing of ideas, and the cooperative construction of informed policy.

The Office of Educational Research and Improvement of the United States Department of Education (OERI) contracted with the Northeast and Islands Regional Educational Laboratory at Brown University (LAB) to create a proof-of-concept pilot for a Web-based environment of best educational practices deployed in the United States. The objectives of this electronic environment are to: Prototype a system of information management and retrieval that is intuitive and serves diverse users and their varied needs; simplify the search by stakeholders for educational programs and methods that deliver proven learning outcomes; assist a broad base of citizens–educational leaders at all levels, classroom teachers, students, and parents–with reaping direct benefit from the substantial investment that OERI and the Department of Education has made to in education initiatives which result in proven practices; setting a new standard that will help to elevate the future educational products and services offered by private industry such as publishers; and, investigate the feasibility of developing a comprehensive electronic resource that moves from information delivery to information creation through collaborative and mutually-supporting activities among participants in a mediated electronic environment. The overarching goal of this entire initiative is first and foremost to change practice in such a way that it positively influences existing educational systems and the teaching and learning outcomes that they produce.

INTRODUCTION TO THE PROBLEM

We were faced with a group of inter-related problems. First, we had to come to some understanding with stakeholders of what is really meant by a 'best' practice; we had to create a Web-based document architecture that expressed both the best practice and our goal of building a collaborative learning community; we had to design a metadata standard in this environment that would underlie the searching, location, and selection of information, as well as support semantic interoperability, resource management and intellectual property.

There is widespread interest in best practices in all sectors of the economy, but especially so in the manufacturing, commercial and military sectors. Best practices in these sectors are usually established by using a set of benchmark data gathered from industrial or commercial practices or processes. That is, benchmarks such as the most throughput per unit of time, lowest cost per unit, highest quality per unit, the best materials to use for a given set of applications, and so on are established by examining practices of organizations within a sector of the economy. For example, 'The Best Manufacturing Practices Program' sponsored by the Office of Naval Research of the United States Department of the Navy surveys companies that use 'best practices' established by panels of experts. Any such organization that employs a best practice must show verifiable quantitative improvement over time, and use up-to-date techniques. The criteria for identifying a best practice are usually unambiguous and quantitative. Because of this, a best practice can be described in a discrete document on the Web and documented using relatively simple metadata for resource discovery.

Best practices in areas outside of industry, such as the work supported by the Arts and Humanities Data Service (*http://www.ahds.kcl.ac.uk*) in the United Kingdom, typically define a clear set of practices, such as the creation and encoding of digital resources of interest and use to scholars and students in the humanities, that can be described in discrete documents which are themselves documented with relatively simple bibliographic metadata and bibliographic information.

Best practice typically describes processes from which there are measurable gains in efficiency or effect, or processes that act upon or affect objects. Compared with such practices, the business of public education is messy. Although there are verifiable quantitative data that indicate increased learning outcomes as well as established practices that have been shown to be successful, for better or for worse, what constitutes a best practice in educational settings is not at all clear. Nor is it clear how one is able to convince another in the field of education that a practice is indeed a best practice.

As part of our work, we convened both face-to-face and electronically-mediated focus groups[1] among stakeholders to help us to understand, among other things, what is a best practice and how can one be measured. The focus groups consistently asked, 'Best practice for whom and for what end?' Although increased test results are usually seen as indicative of increased student achievement among policy makers, a practice that results in increased test result scores but without community involvement is, at best, viewed as problematic. Moreover, many of the nation's schools, and New York City's in particular, hold teaching and learning philosophies that inform all of their practices.

A best practice that is at variance with such a philosophy would be difficult to promulgate and administer in such a setting. Although many best practices are vetted by experts, teachers and many administrators are deeply suspicious of experts, particularly university academics who, in their view, do not understand or appreciate the classroom or the school as a work environment. Although almost all members of the focus groups agree that there needs to be clear and unambiguous evidence of success for a practice, there is no overall agreement on the indicators of success. Teachers are generally suspicious of statistical evidence and rely more on evidence presented by teachers; senior administrators, on the other hand, very much want hard statistical evidence of success coupled with both the direct costs (dollars spent) and ancillary costs (for instance, the number of teachers who need special training, the use of computing facilities, and what not) because such evidence is most useful in staking a claim for resources with politicians and superintendents; managers close to the classroom value both statistical evidence of success as well as qualitative measures (such as a change in classroom climate or improved social behavior among students) so that they can discuss the practice with senior administrators, parents and other localized stakeholders such as bargaining units.

Consequently, despite the current strength of the standards movement, where increased scores on standardized tests are the sole indicators of increased quality in teaching and learning, educational settings are far more complex environments than industrial processes or even some academic processes. Best practices in education-related practices exist within localized social and cognitive settings–they live within cultures and contexts where there are few agreed-upon benchmarks. The localized contexts of school districts, and schools within such a district, may be wildly different–and what may work well in one setting may have little impact in another. Potential users are far more interested in learning how the best practice is established and implemented in real settings, than they are in a description of the practice. Moreover, because the practice directly affects children, not objects, stakeholders maintain a valid concern not only with the outcomes of the practice, but with the process of the practice, as well.

Our focus group discussions demonstrate that the context of the practice–

its setting; its history; its use in real world work environments; participant views; examples of student work; testimonials and views provided by parents, teachers and students; a discussion by interested parties of the practice—are elements that comprise a best practice description in complex educational settings. There are two ways of gathering this information: an expert panel or some other content provider can attempt to build a discrete best practices document that includes this information; or, a base document describing the practice can be created, and ancillary and related documents can be created remotely by practitioners and/or interested content providers. The former allows one centrally to control both for quality and access, while the latter allows one to tap into remote and localized expertise and thereby collect a range of views and experiences. Moreover, by allowing a base document to be 'related' to others on the Web, the best practice logical document itself continually grows and changes. Most important, conversations and debates are more likely to be generated when a document is 'alive' in this way than if it were a static textual object.

A BEST PRACTICES ONLINE DOCUMENT ARCHITECTURE

Because we are primarily interested in creating an online environment within which participants are made aware of best practices, are able to gain a deep understanding of the context within which the practice is used, and who want to communicate with others who share similar experience, we have opted for a distributed document architecture, where the base document is created by a content provider, and related documents are created either by specific content providers (such as technical assistance organizations) or by practitioners in the field. Figure 1 illustrates this document architecture.

The Base Document delineates the best practice itself and points to facts of the practice in the Facts Document, in specific schools and other related information. Based on feedback from our focus groups, we have initially settled on a document structure for the base document that consists of nine elements. The *Header* will provide bibliographic information and be logically attached to the base document through a database link. This allows us to ship metadata independent of the objects they document.

The *Theme document* element describes the overall theme of the practice or intervention, such as 'Professional Development,' or 'Literacy Training.' The *Description document element provides a textual rendition and definition of the practice.* The Questions document element lists the sort of questions that this practice addresses, or questions that readers should bear in mind when considering this practice. The *Policy Alignment document element discusses how this practice aligns with the Secretary of Education's Priority areas for education. The Success Stories Element points readers to*

FIGURE 1. Best Practices Online Document Architecture

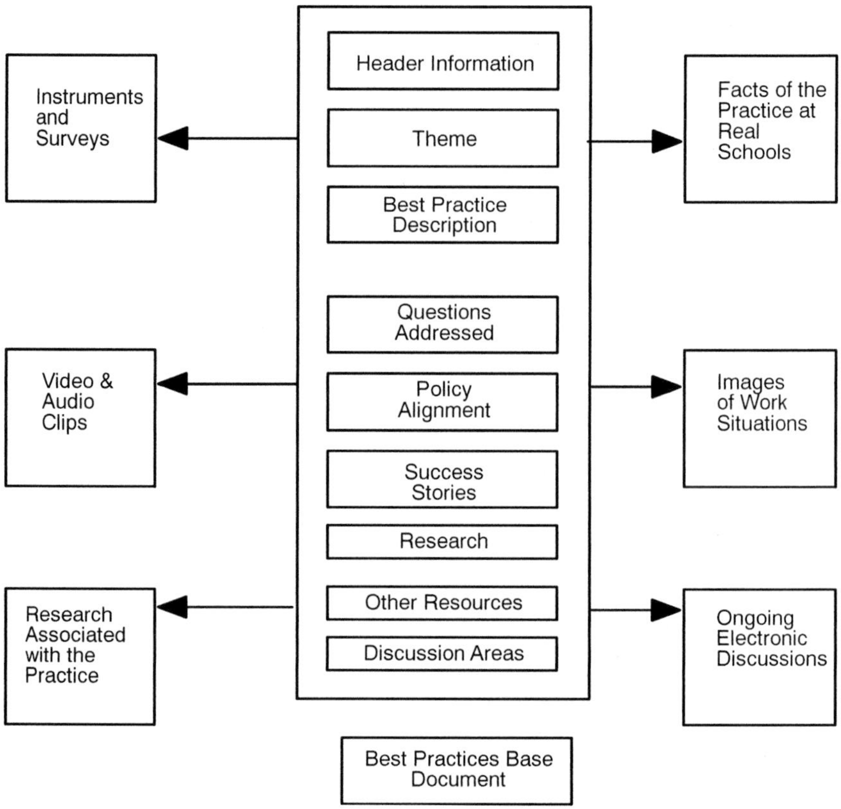

schools that have implemented the practice, as well as facts about the schools and the practice. The Research Document element points to research finds regarding the practice. The Other Resources document element points to resources related to the theme of this practice and other related information. Finally, there is a discussion area regarding the practiced.

The Facts Document delineates the best practice itself and its use in a specific school or schools, and consists of ten document elements. The *Demographics* element will detail the characteristics of the school's population (the number and ratios of various ethnic groups, special needs students, proportion who qualify for school lunches, etc.). The *Background Conditions* describes the context in which the intervention took place–the history of events at the school that lead to the intervention, the deployment of staff, the physical conditions of the buildings, and related material. The *Design and Implementation* element describes the design of the intervention and the techniques used at the school to implement that design. Some specific interventions, for instance, require specific design and implementation methods. This element provides for information on the design methods and implementation techniques required by the intervention, and compares them with the techniques actually used at the school. The *Results* element provides both quantitative and qualitative results of the intervention such as disaggregated longitudinal test scores, anonymous *"report card"* data, truancy rates, graduation rates, student outcomes after graduation and other indicators that depend on the nature of the intervention. Qualitative results, such as changes in school climate, assessment of portfolios, etc., are described by this element. The *Replication Details* element provides information to prospective users of the intervention of just what conditions and resources must be present in their school to replicate the intervention. This element augments the *Costs and Funding* element, as that element is concerned with the dollar costs and access to funding in support of the intervention. *Replication*, on the other hand, discusses the often hidden ancillary costs and resources associated with bringing a specific intervention or practice to a school such as paid time for substitute teachers, a telecommunications and computing infrastructure, special training or group facilitations. *Contact Information* will include contact details of a person who can discuss the intervention with a prospective client in more detail than can be provided in Web-based resources. Finally, *Rating Criteria* provides information on why this intervention and school was chosen as an example of best practice, and why it is included in BPO. For example, a school might be using a best practice in the area of professional development for teachers. The National Partnership for Excellence and Accountability in Teaching (http://www.npeat.org) may have selected this school as one that exemplifies this best practice. The *Rating Criteria* element will provide information on the selection criteria, and how the school met those criteria.

In addition to the Base and Facts documents, there will be a number of documents to the best practice base document. These related documents will not be physically attached to the base document, but may be added to the Web at any arbitrary Web location. The one related document that will always occur is one that delineates facts about the practice in the field (such as the populations that have been subjected to the intervention, demographic information about the schools in which this intervention has taken place, and so on). These are an open set of related documents that may include video clips of the school or work conducted in the school, interviews with parents, teachers and students, examples of student work, underlying research for the intervention, surveys and instruments used during the intervention and online electronic discussions surrounding the practice. A Best Practice Document should thus be thought of as the Base Document, a Facts Document (a document of the facts of the practice), along with none, one or more related documents.

Related documents can occur or be discovered in one of three ways: (1) While constructing a base document the content provider may also construct one or more related documents that can reside in any arbitrary location on the Web; (2) the content provider may discover documents on the Web that are seen related to the best practice, and which should be made known to users of BPO; (3) another content provider may create related documents and inform the base document creator of their existence. Related documents may be freely available to users or they may have copyright restrictions that require payment for use.

Metadata and Resource Discovery

There are three issues attending resource discovery and metadata as they relate to Best Practices Online documents: (1) not duplicating in the Header information already contained in the base or related documents; (2) building upon current metadata standards and practices, especially in the education community; and, (3) providing the means for Web-based resource discovery and documentation for the logical Best Practices Online document (that is, both the base document and related documents).

Our general approach to meeting these issues is to: (1) create a document structure for the base document that is self-indexing; (2) use the Gateway to Educational Materials (GEM) element set whenever possible; (3) to attempt to nest metadata from related documents in a single metadata record so that the base metadata record both points to and documents related documents on the Web. We will discuss these approaches in turn.

THE BASE DOCUMENT AND FACTS DOCUMENT AS SELF-INDEXING OBJECTS

The great weakness of HTML is its inability to express document structure or document function. Roughly speaking, HTML tags generally provide enough information for display, and nothing at all about content. XML allows creators to create explicit document structures and to indicate within those structures specific types of data. Documents properly encoded in either SGML or XML become self-indexing or self-describing objects, and provide far more expression and indexing capabilities than anything encoded in HTML.[2]

The approach we have taken is to encode explicitly each section of the base and facts document, and to store each section (such as 'Demographics,' 'Background Conditions,' 'Results,' etc., from the Facts Document) in a database that can be queried by users. The Base and Facts BPO document are constructed at query time from the database. This arrangement will allow users to build searches that interrogate one or more of the document sections using keywords or more complex search strategies. Thus, for instance, users can search for best practices in schools that, for example, have a relatively large proportion of Mexican students or, to take another example, rural schools whose Native American students' reading test results have increased over a period of three years, or they can search on Theme. Like all database queries, they can be limited to one index or joined across indexes.

Our current pilot work involves the construction a pidgin form of HTML in the form of comments that explicitly encode sections and data within sections. The HTML mimics XML, but is no substitute for it. Our intention is to encode base documents in XML once the pilot project is complete.

THE USE OF THE GEM ELEMENT SET

The GEM element set consists of the fifteen Dublin Core Elements and eight GEM elements.[3] At the outset of our work, we have decided to use the GEM element set for the creation of the Header unless that set proved to be manifestly ill-suited to our needs. Moreover, we want to follow as closely as is practical GEM standards and rules governing Header creation. Although GEM was designed as metadata for lesson plans and other classroom materials, its structure and rules of creation lend themselves to other types of documents. By standardizing on GEM, we can build on their experience in creating a metadata standard, as well as leverage their expertise and resources in training, setting cataloging and documentation standards, and in creating partnerships with organizations that catalog Web objects. By collaborating with GEM, the standard would be informed by our needs, thereby becoming more generalized and useful across a range of education-related materials. Finally, practitioners who are already familiar with GEM would not have to learn yet another standard.

The following is a list of Dublin Core and GEM elements (with HTML 2.0 equivalents) which we have included in our metadata. The semantics of the Dublin Core Elements are defined by the DC Base Semantics of 5 February, 1999; GEM element semantics are defined from the GEM/IMS Documentation of 23 February 1999. We have a special use of the DC.RELATION element, and will reserve discussion of it for the following section.

We do not at this time use the GEM elements GEM.RIGHTS, GEM. SOURCE, GEM.ESSENTIALRESOURCES, GEM.TYPE, GEM.DURATION,

GEM.PEDAGOGY, GEM.QUALITY, and GEM.STANDARDS. Some of the elements, such as DURATION, PEDAGOGY, QUALITY, STANDARDS and TYPE are difficult to map onto Best Practices records, or the information about them is embedded in the text of the base documents. At this time, we have not settled on a rights management policy, so we will defer the use of the RIGHTS element until that policy is established. We expect that all base documents will be freely available but copyrighted by their creators. The ESSENTIALRESOURCES element is subsumed by the REPLICATION element of the best practices base document, and, as we will discuss in the following section, we plan to use the DC.RELATION element to direct users to that information.

Notice that with respect to the Dublin Core elements, our practice conforms well with current GEM practice, but there are some minor variations, particularly in the use of subelements. We do not use any DC elements that are not used by GEM.

DC.CREATOR. The person or organization primarily responsible for creating the intellectual content of the resource. For documents related to the BPO base document, the value for DC.CREATOR will be the person primarily responsible for the intellectual content of that work. In the case of student work, for example, the value for DC.CREATOR would be the student's name.

Subelements: NamePersonal, NameCorporate and Role mandatory only.

GEM example: DC.CREATOR (namePersonal) Pratt, Ian.
                     DC.CREATOR (role) primary.
HTML example:
<meta name='GroupStart' content='1'>
<meta name='DC.CREATOR' content='(type=namePersonal)Pratt, Ian'>
<meta name='DC.creator' content='(type=role)primary'>
<meta name='GroupEnd' content='1'>
Use: Mandatory when known.

DC.DATE. The date that the resource was made in its present form. We will follow the formatting scheme for dates used by GEM (YYYY-MM-DD), an ISO standard.

Subelements: recordCreated, creation, modified,
                     placedOline, validFrom, validTo.

GEM example:
DC.DATE (ISO 8601:1988) (recordCreated) 1994-05-12).

HTML example:
<meta name='DC.DATE' content='(scheme ISO 8601:1988)
(type=recordCreated)1994-05-12.'>
*Use:*Mandatory when known.

DC.DESCRIPTION. A textual description of the source. This will likely be copied from the source document itself. The description will make explicit the phenomena under study (such as an intervention in a school) not a bibliographic description of the source.

Subelements: none.

GEM example:
DC.DESCRIPTION This describes the use of Action Research as a professional development tool at CES 42 (the Claremont School) in the Bronx, New York. The research involved twelve reading teachers . . .
HTML example:
<meta name='DC.DESCRIPTION' content='This describes the use of Action Research as a professional development tool at CES 42 (the Claremont School) in the Bronx, New York. The research involved twelve reading teachers . . . '>
*Use:*Mandatory.

DC.FORMAT. The data format of the resource. The value for the format element will be selected from the Internet Mime Type.

Subelements: Scheme.

GEM example:
DC.FORMAT (IMT) (contentType)text/HTML
HTML example:
<meta name='DC.FORMAT'
content='(scheme=IMT) (type=contentType)text/HTML'>
*Use:*Highly recommended. (In GEM, this is mandatory.)

DC.IDENTIFIER. String or number used uniquely to identify the resource, such as a URL or standard numbers.
Subelements: locSpec (mandatory), public_id (recommended), SID (system generated ID).

GEM example:

DC.IDENTIFIER (URL) (locSpec)http://www.lab.brown.edu/pb/c.htm
HTML example:
<meta name='DC.IDENTIFIER' content' '(scheme=URL) (type=loc-
Spec) http://www.lab.brown.edu/pb/c.htm'>
*Use:*Mandatory.

*DC.LANGUAGE. Languages or writing system of the intellectual content of
the resource.*

Subelements: Code (highly recommended. Use Z39.53 three
                      letter code); Text (required if Code not used).

GEM example:
DC.LANGUAGE (Z39.53) (code)Fre
DC.LANGUAGE (Z39.53) (text)French
HTML example:
<meta name='DC.LANGUAGE'
content='(scheme=Z39.53) (type=code)Fre'>
Use: Mandatory when language of the source is not English.

*DC.PUBLISHER. The entity responsible for making the resource available in
its present form.*

Subelements: Only role is used.

GEM example:
DC.PUBLISHER (name) The LAB at Brown.
DC.PUBLISHER (GEM) (role)onlineProvider.
HTML example:
<meta name='DC.GroupStart' content='1'>
<meta name='DC.PUBLISHER'
    content='(type=name)LAB at Brown'>
<meta name='DC.PUBLISHER'
content='(scheme=GEM) (type=role)onlineProvider'>
Use: Identify only the online provider of the document, not the original
publisher or provider. The value for the role subelement should thus al-
ways be "onlineProvider."

*DC.SUBJECT. The topic of the content or theme of the resource. BPO will
use only controlled vocabularies when using a topic. In addition to standard vocabularies such as ERIC and LCSH, we plan to use a set of BPO
controlled vocabularies. One set would identify the type of school in which*

the intervention takes place; another would identify the theme of the intervention (such as 'Professional Development'), another would map to one of the Secretary of Education's Priority areas and, finally, another would describe the problem or issue that the intervention is meant to address (such as 'low reading scores' or 'poor community involvement.' The focus groups indicated many practitioners prefer to search using the language of the problem rather because that is often all that they know.

Subelements: subjectPath.

GEM example:
DC.SUBJECT (BPO1) (subjectPath) Poor community involvement.
HTML example:
<meta name='DC.GroupStart' content='1'>
<meta name='DC.SUBJECT'
content='(scheme=BPO1 type=subjectPath1)
poor community involvement.'>
<meta name='DC.GroupEnd' content='1'>

Use: Recommended that at least one subject be provided.

DC.TITLE. *The title of the work as provided by the creator, publisher, or cataloger.*

GEM example:
DC.TITLE (BPO1) (subjectPath) Action research at CES 42: Impact on Pre-reading activities.
HTML example:
<meta name='DC.title' content='Action research at CES 42: Impact on Pre-reading activities.'>
Use: Mandatory.

GEM.AUDIENCE. The group or groups that would use or benefit from the intervention. Values for the subelements toolFor and beneficiary would come from either BPO or ERIC controlled vocabularies. Beneficiaries should identify a specific population such as 'learning disabled' or 'second language learners.'

Subelements: toolFor, beneficiary.

GEM example:
GEM.AUDIENCE (toolFor)Secondary school mathematics teachers.
GEM.AUDIENCE (beneficiary) English language learners.

HTML example:
<meta name='GroupStart' content='1'>
<meta name='GEM.audience'
content='(scheme=BPO) (type=toolFor)
Secondary school mathematics teachers'>
<meta name='GEM.AUDIENCE'
content='(scheme=BPO) (type=beneficiary)English language learners.'>
<meta name='GroupEnd' content='1'>
Use: Optional.

GEM.CATALOGING. GEM provides for rich information about the cataloging agency. Although this information might come in handy, we believe that it can be replaced with a simple National Union Catalog (NUC)-like three letter code, as it used on MARC records. The codes would be controlled by BPO, or NUC codes would be used when available.

Subelements: scheme.

GEM example:
GEM.CATALOGING (scheme=BPO)EIC
GEM.CATALOGING (scheme=NUC)NNC
HTML example:
<meta name='GroupStart' content='1'>
<meta name='GEM.CATALOGING' content='(scheme=BPO)EIC'>
<meta name='GEM.AUDIENCE' content='(scheme=NUC)NNC'>
<meta name='GroupEnd' content='1'>
*Use:*Optional.

GEM.GRADE. Where the intervention or practice targets a specific grade or grade range.

GEM example:
GEM.GRADE 8,9,10
HTML example:
<meta name='GEM.GRADE'
content='scheme=GEM) (type=grade)8,9,10'>
*Use:*Optional.

Use of the RELATION Element

As we mentioned at the beginning of this paper, we were guided by the principle of not duplicating, whenever possible, information in the header that is already contained in the base document. Moreover, we need to identify resources on the Web that are related to the base document. We addressed the first principle and the following need through the use of the DC.RELATION element.

In designing the BPO Header, we had originally envisioned that we would create a set of BPO elements that would be appended to the GEM element set. Thus, a BPO metadata package would consist of the Dublin Core Elements used by GEM, the GEM elements used by BPO, elements used only by BPO. These elements included GOALS (the goals and objectives of the intervention); COSTS (the dollar amount of the intervention); EFFECTIVENESS (indicators of success); CONTACT (contact information); and CONTEXT. On advice from our focus groups, however, we developed a document type declaration for the Best Practices Base and Facts document that included this information. The problem was making that information known in the Header without copying it outright from the base document. We were guided primarily by the philosophy of being as parsimonious as possible when creating a best practices Header, and to create common types of information only once in each document. Aside from issues of esthetics (duplicated information violates every data management convention one can imagine), the question of maintenance loomed large. If, for instance, contact information were contained both in the Header and the Base Document, one would have to be sure to make *two* edits in case whenever a change was necessary. We therefore made the decision that where relevant to include any bibliographic information in the Header, and other information (such as contacts, costs, etc.) in the base document.

As we mentioned earlier in this paper, we plan to store the elements of the base and facts documents in a Web-based database. Because of this, we are able to make use of the DC.RELATION element in place of CONTACT, COSTS and ESSENTIALRESOURCES. In the case of ESSENTIALRESOURCES, this information is held in the REPLICATION_DETAILS section of every best practices base document.

The DC.RELATION element consists of an element name followed by a set of attributes and values. A typical DC.RELATION has subelements to delineate the kind of relationship between the source and target objects, a textual description of the relationship and its context, a location specification (such as a URL) and some public standard identifier (such as an ISBN). We use the *text, kind* and *location* subelements to identify and point to sections of the Best Practice Base document. For example, when pointing to contact information, the RELATION element is used like this:

DC.RELATION (description) CONTACT
DC.RELATION (kind) isSiblingOf
DC.RELATION (URL) (locSpec)<*A URL that accesses the database goes here*>

Similarly, we can access ESSENTIALRESOURCES by creating a RELA-TION element like this:

DC.RELATION (description) ESENTIALRESOURCES
DC.RELATION (kind) isSiblingOf
DC.RELATION (URL) (locSpec)*<A URL that accesses the database goes here.>*
Notice that the values of the description subelement have the same name as the GEM element set.

NESTING METADATA FROM RELATED DOCUMENTS ON THE WEB

Because the RELATION element is an object that is related to the base document, we can use a similar construction of the RELATION element for the identification of related Web-based objects as we do for pointing to sections of the base document. The problem, however, is that we not only want to point to the Web-based object, but we want to identify that object in some systematic way within the BPO header by making known the description, creator, title, format, and location specification of the object. This is not easy to do because unlike, for instance, the TEI Corpus Header, there is no way at present to nest bibliographic information in a set of Dublin Core elements. The TEI Corpus Header, for example, allows one to document the entire corpus, as well as each sample text within the corpus, in a single header by allowing each sample text to be nested. As we will illustrate, we plan to use the GEM element names within the RELATION element.[4]

In an ideal world, we would like to have nested full GEM-like bibliographic information about the objects, but in many cases these will not be known. Moreover, the proliferation of cataloging that would attend the cataloging of related objects would probably overwhelm any institution's capacity to cope.

For example, if there a video clip on the Web from a school showing the best practice or intervention in a classroom, we can identify and point to it from the BPO header using a construction like this:

DC.RELATION (description) (element=text) Video of a pre-school class learning reading by photographing a cooking session with a digital camera and making a book from the photographs.
DC.RELATION (description) (element=Creator) David Joseph Adams.
DC.RELATION (description) (element=Title) CES42: Successful Action Research Projects.
DC.RELATION (description) (element=Format) MPEG3

DC.RELATION (description) (element=locspec) http://www.ccm.ny.us/s1c

Its HTML 2.0 equivalent would look like this:

```
<meta name='GroupStart' content='1'>
<meta name='DC.RELATION'
    content='(type=description) (element=text) Video of a pre-school class learn-
    ing reading by photographing a cooking session with a digital camera and
    making a book from the photographs.
<meta name='DC.RELATION'
    content='(type=description) (element=creator) David Joseph Adams'>
<meta name='DC.RELATION'
    content='(type=description) (element=title) CES42: Successful Action Re-
    search Projects.'>
<meta name='DC.RELATION'content=
    '(type=description) (element=format) MPEG3'>
<meta name='DC.RELATION'
    content='(type=description) (element=locSpec) (URL) http://www.ccm.ny.us/
    s1c'>
<meta name='GroupEnd' content='1'>
```

Because the RELATION element can link the Base Document's metadata
to any Web object, we can identify and link to online discussions, chat room,
online seminars and whatnot. For example, identifying and linking to an
electronic discussion of the practice through the DC.RELATION element
would like this in HTML 2.0:

```
<meta name='GroupStart' content='1'>
DC.RELATION (description) (element=text) Online moderated listserv dis-
    cussion of Action Research as a Professional Development tool in urban
    settings.
DC.RELATION (description) (element=Moderator) David Joseph Adams.
DC.RELATION (description) (element=Title)PAR discussion group.
DC.RELATION (description) (element=locspec)
    <http://www.par.cuny.edu>
<meta name='GroupEnd' content='1'>
```

By making use of the DC.RELATION element in this way, we are able to
link to related documents that, when combined as a single logical Best Practices Online document, are able to provide a rich picture of the practice, its
context, practitioner and participant views, as well as ongoing discussions of
the practice.

The weakness with this approach, however, is that it is an improvisation, a kludge that attempts to make Web sources available in a systematic way when, of course, the tools for doing so are only just emerging. Without the judicious use of a URL or a URC (or some equivalent mechanisms), the approach will fail as soon as the location of the Web object is moved, and it will become frustrating and difficult to maintain over time.[4] Having said this, the benefits of creating a rich picture of the practice, and building discussions and debates around the practice, argue that we do not wait for the appropriate technologies to mature.

CONCLUSIONS

Although best practices are relatively easy to characterize in industrial, commercial settings, or where the practice (or process) affects an object, such a simple world does not exist in the education community. Stakeholders maintain different views of the efficacy of the practice, expert opinion counts for only so much, and the evaluation of evidence is not uniform. Moreover, the context of the practice, and a wide contribution of views, evidence and discussion, are needed not only to make the practice understandable, but acceptable to the community.

The approach we took in making best educational practices known to a wide audience is to construct a document architecture of a base document that provides baseline evidence and information of the practice, and documents related to the base document. Related documents can take the form of video files, testimonials, statistical data or online discussion groups, to name a few. The base document and its open set of related documents compose a logical best practices record.

We have found that the Dublin Core and GEM element set are able to provide most of what is needed in creating metadata for this sort of record architecture. The weakness, however, is that GEM metadata (and the Dublin Core) do not lend themselves to the nesting of metadata. We have found a solution using the DC.RELATION element, but this is a partial solution. While we are able to identify, document and locate Web sources through this element, it is, in effect, a static pointer in a dynamic world.

NOTES

1. For the preliminary results of this focus group, see Richard Giordano, "Focus Group Summary," <http://www.lab.brown.edu/bpo/focus/welcome.shtml>

2. For an excellent introduction to why XML is needed for the next generation of Web-based documents and interactivity, see Jon Bosak & Tim Bray, "XML and the Second-Generation WEB," *Scientific American* v2330, n5 (May, 1999), pp. 89-93.

3. See Stuart Sutton, "Gateway to Educational Materials (GEM): Metadata for networked information discovery and retrieval," *Computer networks and ISDN systems*, v.30, issue 1-7 (April, 1998), pp. 691-693.

4. See "The Corpus Header" in Michael Sperberg-McQueen and Lou Burnard, eds. *Guidelines for Electronic Text Encoding and Interchange* (P3). (Chicago & Oxford: ACH/ALLC/ACL), pp. 643-664. For an analysis of the problems of maintaining Web objects in real time, see Giordano, Richard, Carole Goble and Gunnell Kallgren, "Problems of Multidatabase Construction for Literary and Linguistic Research," in Ide, Nancy and Susan Kockey, eds., *Research in Humanities Computing* (Oxford: Oxford University Press, 1996).

Structured Metadata Spaces

Thomas D. Wason
David Wiley

SUMMARY. This paper presents the concepts of a *metadata space* as it relates to cataloging and discovery. A space has multiple dimensions; in the case of resource metadata, these *are descriptive dimensions*. We explain the needs for orthogonal descriptive dimensions, and present a method for achieving maximally efficient, independent dimensions using *semantic structures* realized in *structured metadata*. A specific example of this system as developed in the IEEE Learning Technology Standards Committee (LTSC P1484) Learning Object Metadata (LOM) is presented. The LOM is the collaborative work of many organizations including ADL, AICC, ARIADNE, GESTALT, and IMS (see acronym list at the end of the article, following references). The scope of the concepts presented in this paper encompasses general concepts of metadata systems. *[Article copies available for a fee from The Haworth Document Delivery Service: 1-800-342-9678. E-mail address: <getinfo@haworthpressinc.com> Website: <http://www.HaworthPress.com>]*

KEYWORDS. Metadata, resource discovery, descriptive metadata

THE PROBLEMS

In order to understand the requirements for a metadata system, the nature of the problems such a system addresses needs to be understood. The user

Thomas D. Wason is affiliated with the IMS Project and GEM.
David Wiley is DLE Group Technical Lead, Brigham Young University.

[Haworth co-indexing entry note]: "Structured Metadata Spaces." Wason, Thomas D., and David Wiley. Co-published simultaneously in *Journal of Internet Cataloging* (The Haworth Information Press, an imprint of The Haworth Press, Inc.) Vol. 3, No. 2/3, 2000, pp. 263-277; and: *Metadata and Organizing Educational Resources on the Internet* (ed: Jane Greenberg) The Haworth Information Press, an imprint of The Haworth Press, Inc., 2000, pp. 263-277. Single or multiple copies of this article are available for a fee from The Haworth Document Delivery Service [1-800-342-9678, 9:00 a.m. - 5:00 p.m. (EST). E-mail address: getinfo@haworthpressinc.com].

© 2000 by The Haworth Press, Inc. All rights reserved.

community encompasses a wide variety of needs, not all of which can be predicted by the cataloging community. The user may be a teacher searching for individual resources or complete courses. It may also be a student looking for references for a paper or doing research for a project. (A data management system may be considered a special form of user.) Metadata can be considered a system that supports communications between two very diverse user communities. As a *communications system* it must have a well-defined vocabulary and syntax to support a wide variety of semantic needs. There is inherent variability in the use of a communication system: interpretation of the language may vary with individuals and/or may drift over time. This variability creates a certain lack of clarity in the communications, or "fuzziness." Additionally, the purposes filled by the system may change, causing the system itself to change to fulfill these new requirements.

Communication

Bibliographic metadata can be considered to be a system of communication between the *cataloging community* and the *user community*. The cataloging community ranges from the professional cataloger who describes a large number of resources on a daily basis to the casual creator of metadata who may want to provide some meaningful labels for a Web page. Together, the community of catalogers creates a corpus of metadata.

There is a strong need for a common language that has adequate richness but will not fall apart due to the noise inherent in the system. Metadata is a poor personal communications system, as the cataloger cannot know exactly for what purpose every user will want a resource. Additionally, the user cannot ask for information that does not exist. As the communication becomes more uni-directional, the requirement for unambiguous messages increases. The need for a common, robust communications system is clear, but what are its characteristics? The purpose of the system, as with normal human language, is to enable the communication of meaning. Metadata should describe resources in ways that will be useful to the user. The user communicates with the cataloger in an abstract fashion: the user asks the cataloger to describe the resource in the same manner that the user does. There is a communications expectation created by the user, but the communications channel is restricted. Formative feedback from the user to the cataloger is diffuse, either through complaints or from lack of use of the resources. An effective metadata communications system must have some mechanism for providing this feedback. *An effective metadata system should provide good correspondence between the description of the resource by the cataloger and the strategies of the searcher.*

Description and Discovery

Discovery is the process of finding a previously unknown resource that satisfies a particular need. The discovery process itself may serve to sharpen the definition of that need. The definitions that underlie the description of a resource may not reveal the purpose of the resource. The searcher has a purpose for his or her discovery process. Some purposes can be clearly articulated in terms of the information needed. The definitions of the terms of description should be as free of implied purpose as possible. *In an efficient metadata system, the resource description should be as objective as possible, but provide enough information for a user to determine if the resource is appropriate for his or her purposes.*

Fuzziness

Ask ten catalogers to provide descriptions of a resource using an unrestricted vocabulary. Ask ten searchers to find the resource, again, using an unrestricted vocabulary. A perfect system would have the resource descriptions provided by all ten catalogers found in the searches by all ten searchers. This is highly unlikely, however, because the catalogers will differ in their descriptions of the resource and the searchers will differ in their search strategies and terminology. The lack of correspondence between the user community and the cataloging community creates a system with noise or *fuzziness.* Fuzziness can be considered from a statistical standpoint: it is the variability in repeatedly assigning the same values to the same resource over repeated trials. The same person may not produce exactly the same metadata for a resource now that he or she might have a month earlier. Descriptions that overuse multiple terms in a single field may create another kind of fuzziness.

Change

Metadata systems change. The fields used, the definitions of the fields, and the vocabularies used have changed and will change again. Some changes will be evolutionary, some revolutionary. *A metadata system must do more than contend with changes, it must manage them.*

METADATA SPACE

Metadata spaces provide an analogy for thinking about, describing, and creating effective metadata systems. The following is adapted from Wason (Wason, 1998).

Precision, Resolution, and Repeatability

Precision is the degree of fidelity with which something can be represented. *Resolution* is the ability to differentiate between two similar items. *Repeatability* is the ability to have the same resource described the same way on two or more occasions.

If one has a green square, it is possible to describe that *color* from a fixed vocabulary. If the vocabulary contains only *colored*, *black*, and *white* as terms, then one can describe the square as "colored." This is a low degree of fidelity, however. The *precision* is low. Next introduce a blue octagon to the collection. The vocabulary does not permit the two items to be separated in a search; the *resolution* is low. Now suppose two different people search for the green square. Both will probably pick "colored." The colored descriptor *repeatability* is high.

Continuing with the green square example, what if we change the color palette: black, white, red, orange, yellow, green, blue-green, blue, and violet. We have increased the potential precision of the descriptive field. Again, we have people independently categorize the square and the octagon. For the square, most will pick "green," but a few will pick "blue-green" or "yellow." For the octagon, most will pick "blue," but some will pick "blue-green," some "violet." The larger vocabulary has increased precision and resolution at the cost of lower repeatability. The variability among all of the catalogers has a *probability distribution*. This is the *fuzziness* referred to above. The searcher selecting a blue-green shape will get back a mix of shapes. The searchers also have some variability in their personal color interpretations. Thus the searchers have a probability distribution. Skilled catalogers may have a smaller distribution than searchers, but beyond a certain point the increased cataloging precision has no value in the meaningful resolution among instances. The variability of the searchers overwhelms the precision. As a consequence, the probability of the searcher discovering appropriate materials while excluding intrusions has a finite limit.

Different fields can support different size vocabularies. Well-structured vocabularies, including taxonomies, may support many more levels of precision, particularly if both catalogers and searchers agree upon the terms and definitions. But eventually the fuzziness overwhelms the precision such that increased vocabularies provide no increase in performance. Rather this activity decreases performance with the increase in intrusions due to a reduced capability to provide meaningful resolution among items. At a certain point it is simply not possible to resolve the differences between two very similarly colored polygons based on the description in this field (the "color" metadata). It is necessary to turn to some other feature to discover the differences between these polygons.

Attempts to reduce system fuzziness usually focus on controlling the vocabularies used by the different communities. If the catalogers and searchers can agree on a common vocabulary with consistent definitions, fuzziness is reduced. Restricted vocabularies have narrower *resolution* and *precision*. The two concepts are closely related. When an online search produces a large number of hits that are poor matches for the user's needs, it is frequently due to failures in resolution and/or precision in the metadata. *An efficient metadata system should reduce fuzziness without unnecessarily reducing resolution or precision.*

Dimensions

Differentiation is the ability to separate two items that appear identical along one dimension by using another dimension. If resources are described from different standpoints with smaller vocabularies, the chances of agreement on terms in any given field are higher, and the possibility of discovering a resource is greater. For our polygons above, if we use shape as a descriptor it is possible to reliably differentiate the polygons by the number of sides. Figure 1 demonstrates the manner in which different dimensions are combined to form a space.

The number of sides is independent of the colors of the polygons. We can say that they are *orthogonal* dimensions. If we know the number of sides of a polygon, then we may know the relationship between its size and area. They are not completely dependent, nor are they orthogonal. The most efficient method for describing a space is with orthogonal vectors or dimensions. If the vectors are not independent, then more must be used to fully define the space. *An efficient metadata system strives to have as nearly independent dimensions as possible.*

FIGURE 1. Space defined by multiple dimensions.

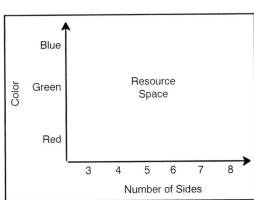

Metadata Space Concepts

Here we present the underlying concepts of a *metadata space*, a geometrical analogy that will allow us to speak, albeit indirectly, about the properties of a metadata system.

Points, Lines and Spaces

We can consider resource discovery a process that explores geometrical space. The potential for unique identification of a resource is proportionate to the number of available *dimensions*. The more dimensions available, the more unique possibilities exist (e.g., a $10 \times 10 \times 10$ cube has 1,000 unique addresses while a flat 10×10 grid has only 100). Thus, spaces can easily differentiate more items than lines, and points don't differentiate with respect to any sort of continua. The more uniquely defined an object is relative to other objects, the more easily it can be differentiated from others.

Dimensions. Dimensions are analogous to the resource metadata *fields*. A dimension is a measurement in a direction. The vocabulary terms used in the metadata fields are the metrics. For example, a ruler is able to measure along a line in some sort of standardized units, such as millimeters. Metadata can be analyzed according to its dimensions.

Metrics. Specific points along a dimension are defined by metrics. One centimeter (1 cm.) is a specific location relative to 0. The metrics that specify locations along the metadata field dimensions are not always ordinal. For example, learning style does not have an inherent order of terms. If there is no particular order to the dimension, then how is one to locate an object along it? Restricting the number of points on the dimension simplifies the task. For metadata fields, this means using finite, known vocabularies. If all resources are defined with a common set of terms, and if there are enough terms and dimensions to differentiate the resource well, then powerful discovery methods yielding small, focused sets of results are possible.

Points. Imagine that someone asked where a particular rock was, and you responded by saying "Oak." If you are standing in a field with a single oak tree in it, one can presume the rock is near the oak tree. The oak tree is a single point. If you don't know its context, it doesn't provide much information. Each word in a document can be considered a point of information. For example, if one searches for all content with the word "the," the return will be huge, but will provide little specificity. Sorting by selecting various points (terms) for filtering may allow one to access the largest number of resource items, but it provides no specificity, as the words are not metrics for any dimension. As Paul Saffo said, "It's the context, stupid" (Saffo, 1994).

Lines. A line has a single dimension and can be resolved into smaller pieces or segments. One method of resolving a dimension is through hierarchies. Each finer level of granularity further resolves the dimension into finer levels, thus creating a hierarchy. A library can be considered to be one long shelf of books. The shelf is broken down into major sections that are further subdivided into minor sections, and so on. Hierarchies are logical structures for resolving dimensions. Hierarchies are useful methods of storing and retrieving information. The location on the "line" can be defined with increasing precision until the object is uniquely located. The Dewey Decimal Classification (DDC) system is a fairly hierarchical system.

Hierarchies have limitations. For instance, a book on armaments of World War II could be located under history (WWII) or under technology (armaments). A person wanting to locate information on WWII armaments must decide how the "line" is resolved, and follow that hierarchy to locate the book. Libraries solve this problem through cataloging systems that cross-reference though subject descriptors.

Spaces. Resources can also be described by multiple dimensions. For example, a polygon may have a certain number of sides and be of a certain color. The number of sides can be varied independently from the color. Independent dimensions are *orthogonal*.

Obviously, the more orthogonal the dimensions, the more potentially differentiable positions are possible in the resulting space. The more dimensions one uses to define a space, the more likely one is to find that they are not truly independent. *An effective metadata system will utilize the right number of dimensions.*

Sub-Spaces. Orthogonal metadata fields serve the process of discovery. One may choose not to use all of the available metadata fields. For instance, one may search using only the fields of Subject, Content Type and Learning Level and a few key words to be used against the ABSTRACT. As all of the other fields are not specified, such as Creator (e.g., author), the search takes place against all creators. Selecting values for some of the dimensions while ignoring others creates a sub-space. Thus, having fields that are not used by the searcher is not a penalty as the objects in the space are still accessible. If there are a large number of "hits," the searcher may choose to include additional fields to refine the search.

DEFINITION MANAGEMENT

Stable definitions that can be commonly agreed upon are the basis of interoperability. Both fields and vocabularies need consistent definitions. Here we will address the creation of definitions for dimensions to create as nearly orthogonal dimensions as possible. Vocabulary definition is not addressed in this paper.

Semantic Structures

The following is adapted from Wiley (Wiley, 1999a, 1999b). A semantic structure is an organization that represents *meaning*. For example, an English sentence is a semantic structure. Consider the sentence structure: subject–verb–object. Before objecting by saying something like "the words have meaning, not the structure," consider two examples of the previous structure: (1) Dog bites man. (2) Man bites dog.

Obviously the words have meaning. But, two sentences containing the same words in the same structure can have very different meanings–depending on *where* in the structure the words appear. How do you know which position means what? Systems that use semantic structures (like languages) must supply a grammar, or way of interpreting meaning based on structure, in order to be useful.

You are asked to build a house out of blocks and given your choice of two different sets of blocks. The first set only contains five pieces: three walls, a wall with a door, and a roof. The second set is like Lincoln Logs, i.e., several different small pieces which can be hooked together by lining up the ends in a certain way. Consider the answers to the following questions: With which set could you build a house the quickest? With which set could you most easily add a new wing or garage if the need arose? Clearly, the Lincoln Logs allows you the highest degree of individuality and flexibility, as well as the greatest possibility for future expansion.

The Learning Object Model (LOM) metadata standard is written like a set of Lincoln Logs. There is a dictionary of terms, like a bag of differently shaped logs, there is a grammar, like the rules for stacking the logs, and there is a schema, like a blueprint (one possible way of organizing the logs).

The LOM metadata standard contains a Master schema, or listing of many possible cabin features like walls, doors, windows, hot tubs, covered porches, tennis courts, etc. The schema is a hierarchical structure created from the elements in the dictionary. The dictionary is a list of elements with brief, non-contextualized definitions. We shall use the IEEE LOM *preliminary* draft metadata standard for examples.

There is a term in the LOM metadata dictionary called "person," meaning, "a specific human being." As in the dog bites man example, the term "person" itself has some meaning. However, it gets greater meaning by being placed in the following context:

Meta-metadata.Contribute.Person

The context, or structure, tells us that this particular person is the "specific human being who contributed to the metadata." In another position in the metadata structure, such as:

LifeCycle.Contribute.Person

Person now means the "specific human being who contributed to this version of the resource."

One may ask, "if the LOM is recommending a specific metadata schema, then why doesn't it just provide three walls, one wall with a door, and a roof instead of forcing us to build a metadata implementation from small, recombinant terms organized in semantic structures?" While the five-piece approach is the fastest, it is also a dead end. If we want to leave room for ourselves to improve the LOM metadata house in the future we need to build it from little blocks. There are a number of benefits to be reaped by utilizing a semantic structure approach to metadata–many more than the extensibility issue addressed above.

An organization may extend the Master metadata set in some way. If that extension is done using terms from the LOM dictionary, a search agent that has never before encountered your particular metadata set could still understand it. How? Because it knows the meaning of the dictionary terms and the rule by which they are structured, it can infer meaning from a previously unencountered metadata schema. When you saw the example Meta-metadata.Contribute.Person above, if you knew the meanings of the words meta-metadata, contribute, and person, you probably had a pretty good idea what it meant even before we explained it.

You may extend the metadata set using terms outside the IMS dictionary, or structures other than those in the grammar. As long as you provide a dictionary and grammar that the search agent can access in order to learn the "meanings" of your terms and structure (link types), the agent could again infer meaning from the structure and interpret your metadata accordingly. The degree to which the elements in the dictionary have well-differentiated definitions will be reflected in the orthogonality of the dimensions. A major reason for using semantic structures is to manage the dimension (field) definitions.

Evolution

Evolution is not just about change. It is about change based on an underlying stability. Evolution has three main factors: change, stability, and selection.

The process of evolution may be summarized:

- An evolving system does *not* have a *goal*.
- It *may* have a *purpose*.
- Evolution produces an improvement in quality according to some *metric*.
- Adherence to the *metric* controls the *purpose*.

A brief summary on current thinking in evolution provides a useful model. The following is adapted from Wason (Wason, 1997). In the paleontological record, species appear to change in steps, rather than in a slow, continuous process. This step model is called "saltatory change."

In the natural, real-world process of evolution, one theory (e.g., Gould et al.) states that evolution does not occur in the main population, but occurs in pioneer populations that splinter off from the main population. The pioneer populations are fairly isolated from the main population for some period. There may or may not be a connection for genetic communication between the main and pioneer populations.

A pioneer population will frequently occupy some *niche*. This may be by choice or due to external factors (e.g., a landslide blocks a mountain pass). The pioneer population is small, so the probability that a mutation will *persist* is increased relative to that in the main population. In addition, the pioneer population probably occupies an environment that differs from that of the main population. Mutations are of great value if they provide a survival advantage. If the pioneer population becomes re-connected to the main population, the pioneer population may serve to infect the main genetic pool with variant information that has been hammered out on the hard anvil of local survival. Or, in a more sinister fashion, the pioneer population may be so superior to the main population that it replaces it. This may occur through direct conflict or by more successfully competing for resources.

How does this all relate to the management of metadata? There are to be well-defined populations or communities of practice that may create changes in their own systems of metadata. These changes may propagate within the population. These populations interact with other populations in a well-controlled manner to select the best quality components for a continually improving system of metadata. Quality is defined as that which best fills the needs of the relevant population.

The metadata system is intended to support the entire evolutionary process in a state of control. The relationship between the main and pioneer populations will be illustrated in the IEEE LOM implementation, summarized below.

RELATIONSHIP BETWEEN SEMANTIC STRUCTURES AND METADATA

Structured Metadata

The metadata encoding, or binding, should reflect the definition structure. In this way the structure of the metadata directly reflects the semantic structure that defines the fields. Thus, it is interpretable by applications that have the semantic structure syntax and dictionary available. This supports both interoperability and extensibility.

Interoperability

Interoperability relies on the accessibility of stable definitions that are generated by a common method. Systems of structured metadata that use a well-defined binding, or method of encoding, that directly reflect a common semantic structure or method can be interpreted relative to each other. This provides the ability to map from one system into another, or create a cross-walk between the two. The two metadata systems do not need to be identical; they need to have non-conflicting dictionaries with as many common terms as possible, and adhere to a common syntax.

FILTERING MODEL

The following is adapted from Wiley (Wiley, 1999c, 1999d). Most search interfaces do not take advantage of the multidimensional nature of metadata, providing nothing more than an open-ended, full-text search of the available metadata. And many of those search engines that do provide multidimensional resolution provide it a very unnatural way: they force simultaneous multidimensional resolution. For example, let's say that Jill is shopping for a house online. She may be able to search dimensions like location, number of bedrooms, square footage, and price range. The unnaturalness of the search comes from the way she is forced to make these many decisions at once. In the real world, most people probably go through an iterative process in which the resolution of the various dimensions (metadata fields) is spread out temporally. In Jill's case, perhaps she would decide first on a city and then view what is available. After observing current prices on homes in that area, she may next select a price range and see what is available within it. Each time she selects a value for a given metadata field, she reduces the metadata space in one dimension to a subregion of values, creating increasingly smaller and more relevant subsets. Four points merit special attention here.

First, Jill is creating a path by traversing a series of options. If she hits a dead end, instead of completely recreating the search she simply traverses up the path to the previous fork in the road, and heads another direction. All of the pertinent search information, i.e., the set of values creating the path to the fork where the ineffective decision was made, is preserved.

Second, a search that unfolds over time in this manner provides a greater opportunity for multiple metadata repositories to provide meaningful information to the searcher. For example, if Bill goes to the local mall to purchase a pair of shoes, he may not know exactly what he is looking for. Bill would probably not approach the information desk and say, 'I would like a pair of white and blue high top shoes.' He might ask the person at the information desk what stores sell athletic shoes. Once at a sporting goods store, he would ask the clerk where athletic shoes are on display. Bill would then look for a pair of shoes that appeals to him. If he doesn't find a pair, he simply moves on to another store. Once he finds a pair, he checks the price to see whether or not he can afford them.

Third, inherent in this last example is the notion that the discovery process is only partially a search process, as opposed to the retrieval process, which is solely a search process. The *discovery* process is always part search, part browse. Once Bill reaches the athletic shoe section of the store, i.e., once he has collapsed the metadata space to a sufficiently small and relevant sub-space, he stops searching *per se* and begins browsing.

Finally, also inherent in the shoe example is the potential economic characteristic of the iterative filtering model. When Bill arrives in the shoe section of the store, he is surrounded by a number of items relevant to his interest that he did not initially intend to purchase. Once he enters the subregion he is browsing not only shoes, but also other relevant resources such as shoelaces, T-shirts, shorts, water bottles, etc. This replicates point-of-purchase and other successful in-store advertising models.

IMPLEMENTATION

What organizations are using structured metadata spaces? There is a combined effort by a number of educational organizations to create a common educational metadata standard, and common method of managing metadata definitions.

Organizations

The IEEE Learning Technology Standard Committee (P1484) (see acronym list at the end of the article, following references) is working to create a standard for Learning Object Metadata (LOM) using metadata spaces and semantic structures. Organizations participating in the effort include:

- ADL (Advanced Distributed Learning Initiative of the U.S. Dept. of Defense),
- AICC, (Aviation Industries CBT Committee),
- ARIADNE (Alliance of Remote Instructional Authoring and Distribution Networks for Europe),
- GESTALT (Getting Educational Systems Talking Across Leading-Edge Technologies), and
- IMS (IMS Project)

Audience

The IEEE LTSC LOM is designed to serve educators, learners, coordinators, and providers. Educators included teachers, tutors and trainers. Learners include K-12 students, home school students, college and university students, employees, military members, retirees, and other life-long learners. Coordinators include colleges and universities, public and private K-12 schools, the military, departments of labor, parents delivering home schooling, assessment specialists, and learners who are self managing. Providers include anyone that creates or edits materials, such as professors, teachers, publishers, and students. The purpose of metadata is to help this audience discover and assess the appropriateness of resources.

Duplication

Duplication means that there are some fields that duplicate the information in other fields. The metadata space model encourages the creation of independent fields, or dimensions of the space. However, there is also a need to provide for the evolution of metadata. The model of evolution presented above features a main, stable population and one or more pioneer populations that differ from the main population. These pioneer populations in metadata may wish to create new fields and new vocabularies and taxonomies. How are stable metadata fields and evolving metadata fields managed together?

An overdetermined system is used to support evolution. IEEE LOM uses *Classification* to allow specialized taxonomies and vocabularies that may duplicate the field definitions elsewhere in the metadata hierarchy. For example, the IEEE LOM has a top-level element, called a "category," of *Educational*. This has a definition of "Educational or pedagogic features of the resource." *Educational* contains the following fields:

Educational
    Typical Age Range
    Difficulty

Difficulty is considered by many not to be independent of *Typical Age Range*. There is no standard taxonomy of difficulty and there is no standard method for defining an age range. *Educational Difficulty* and *Educational Typical Age Range* are considered by this community to be too important to be omitted. There is a desire to move slowly toward some standard taxonomy.

The IEEE LOM takes a two-pronged approach: (1) it created the two simple fields above, with limited controlled vocabularies, (2) it created an additional structure under a category element of *Classification*. The controlled vocabularies of the predefined fields are quite simple: *Typical Age*

Range as values of one or two integers, and *Difficulty* has integer values of 0 to 4, with 0 being "Very Easy," and 4 being "Very difficult." These vocabularies are inadequate, but provide a consistent starting point.

Classification can be defined as a description of a characteristic of the resource by entries in classifications. This is a structure that does not directly create a specific definition. Instead, it contains a sub-element of *Purpose* to specify the type of classification. It has an unrestricted vocabulary including: *Discipline, Idea, Prerequisite, Educational Objective, Accessibility Restrictions, Educational Level, Skill Level,* and *Security Level.*

Classification has the structure:

Classification (unordered list)
   Purpose (Single)
   Description (unordered list of LangStrings)
   Keywords (unordered list of LangStrings)
   Taxonpath (unordered list)
      Source (single)
      Taxon (ordered list)

Instead of the completely defined definition that is created by other parts of the semantic structure, this uses a dependent "clause" (i.e., *Purpose*) to create the full definition.

This is effectively an extension without requiring an extension to be created; new classification systems can readily be added, such as security or skill level, without the need to extend the metadata structure. More than one instance of *Classification* and its structure can be used (an unordered list). Referring to the evolutionary model above, *Classification* becomes a potential mechanism for the "pioneer" efforts in using new taxonomies and vocabularies, while the controlled vocabularies elsewhere in the structure provide stability.

The IEEE LOM standard should be submitted for vote by the publication of this paper; it is slated for a 19 July 1999 submission. This standard will be available for use by anyone. The organizations listed above will all be subscribing to this standard, providing a truly international standard for educational metadata that will support future growth.

CONCLUSION

Thinking about metadata as a space having structure provides a model for creating and using metadata fields. Orthogonal metadata fields provide the most efficient use of that space. Semantic structures provide a method of managing the definitions of the fields. Semantic structures provide a basis for interoperability among metadata systems, as interoperability is largely a matter of determining equivalence between metadata fields in different systems. Metadata encoding that captures the semantic structures helps to convey the field definitions among applications.

REFERENCES

Saffo, Paul. (1994). *It's the context, stupid* [On-line]. Available: http://www.saffo.org/contextstupid.html

Wason, Thomas D. (1998). *Metadata spaces* [On-line]. Available: *http://www.imsproject.org/technical/metadata/History/did054.html*

Wason, Thomas D. (1997). *An evolutionary model for TIERS* [On-line]. Available: *http://www.imsproject.org/technical/metadata/Tiers/did159.html*

Wiley, David A. (1999a). *Why semantic structures?* [On-line]. Available: *http://ims.byu.edu/semantics.html*

Wiley, David A. (1999b). *My, what an intelligent tool you have!* [On-line]. Available: *http://ims.byu.edu/intelligent.html*

Wiley, David A. (1999c). *An intelligent method for searching metadata spaces* [On-line]. Available: *http://wiley.byu.edu/search/if-search.pdf*

Wiley, David A. (1999d). *Metadata mall: Two arguments for the IF-search technique* [On-line]. Available: *http://wiley.byu.edu/search/mm.html*

ACRONYMS

ADL: Advanced Distributed Learning Initiative, *http://www.adlnet.org*
AICC: Aviation Industries CBT Committee, *http://aicc.org*
ARIADNE: *http://ariadne.unil.ch/*
DC: Dublin Core, *http://purl.org/DC*
IMS: *http://www.imsproject.org*
IEEE (Institute of Electrical and Electronic Engineers) LTSC (Learning Technology Standards Committee, P1484), *http://ltsc.ieee.org/wg12/*
GEM: Gateway to Educational Materials, *http://gem.syr.edu/*
GESTALT: *http://www.fdgroup.co.uk/gestalt/metadata.html*
GILS: *http://fiat.gslis.utexas.edu/~ssoy/pubs/1391d2a.htm*
MARC: *http://lcweb.loc.gov/marc/marbi/dp/dp86.html*

Discovering and Using Educational Resources on the Internet: Global Progress or Random Acts of Progress?

William H. Graves

THE FUTURE OF EDUCATION

What will be the strategic impact of the Internet on education? This article addresses that question and in the process also addresses the resource discovery themes that inform this volume. Indeed, recent progress in disintermediating the cataloguing and indexing of educational resources portends a future in which indexing and cataloguing professionals will work at the boundary of mediation/disintermediation by contributing to the formulation of Internet standards that enable disintermediation.

THE ROLE OF THE INTERNET IN EDUCATION

Education at its core is about the creation, classification, and sharing of knowledge. These knowledge activities rely heavily on human communication and resource sharing, which are the major beneficiaries of the Internet revolution. As soon as e-mail and lists became broadly available, learned communities of scholars and researchers and their graduate students went

William H. Graves is Chairman and Founder of EDUPRISE.COM, Morrisville, NC (e-mail: wgraves@collegis.com).

[Haworth co-indexing entry note]: "Discovering and Using Educational Resources on the Internet: Global Progress or Random Acts of Progress?" Graves, William H. Co-published simultaneously in *Journal of Internet Cataloging* (The Haworth Information Press, an imprint of The Haworth Press, Inc.) Vol. 3, No. 2/3, 2000, pp. 279-287; and: *Metadata and Organizing Educational Resources on the Internet* (ed: Jane Greenberg) The Haworth Information Press, an imprint of The Haworth Press, Inc., 2000, pp. 279-287. Single or multiple copies of this article are available for a fee from The Haworth Document Delivery Service [1-800-342-9678, 9:00 a.m. - 5:00 p.m. (EST). E-mail address: getinfo@haworthpressinc.com].

© 2000 by The Haworth Press, Inc. All rights reserved.

online. While not replacing other forms of scholarly communication, e-mail and lists were readily accepted by these narrowly focused learned communities as a new and convenient means of informal scholarly communication.

In contrast, instructors have only recently begun to take advantage of the Internet in meeting their broader instructional obligations. But there is a reason for this seemingly tardy response to the broad educational potential of the Internet. For example, in the higher education environment, teaching a typical undergraduate course involves creating a new learning community in which the participants generally do not know each other and do not necessarily share with the instructor a steadfast dedication to the advancement of the body of knowledge that is at the heart of the course. It is more difficult to create a new online learning community involving ordinary students than to participate in an online learned community defined by a shared and highly developed scholarly interest. This distinction between facilitating the creation of a new learning community representing different levels of interest and preparation and participating as an expert or an expert's apprentice in a well defined learned community is one reason why it has taken longer for the Internet to become a major force in the instructional enterprise than in scholarship and research. But technology has also been a factor. The passion of scholarly collaboration is a better palliative for the pain of managing e-mail and list messages than is the task of managing instruction.

Recent advances in online communication and publication tools are now making it easier to create learning communities among groups of novice students and geographically dispersed students. Web-based threaded discussions and tools for publishing and organizing content–class notes, a syllabus, etc.–are being used to enhance classroom-based courses and to offer courses without classrooms. The resulting online learning materials and threaded discussions are easier to manage than e-mail and list messages. These advances in tools that facilitate online collaboration and information sharing have led to intense interest in new student-centered instructional models that remove many of the constraints of teacher-centered and institution-centered education, along with the constraints of time and place. Other constraints remain, however. For example, it is not easy for instructors and students to locate educational resources on the Web–searches yield too many hits with too little information about each. Metadata specifications, such as the IMS Meta-data Specification,[1] recently adopted by the Instructional Management Systems Cooperative, have the potential to advance the arts of cataloguing and discovering educational resources on the Web.

The ultimate result of the increasing ease with which interested parties can attempt to create online learning communities is likely to be the deregulation of education in favor of a free-market approach in which highly differentiated nonprofit and commercial education providers offer a rich array of cradle-tograve educational services. The residential campus offering a coming-of-age education to 18-22-year-olds will represent but one model among many others that are more focused on convenience (increased access) or the continuing education needs of a knowledge economy.

Speculating on the future of public support for the "right" to an education is foolhardy. It is conceivable, however, that the deregulation and differentiation encouraged by the technology-enabled disaggregation of educational services will shift tax dollars away from the direct support of public schools, colleges, and universities and toward a voucher system that directly supports the student rather than the institution while leaving it to the institution, non-profit or profit, to compete for and qualify students in its market niche. A trend toward deregulation is already apparent in new constructs such as the Western Governors' University and in a recent legislative pilot that relaxes residency requirements for financial aid to encourage distance education. What is clear is that the education marketplace will be in a state of churn for the foreseeable future. It is also clear that the Internet and its World Wide Web have become today's primary levers for increasing the effectiveness of education providers and extending their reach–and that the development and implementation of an effective metadata schema is critical to employing the Web as an educational tool.

THE BASIC IMS CONCEPT AND ITS CONTEXT

Five years ago when what is now the EDUCAUSE National Learning Infrastructure Initiative (NLII) was organized and rolled out, two exciting instructional technology tracks had barely begun to intersect.[2] Advances in microcomputer-based multimedia technology had enabled the development of media-rich, interactive learning materials in the stand-alone medium of the microcomputer with a CD-ROM drive. In a separate but parallel track, the introduction of the HyperText Transfer Protocol (HTTP), the HyperText Markup Language (HTML), and the Web browser had made it possible to deliver learning materials for "anytime, anyplace" study by students who had access to an Internet-connected microcomputer and a Web browser. Similarly, Internet-based e-mail (and lists) were enabling "anytime, any-place" communications within learning communities of students and instructors.

The Internet and its Web protocol (HTTP) were promising to resolve the distribution and revision bottlenecks inherent in providing instruction through CD-ROMs and floppy disks–and books. And the Web browser, supporting HTTP and HTML, was becoming a standard for gaining access to learning materials "published" on the Web using HTML tags, obviating the need for students to have any software more specialized than a Web browser. But the Web was not then, and still is not, as rich as the stand-alone multimedia microcomputer environment in the potential to focus the full range of human senses on decisions and actions that lead to learning.

Some nevertheless thought that a national learning infrastructure would inevitably emerge with the commercial evolution of the Web. The Web, they argued, would surely become a more interactive, media-rich environment in which innovative instructors would "author" Web-based courses richer and more immersive than any collection of linked HTML files. They were partly right. Technologies such as Java now hold this promise, but their broad educational potential has yet to be realized. Progress to date owes mostly to the work of individual instructors using a variety of technologies that either do not scale or have not met with the universal acceptance accorded HTTP and HTML. Indeed, progress thus far might best be described as *random acts of progress*. The larger purpose of the EDUCAUSE Instructional Management Systems (IMS) Cooperative is to channel the necessary bottom-up innovation and progress into national and global progress that can be understood and supported from the top down.[3] A critical component of this effort has been creating metadata standards for describing and discovering educational resources on the Internet.

The IMS Cooperative is trying to provide synchronizing, technical leverage for the forward-looking initiatives of all stakeholders in education and training. At stake are the interests of

- organizations that sponsor and deliver instruction and/or certify its outcomes,
- educational policy and standards bodies,
- instructors,
- developers of instructional resources,
- commercial and noncommercial providers of instructional resources and other suppliers to the education and training "industry,"
- learners, and
- the commercial and societal groups that expect some form of quality assurance in the education and training marketplace.

The IMS Cooperative is not about a single piece of instructional management code or a single functional standard for instructional management systems. The IMS Cooperative is trying to build the "Internet architecture for learning." An architecture requires a blueprint that conforms to a set of building codes. One such architecture is that promoted by the IMS Meta-data Specification.

The IMS Cooperative gathers ideas about what kind of functionality will be needed in the online components of a global learning infrastructure. The IMS technical team then designs and vets technical specifications to support that functionality, with the ultimate goal of facilitating the acquisition of component parts from a range of suppliers in the educational value chain of nonprofit and commercial interests. These technical specifications are the IMS candidates for industry-wide de facto standards that will enable different software technologies in the various online instructional infrastructure and application layers to exchange information and otherwise to interoperate. They are offered publicly as de facto standards for interoperability among learning systems, management systems, content, and discourse. The intent is to promote broad adherence to the open IMS specifications. If any become formal standards, so much the better.

THE CHALLENGES INHERENT IN ONLINE EDUCATION

There are many reasons why progress toward a global learning infrastructure has not been systemic. Many of these reasons illustrate both the need for and the complexity of an agenda such as that put forth by IMS, and are given below.

Content Is More Than Lecture Notes

The textbook has long been a mainstay of instruction. It is used by instructors to organize a course of study and to provide students with material for self-study. Few instructors are textbook authors. Instead, most instructors select a textbook and prepare syllabi and lecture notes to reorganize and supplement that textbook with their insights and expertise. Because syllabi and lecture notes can easily be published on the Web, that act is often confused with the electronic equivalent of authoring and publishing a textbook. But the posting of syllabi and notes on the Web usually happens without the peer review and professional editing associated with the publication of a textbook. The true technology-enhanced counterpart to the textbook is, instead, *learningware*–carefully designed and reviewed interactive software environments that organize and deliver not only knowledge but the means to participate actively in the creation of knowledge through simulations, modeling, tutoring, and the like. There is as yet no significant higher education marketplace in learningware. Moreover, instructors and their institutions are no more likely to succeed in the business of creating reusable, nationally or globally reviewed learningware than they would be if together they organized a business for refining class notes into published textbooks to compete against commercial publishers in the textbook market. The IMS specifications can help create a sorely needed commercial infrastructure for developing, selling, and distributing learningware that can be used interchangeably in a global learning infrastructure.

A Course Is More Than Content

Even when the acquisition of "content" is designed on the constructivist model to engage multiple senses and learning styles–as with exploratory multimedia learningware–most students need the guidance of an instructor. Instructors help learners acquire knowledge and assimilate that new knowledge in the larger context of a coherent body of knowledge that constitutes a "way of knowing": a curriculum, a liberal education, the scientific method, a body of professional knowledge and skills, or other educational constructs. Instructors accordingly are responsible for much more than the delivery of content, and the IMS specifications offer the prospect of seamless technical integration for instructors who use a variety of technologies to amplify their effectiveness and efficiency as they fulfill their responsibilities in the instructional process. Those responsibilities include the following:

- Select and sequence the content to be studied
- Organize discussions and other class group activities to encourage and facilitate collaborative learning
- Guide students' self-study–advise, tutor, and assign readings, papers, projects, etc.
- Critique and measure (grade) students' individual progress
- Manage and report students' progress within an institutional or interinstitutional process that leads to the certification of students' individual accomplishments

A Student's Education Involves More Than a Single Course and Instructor

An education is earned by successfully navigating multiple learning events, typically organized as courses and orchestrated by different instructors working in complex organizational settings. These settings are sometimes interinstitutional–as is often the case when the context is "K-grave" lifelong learning. In this broader view of what constitutes a formal education, little institutional and interinstitutional progress has been made in using online technologies to enhance the instructional process and to record the learning accomplishments that should be its goal. The IMS Cooperative encourages the coherence of pockets of progress into a systemic global learning infrastructure. Initially focused on higher education, the IMS founders envisioned a future in which postsecondary students would select their educational opportunities in a competitive education marketplace. Students would have choices as they tried to balance a variety of individual educational requirements, including, especially, individual requirements for convenience and quality. This open education marketplace would be defined by thousands of competing offerings that would aggregate the work of expert content organizers and learning mentors (instructors), content authors and publishers, and providers of education and educational infrastructure (institutions). The IMS specifications can be the technical glue that will integrate these components, to the mutual benefit of the student, the instructors, the institutions, and the companies involved in a student's education.

Convenience Is Important for Both Students and Instructors

Students who seek educational opportunities at a distance often raise a variety of convenience issues. Is communication primarily asynchronous, or are there requirements for real-time class participation or location-based participation? Can admission and registration, academic advising, book purchases, library research, and assignment submission be accomplished online? These are issues mostly of convenience, not of distance. Even students who seek a residential educational experience often enroll in Web-based courses or utilize online administrative and student services for reasons of convenience. Whatever the context, online communication, study materials, and instructional processes will not be perceived as convenient unless they are seamlessly woven together to obviate the need for multiple application interfaces and navigational rules that vary significantly from course to course, department to department, and institution to institution. Metadata plays an important role in the development of a good interface, and an extensible metadata schema can support a more-or-less seamless access interface, further supporting convenient access. Moreover, instructors who do not count themselves among the early adopters of technology-enhanced instructional methods are not likely to participate in online educational environments unless it is convenient to do so–or they are forced to do so. Overall, the Internet can be a convenient medium in which to conduct education and training–from the perspective of all the stakeholders involved.

Quality Assurance Is Difficult

The considerations described above reveal the complexity of the online instructional environment with its many stakeholders–learners, instructors, authors, publishers, institutions, and the external commercial and societal beneficiaries of education and training. In the face of such complexity, there is strong need to monitor and negotiate the overall quality of the enterprise. In this context, the IMS Cooperative is working to ensure interoperability and competition within the enterprise and thus choice in the value chain of developing, purchasing, delivering, and certifying education and training. The application of the IMS Meta-data Specification will assist in assuring that quality data about IMS-tagged resources is recorded. Overall, choice permits

the exercise of judgment and provides a framework for pursuing and nego-
tiating quality assurance from a variety of perspectives.

Discovering and Using Educational Resources Is Difficult

And finally, the organic nature of the Web will render futile any scheme
for cataloguing Web content that depends on the intervention of indexing
professionals. Even Web crawlers have not been able to keep pace with the
exponentially increasing mass of the Web. Cataloguing will have to be left to
the developers of Web content via easy-to-use indexing standards that have
been designed with input from indexing professionals. But developers of
educational resources have to date had no standard process for providing a
high-level description of their resources. This has contributed to the problems
that instructors and students experience today in trying to discover educational resources on the Web. The recently approved IMS Meta-data Specification
for tagging educational resources is a first step in resolving these issues. But
even when good educational resources are located, using those resources may
be difficult. That difficulty is often present in resources that are not just
textual materials published to the Web, such as resources that require plug ins
or even special client software on the instructor's or student's machine.
Interactive resources designed as courseware often fall into this category.
Future IMS specifications will address these difficulties.

CONCLUSION

The Internet is a force that is reshaping education as it relentlessly re-
shapes the larger socio-economic context for education. These changes beg for
a reshaping of the public policies and professional and institutional practices
that prescribe the pre-Internet educational environment and that persist in
education today. But such a reshaping will require more than political will. It
will require a globally coordinated "Internet architecture for learning," as
outlined in the goals of the IMS effort. And associated with these goals is the
development and implementation of a flexible and effective metadata schema.

No aspect of any such effort, including that put forth by IMS, is more
important than the work to ease the difficulty of describing or cataloguing
and discovering educational resources. Indeed, the first IMS specification to
be approved was the IMS Meta-data Specification. At the heart of the IMS
metadata work is the proposition that indexing must be disintermediated and
left to the developers of educational resources. But that democratizing concept will lead to chaos without the involvement of cataloguing and indexing
professionals in formulating emerging standards, such as the IMS Meta-data

Specification. Professionals with expertise in this area of knowledge organization and discovery will work at the boundary of mediation/disintermediation, helping to formulate the standards that enable effective, rather than chaotic, disintermediation. Major contributions to online education can flow from their future work.

NOTES

1. IMS Meta-data Specification. (1999). Available via the Internet at: *http://www.imsproject.org/metadata/index.html*

2. Dr. Robert Heterick, in his role as president of Educom, invited Dr. Carol Twigg and the author to collaborate with him, under Educom's sponsorship, to conceive and roll out the Educom National Learning Infrastructure Initiative. Twigg subsequently joined Educom as a vice-president to lead the initiative. The author continues to chair the Planning Committee for the initiative, which is now led by EDUCAUSE Vice-President Dr. Carole Barone.

3. The IMS Cooperative is a project of the NLII. A wealth of information and a formal statement of IMS goals and objectives are online at http:/www.imsproject.org.

Index

090 field (MARC format), 220-221
100 field (MARC format), 220-221
245 field (MARC format), 29-30,221
246 field (MARC format), 221
300 field (MARC format), 29
490 field (MARC format), 221
4th Dimension (database software),
174-189
500 field (MARC format), 27-29,221
505 field (MARC format), 33,221
506 field (MARC format), 221
516 field (MARC format), 221
520 field (MARC format),
21-23,29,33-34,131-132,221
521 field (MARC format),
13-14,21-27,131-132
526 field (MARC format),
13-14,21,24-27,132
538 field (MARC format), 29
658 field (MARC format),
13-14,21,24-27,132
6*XX* fields (MARC format), 221
740 field (MARC format), 221
856 field (MARC format), 13-14,
19-22,32,86-87,218,221

A-G Canada, 79-92
*AACR. See Anglo-American
Cataloguing Rules* (AACR)
and revisions
ACCESS (database software), 46-47
ACM. *See* Association for Computing
Machinery (ACM)
Computing Reviews
classification
ADL. *See* Advanced Distributed
Learning Initiative (ADL)

Adult Learning Documentation and
Information Network
(ALADIN)
data organization and, 49-40
databases with external online
access, 51-52
introduction to, 3,8,41-44
mapping adult learning
documentation and information
services and, 44-49
strategic planning and, 50
work of, 44-49
Advanced Distributed Learning
Initiative (ADL), 263-277
AGLS. *See* Australian Government
Locator Service (AGLS)
AICC. *See* Aviation Industries CBT
Committee (AICC)
ALA. *See* American Library
Association (ALA)
ALADIN. *See* Adult Learning
Documentation and
Information Network
(ALADIN)
ALLEGRO (database software), 46-47
Alliance of Remote Instructional
Authoring and Distribution
Networks for Europe
(ARIADNE) metadata
schema and project
community and experience of,
167-169
elements, lists of, 150,153,156,
158-160
importance of, 170
infrastructure, schematic of, 147f
introduction to, 4,9,145-148
metadata schema, detailed
description of, 148-161
metadata tools, 161-167

© 2000 by The Haworth Press, Inc. All rights reserved.

related work, 169-170
research about, 171
structured metadata spaces and,
       263-277
American Library Association (ALA)
   Machine Readable Bibliographic
       Information Committee
       (MARBI). *See* Machine
       Readable Bibliographic
       Information Committee
       (MARBI), American Library
       Association (ALA)
   Resources and Technical Services
       Division (RSTD). *See*
       Resources and Technical
       Services Division (RSTD),
       American Library
       Association (ALA)
American Memory: Historical
       Collection for the Digital
       Library, Library of Congress,
       128
*Anglo-American Cataloguing Rules
       (AACR)* and revisions
   metadata cataloging and, 5,15-16,
       18,27,29,48,54,205
   Web site cataloging and, 79-92
Architecture, document, 243-261
ARIADNE. *See* Alliance of Remote
       Instructional Authoring and
       Distribution Networks for
       Europe (ARIADNE)
       metadata schema and project
ARL/EDUCAUSE CNI. *See* Coalition
       for Networked Information
       (CNI)
Arts and Humanities Data Service,
       245-246
AskERIC (online service), 109-129
Association for Computing Machinery
       (ACM) Computing Reviews
       classification, 152
Association of Research
       Libraries/EDUCAUSE CNI.
       See Coalition for Networked
       Information (CNI)

AT&T Education Foundation, 120-121
Atomic Web-based objects for lesson
       plan construction, 127-144
Australian Digital Theses Project,
       207-208
Australian Government Locator
       Service (AGLS), 208-210
*Australian Thesaurus of Education
       Descriptors* (controlled
       vocabulary), 47-48
AUTOCAT (electronic discussion list),
       13-38,193-194
Aviation Industries CBT Committee
       (AICC), 263-277

Bern Dibner Library of Science and
       Technology, Polytechnic
       University, 3,9,217-225
Best educational practices and
       metadata issues, 243-261
*Black Studies Database: Kaiser Index
       to Black Periodicals*
       (publication), 97
Borgman, C.L., 35
Bowers, F., 88
Brown University, 244

Campbell, D.G., 8,79-92
Canadian Literacy Thesaurus
       (controlled vocabulary),
       47-48
Cardinaels, K., 145-171
CARL-AUCC Taskforce on Academic
       Libraries and Scholarly
       Communication, 83
Carnegie Corporation, 94
Carnegie Mellon University, 128
Cataloging Internet Resources Project,
       79-92
*Cataloging Internet Resources: A
       Manual and Practical Guide*
       (cataloging tool and
       standard), 5,89

Cataloging the Chameleon (publication), 80
Cataloging tools and standards
  Anglo-American Cataloguing Rules (AACR) and revisions, 5, 15-16,18,27,29,48,54,79-92, 205
  Association for Computing Machinery (ACM) Computing Reviews classification, 152
  Cataloging Internet Resources: A Manual and Practical Guide, 5,89
  Curriculum-Enhanced MARC (CE-MARC), 13-38,131-140
  Dewey Decimal Classification (DDC), 5,8,27,46-47,67-77, 95-99,151-152,269
  Guidelines for Standardized Cataloging of Children's Materials, 27,36
  International Standard Bibliographic Description for Computer Files (ISBD/CF), 5
  International Standard Bibliographic Description for Electronic Resources (ISBD/ER), 5,89
  Journal of Economic Literature (JEL) classification code, 236
  Library of Congress Classification (LCC), 27,30,46-47
  Library of Congress Subject Headings (LCSH), 4,30, 75-77,98-99,169-170, 199-202
  MAchine-Readable Cataloging (MARC), 4-6,74,89-90, 114-124,195-202,217-225
  Medical Subject Headings (MeSH), 5
  metadata schemas. *See* Metadata schemas

Sears List of Subject Headings, 47-48
Swedish cataloging system (SAB), 48
Universal Decimal Classification (UDC), 46-47,151-152
USMARC documentation, 23-26
Catalogs, online
  metadata and (general information about), 1-11
  publishing source, as a, 217-225
CDL. *See Courseware Description Language (CDL) Descriptors Key Index*
CDS/ISIS (database software), 46-47
CE-MARC. *See* Curriculum-Enhanced MARC (CE-MARC)
Changing World of Scholarly Communication: Challenges and Choices for Canada (publication), 84
Clarke, R., 115,117
Clinton,W., 243-244
CNI. *See* Coalition for Networked Information (CNI)
Coalition for Networked Information (CNI),9-10,281-287
Colleges and universities. *See* Universities and colleges
Controlled vocabularies
  Australian Thesaurus of Education Descriptors, 47-48
  Canadian Literacy Thesaurus, 47-48
  Courseware Description Language (CDL) Descriptors Key Index, 133
  Eisenhower National Clearinghouse for Mathematics and Science Vocabularies, 25
  Engineering Information (EI) Thesaurus, 199-202
  European Education Thesaurus, 47-48
  Feminist Thesaurus, 47-48

Human Rights Thesaurus, 47-48
*Library of Congress Subject
    Headings (LCSH)*, 4-5,30,
    75-77,98-99,169-170,
    199-202
Medical Subject Headings (MeSH),
    152
*Multilingual Thesaurus of
    Vocational Training*, 47-48
OECD Macro-thesaurus, 47-48
Sears List of Subject Headings,
    47-48
Tesauro Colombiano Educación,
    47-48
Thesaurus of ERIC Descriptors, 25,
    47-48
*UNESCO IBE Education
    Thesaurus*,47-48
UNESCO Thesaurus, 47-48
World Bank Thesaurus, 47-48
Course materials (higher education),
    providing access to
importance of, 212-213
introduction to, 203-206
metadata
    conversion process and
        procedures, 210-212
    standards for teaching and
        learning, 213
problems and issues associated
    with, 206-210
research about, 214
sample records, 215-216
*Courseware Description Language
    (CDL) Descriptors Key
    Index*, 133
Cox, J.P., 79-80,89
Crane, G., 174-175
Crowston, K., 83
Cruz, J.M.B., 4,9,227-241
Curriculum resource cataloging
    criteria and procedures
        abstracting, 61-64
        cataloging, 58-61
        collection development, 55-58
    Curriculum-Enhanced

MAchine-Readable
    Cataloging (CE-MARC) and.
    See Curriculum-Enhanced
    MAchine-Readable
    Cataloging (CE-MARC)
importance of, 64
introduction to, 2-3,8,53-55
research about, 64-65
ScienceNet and, 67-77
Curriculum-Enhanced MARC
    (CE-MARC), 13-38,131-140
Cutter, C.A., 82

Daniels, W., 8,67-77
Database Management Systems
    (DBMS), 149
Database software
    4th Dimension, 174-189
    ACCESS, 46-47
    ALLEGRO, 46-47
    CDS/ISIS, 46-47
    EndNote, 174-189
    FileMaker, 174-189
    LARS, 46-47
    LOTUS, 46-47
    ORACLE, 46-47,164
    SQL, 238-241
DBMS. *See* Database Management
    System (DBMS)
DCMI. *See* Dublin Core Metadata
    Initiative (DCMI) (metadata
    schema)
*DDC. See Dewey Decimal
    Classification (DDC)*
Deakin Australia, 203-216
Deakin University, 203-216
Dekker, J., 80,89
Delsey, T., 82
Dewey Decimal Classification (DDC),
    5,8,27,46-47,67-77,95-99,
    151-152,269
Deyoe, N., 15
*Dictionary Catalog of The Schomburg
    Collection of Negro
    Literature and History*
    (publication), 96-97

Digital libraries
  Adult Learning Documentation and
    Information Network
    (ALADIN), 41-52
  Alliance of Remote Instructional
    Authoring and Distribution
    Networks for Europe
    (ARIADNE) metadata
    schema and project,
    managing resources with,
    145-171
  course materials (higher education),
    providing access to, 203-216
  Digital Library Project, Bern
    Dibner Library of Science
    and Technology, Polytechnic
    University, 217-225
  Digital National Library (DNL),
    200
  Digital Schomburg, The
    (Schomburg Center for
    Research in Black Culture),
    93-108
  discovering and using educational
    resources on the Internet,
    impact of, 279-287
  document architecture and best
    practices and, 243-261
  Internet-based educational terrain,
    introduction to, 1-11
  link libraries and, 67-77
  National Engineering Education
    Delivery System (NEEDS),
    Synthesis Coalition, 191-202
  Pennsylvania Education Digital
    Object Repository
    (PEN-DOR), 127-144
  Perseus Project, 173-189
  ScienceNet, 67-77
Digital Library Project, Bern Dibner
    Library of Science and
    Technology, Polytechnic
    University, 217-225
Digital National Library (DNL), 200
Digital Schomburg, The. See
    Schomburg Center for

Research in Black Culture,
    The Digital Schomburg
Dillon, M., 82
DNL. *See* Digital National Library
    (DNL)
Document architecture
  base and fact documents, 250-251
  best practices, 247-250
  Gateway to Educational Materials
    (GEM) Element Set and
    project and, 109-126,251-258
  importance of, 260
  introduction to, 243-247
  metadata cataloging and, 6,8-9,
    67-77,131,151-152,169-170,
    208-214
  nesting metadata from related
    documents, 258-260
  research about, 260-261
Document Type Definition (DTD). *See*
    Standard Generalized
    Markup Language (SGML)
Dodson, H., 98-99
DTD. *See* Standard Generalized
    Markup Language (SGML)
Dublin Core Metadata Initiative
    (DCMI) (metadata schema)
  document architecture and best
    practices and, 243-261
  examples of, 106-108,215-216
  Gateway to Educational Materials
    (GEM) Element Set and
    project and, 109-126
  metadata cataloging and, 6,8-9,
    67-77,131,151-152,169-170,
    208-214
Duval, E., 4, 145-171

EAD. *See* Encoded Archival
    Description (EAD) (metadata
    schema)
EBSS, 22
Economic research preprints,
    cataloging of, 227-241
ED's Oasis (online service),
    120-124,126

Eden, B., 9,191-202
Edmonds, L., 35
EdNA. *See* Education Network
    Australia (EdNA) (metadata
    schema)
Education Network Australia (EdNA)
    (metadata schema), 6
EDUCAUSE CNI. *See* Coalition for
    Networked Information
    (CNI)
EI. See Engineering Information (EI)
    Thesaurus (controlled
    vocabulary)
Eisenhower National Clearinghouse
    for Mathematics and Science
    Education (ENC), math and
    science curriculum resource
    cataloging project
  criteria and procedures
    abstracting, 61-64
    cataloging, 58-61
    collection development, 55-58
  importance of, 64
  introduction to, 2-3,8,53-55
  research about, 64-65
Eisenhower National Clearinghouse
    for Mathematics and Science
    Vocabularies, 25
Eiteljorg, N., 176-178
ENC. *See* Eisenhower National
    Clearinghouse for
    Mathematics and Science
    Education (ENC), math and
    science curriculum resource
    cataloging project
Electronic discussion list, AUTOCAT,
    13-38,193-194
Encoded Archival Description (EAD)
    (metadata schema), 131
EndNote (database software), 174-189
Engineering Information (EI)
    Thesaurus (controlled
    vocabulary), 199-202
Engineering resources, cataloging of,
    191-202
ERIC

AskERIC (online service), 109-129
Clearinghouse of Information and
    Technology, 109-129
Thesaurus of ERIC Descriptors.
    See Thesaurus of ERIC
    Descriptors (controlled
    vocabulary)
EUN. *See* European School Net
    (EUN) (metadata schema), 6
European Commission, Telematics
    Applications Program,
    145-171
European Education Thesaurus
    (controlled vocabulary),
    47-48
European School Net (EUN)
    (metadata schema), 6
Everhart, N., 25,35
Extensible Markup Language (XML),
    102-103,149,207-213,
    233-234,250-251

Feminist Thesaurus (controlled
    vocabulary), 47-48
FileMaker (database software),
    174-189
Follet Software Company, 25
Forte, E., 145-171
Fullerton, K., 127-144

Gateway to Educational Materials
    (GEM) Element Set and
    project
  case studies of, 120-123,126
  document architecture and best
    practices and, 243-261
  evaluation form for collection
    holders membership, 125
  introduction to, 6,8-9,75,109-110
  metadata, importance of, 114-117,
    123-124
  project description, 110-114,125
  research about, 124
  research foundations of, 117-120
GEM. *See* Gateway to Educational

Materials (GEM) Element
Set and project
German Federal Ministry of
Education, Science, Research
and Technology, 41-52
GESTALT, 263-277
Giere, U., 3,8,41-52
GILS. *See* Government Information
Locator Service (GILS)
(metadata schemas)
Giordano, R., 9,243-261
Gorman, M., 83,88
Government Information Locator
Service (GILS) (metadata
schema), 131
Graves, W.H., 9,279-287
Greek sculpture, digital catalogs of,
173-189
Greenberg, J., 1-11,127-144
*Guidelines for Standardized
Cataloging of Children's
Materials* (cataloging tool
and standard), 27,38
Guildford protocol, 231-233

Haenni, F., 145-171
Heery, R., 115
Hendrikx, K., 145-171
Herrera, T., 56
Historical resources, cataloging of,
93-108
Howarth, L., 82
Human Rights Thesaurus (controlled
vocabulary), 47-48
Hutson, J.B., 95-96

IASL. *See* International Association of
School Librarianship (IASL)
*IBE Education Thesaurus. See
UNESCO IBE Education
Thesaurus*
ICAE. *See* International Council for
Adult Education (ICAE)
IEEE Learning Technology Standards

Committee (LTSC), Learning
Object Metadata (LOM)
(metadata schema), 6,9,
145-171,263-277. *See also*
Alliance of Remote
Instructional Authoring and
Distribution Networks for
Europe (ARIADNE)
metadata schema and project
IMS. *See* Instructional Management
Systems (IMS) Metadata
Specification (metadata
schema)
Indexing tools. *See* Controlled
vocabularies
*Information Power: Building
Partnerships for Learning*
(publication), 22-23
Informedia Digital Video Library,
Carnegie Mellon University,
128
Instructional Management Systems
(IMS) Metadata
Specification (metadata
schema), 6,133,279-287
INTERCAT (database), 89-90
International Association of School
Librarianship (IASL), 80-82
International Council for Adult
Education (ICAE), 48
International Federation of Library
Associations (IFLA)
metadata cataloging and, 82
*International Standard Bibliographic
Description for Computer
Files* (ISBD/CF) (cataloging
tool and standard), 5
*International Standard Bibliographic
Description for Electronic
Resources (ISBD/ER)*
(cataloging tool and
standard), 5,89
Internet-based educational terrain
definition of, 2-4

discovering and using educational
resources on the Internet,
impact of, 279-287
importance of, 10
introduction to, 1-4
metadata issues and, 4-10,243-261
research about, 10-11
Iowa State University, 191-202
ISBD/CF. See International Standard
Bibliographic Description
for Computer Files
(ISBD/CF) (cataloging tool
and standard)
ISBD/ER. See International Standard
Bibliographic Description
for Electronic Resources
(ISBD/ER) (cataloging tool
and standard)

JEL. See Journal of Economic
Literature (JEL)
classification code
Journal of Economic Literature (JEL)
classification code, 236
Jul, E., 82

Kartus, E., 9,203-216
Knowledge Pool System (KPS),
4,146-171. *See also* Alliance
of Remote Instructional
Authoring and Distribution
Networks for Europe
(ARIADNE) metadata
schema and project
Kohn, M., 176
Kolb model of experimental learning,
192-193
KPS. *See* Knowledge Pool System
(KPS)
Kranz, J., 22
Krichel, T., 4,9,227-241
Kulthau, C.C., 81
Kupidura, E., 3,8,41-52

Lamb, A., 22-23
LARS (database software), 46-47
Laws and legislation, P.L. 101-589,
54-65
LCC. See Library of Congress, *Library*
of Congress Classification
(LCC)
LCNAF. *See* Library of Congress,
Library of Congress Name
Authority File (LCNAF)
LCSH. See Library of Congress,
Library of Congress Subject
Headings (LCSH)
Learning Object Metadata (LOM). *See*
IEEE Learning Technology
Standards Committee
(LTSC), Learning Object
Metadata (LOM) (metadata
schema)
Lesson plan construction, atomic
Web-based objects for,
127-144
Letarte. K., 8,13-38
Levoy, M., 186-187
Lewis, R.W., 22-23
Library of Congress
American Memory: Historical
Collection for the Digital
Library, 128
Library of Congress Classification
(LCC), 27,30,46-47
Library of Congress Name
Authority File (LCNAF),
98-99
Library of Congress Subject
Headings (LCSH),
4,30,75-77,98-99,
169-170,199-202
Link libraries,67-77
Link-2-Learn initiative, 3,129-144
LOM. *See* IEEE Learning Technology
Standards Committee
(LTSC), Learning Object
Metadata (LOM) (metadata
schema)

LOTUS (database software), 46-47
Lowe, C., 8-9,109-126
Lowry, L., 26
LTSC LOM. *See* IEEE Learning
Technology Standards
Committee (LTSC), Learning
Object Metadata (LOM)
(metadata schema)
Lundgren, J., 88

MacArthur Foundation, 98
Machine Readable Bibliographic
Information Committee
(MARBI), American Library
Association (ALA), 21-25
MAchine-Readable Cataloging
(MARC)
090 field, 220-221
100 field, 220-221
245 field, 29-30,221
246 field, 221
300 field, 29
490 field, 221
500 field, 27-29,221
505 field, 33,221
506 field, 221
516 field, 221
520 field, 21-23,29,33-34,
131-132,221
521 field, 13-14,21-27,131-132
526 field, 13-14,21,24-27,132
538 field, 29
658 field, 13-14,21,24-27,132
6*XX* fields, 221
740 field, 221
856 field, 13-14,19-22,32,86-87,
218,221
Curriculum-Enhanced MARC
(CE-MARC), 13-38,131-140
Gateway to Educational Materials
(GEM) Element Set and
project and, 109-126
metadata cataloging and, 4-6,74,
89-90,195-202

online catalogs as publishing
sources and, 217-225
sample records, 225
MARBI. *See* Machine Readable
Bibliographic Information
Committee (MARBI),
American Library
Association (ALA)
MARC. *See* MAchine-Readable
Cataloging (MARC)
Martin, C., 8,67-77
Math curriculum resource cataloging,
53-65
Medical Subject Headings (MeSH)
(controlled vocabulary), 152
Meekley, F., 242
*MeSH. See Medical Subject Headings
(MeSH)* (controlled
vocabulary)
Meta-metadata, 117,158-160
Metadata and Internet-based
educational terrain (general
information about)
document architecture and,
243-261
introduction to and definition of,
1-11
metadata schemas. *See* Metadata
schemas
structured metadata space, 263-277
Metadata schemas
Alliance of Remote Instructional
Authoring and Distribution
Networks for Europe
(ARIADNE), 4,9,263-277
cataloging tools and standards. *See*
Cataloging tools and
standards
*Courseware Description Language
(CDL) Descriptors Key
Index*, 133
discovering and using educational
resources on the Internet,
impact of, 279-287
document architecture and,
243-261

Dublin Core Metadata Initiative
(DCMI), 6,8-9,67-77,
109-126,131,151-152,
169-170,208-216,243-261
Education Network Australia
(EdNA), 6
Encoded Archival Description
(EAD), 131
European School Net (EUN), 6
Gateway to Educational Materials
(GEM) Element Set and
project, 6,8-9,109-126, 243-261
Government Information Locator
Service (GILS), 131
IEEE Learning Technology
Standards Committee
(LTSC), Learning Object
Metadata (LOM), 6,9,
145-171,263-277
importance of, 114-117,123-124
Instructional Management Systems
(IMS) Metadata
Specification, 6,131,279-287
introduction to, 130-132
Pennsylvania Educational
Network-Digital Object
Repository (PEN-DOR)
Element Set and project, 3,
6,8-9,127-144
structured metadata space, 263-277
Miksa, F., 81,83
Miller, M.L., 15-16
Miller, P., 114,116
Minier, R., 22,24
*Multilingual Thesaurus of Vocational
Training* (controlled
vocabulary), 47-48
Multimedia catalogs, 173-189
Murphy, C., 22-24
Murray, J.B., 8,93-108
Myers, N., 15
Mylonas, E., 176

National Center for Education
Statistics (NCES), 16

National Council of Teachers of
Mathematics, 63-64
National Endowment for the
Humanities (NEH),
98-99,101
National Engineering Education
Delivery System (NEEDS),
Synthesis Coalition
cataloging project
cataloging criteria and procedures,
195-200
future work of, 200
importance of, 200-201
introduction to, 9,191-193
remote cataloging of digital
resources, introduction to,
193-195
research about, 201
subject cataloging, 200
National Library of Australia (NLA),
207-208
National Science Foundation (NSF),
191-202
NEEDS. *See* National Engineering
Education Delivery System
(NEEDS), Synthesis
Coalition cataloging project
NEH. *See* National Endowment for the
Humanities (NEH)
New York Public Library (NYPL),
Schomburg Center for
Research in Black Culture.
See Schomburg Center for
Research in Black Culture,
The Digital Schomburg
NLA. *See* National Library of
Australia (NLA)
Nordic Metadata Project, 73
NSF. *See* National Science Foundation
(NSF)
NYPL. *See* Schomburg Center for
Research in Black Culture,
New York Public Library
(NYPL)

OCLC
　　Dublin Core Metadata Initiative
　　　　(DCMI). *See* Dublin Core
　　　　Metadata Initiative (DCMI)
　　INTERCAT database. *See*
　　　　INTERCAT database
　　metadata cataloging and, 89
Oddy, P., 83
OECD Macro-thesaurus (controlled
　　vocabulary), 47-48
OERI. *See* Office of Educational
　　Research and Improvement
　　(OERI), U.S. Department of
　　Education
Office of Educational Research and
　　Improvement (OERI), U.S.
　　Department of Education,
　　53-65
Ohio State University, 55-65
Olivié, H., 145-171
Online catalogs. *See* Catalogs, online
OPACs. *See* Catalogs, online
ORACLE (database software), 46-47,
　　164

P.L. 101-589 (legislation), 54-65
PEN-DOR. *See* Pennsylvania
　　Educational Network-Digital
　　Object Repository
　　(PEN-DOR) Element Set and
　　project
Pennsylvania Educational
　　Network-Digital Object
　　Repository (PEN-DOR)
　　Element Set and project
　　description of, 137-138
　　development and design of,
　　　　132-137
　　examples of, 142-144
　　future challenges for, 138-140
　　introduction to, 3,6,8-9,127-130
　　metadata, introduction to, 130-132
　　research about, 140-141
Perseus Project, Greek sculpture
　　catalog

adapting catalogs to the Internet,
　　177-184
future work, 184-187
HyperCard CD-ROM catalog,
　　174-177
importance of, 187
introduction to, 173-174
research about, 187-189
Plummer, K.A., 3,8,53-65
Polytechnic University, Bern Dibner
　　Library of Science and
　　Technology, 3,9,217-225
Preprints (economic research),
　　cataloging of, 227-241
Publications
　　*Black Studies Database: Kaiser
　　　　Index to Black Periodicals*,
　　　　97
　　Cataloging Internet Resources, 89
　　Cataloging the Chameleon, 80
　　cataloging tools and standards. *See*
　　　　Cataloging tools and
　　　　standards
　　*Changing World of Scholarly
　　　　Communication: Challenges
　　　　and Choices for Canada*, 84
　　*Dictionary Catalog of The
　　　　Schomburg Collection of
　　　　Negro Literature and History*,
　　　　96-97
　　*Information Power: Building
　　　　Partnerships for Learning*,
　　　　22-23
　　metadata schemas. *See* Metadata
　　　　schemas

Rasmussen, E., 127-144
RDF. *See* Resource Description
　　Framework (RDF)
ReDIF template metadata format,
　　231-241
RePEc. *See* Research Papers in
　　Economics (RePEc) project
Research Papers in Economics
　　(RePEc) project
　　archive structure, 231-234

dataset, 234-238
Guildford protocol, 231-233
importance of, 240
introduction to, 4,9,227-231
ReDIF template metadata format,
    231-241
research about, 241
user services, 238-240
Resource Description Framework
    (RDF), 149
Resources and Technical Services
    Division (RSTD), American
    Library Association (ALA),
    27
Richmond, C., 9,203-216
Roempler, K.S., 55-56
Role of the Internet on education,
    279-287
Rottenbucher, A., 22-23
RSTD. *See* Resources and Technical
    Services Division (RSTD),
    American Library
    Association (ALA)

Saffo, P., 268
Schemas, metadata. *See* Metadata
    schemas
Schomburg Center for Research in
    Black Culture, *The Digital
    Schomburg*
    cataloging of resources
        criteria and procedures and,
            101-104,106-108
        historical perspectives of, 94-101
        sample records, 106-108
    content of, 104-105
    description of, 100-101
    introduction to, 8,93-94
Schomburg, A.A., 93-96,98-99,
    101-102
School library media centers,
    cataloging issues and
    Curriculum-Enhanced
        MAchine-Readable Cataloging
        (CE-MARC) and, 19-27

electronic access, direct, 15-18,
    27-31
electronic access, remote, 15-16,
    18-19,31-34
importance of, 34-36
introduction to, 13-14
MAchine-Readable Cataloging
    (MARC) and, 19-27
research about, 36-40
surveys about, 13-40
Science curriculum resource
    cataloging, 53-65,67-76
Science Net
    access issues and, 72-75
    importance of, 76-77
    introduction to, 8,67-70
    research about, 77
    sites, cataloging of, 75-76
    structure of, 70-73
Sculpture (Greek), digital catalogs of,
    173-189
Sears List of Subject Headings
    (controlled vocabularies),
    47-48
SGML. *See* Standard Generalized
    Markup Language (SGML)
Shepherd, M., 83
Shontz, M.L., 15-16
Simillion, F., 145-171
Simpson, B., 88
Small, R., 117
Smith, A.C., 3,9,173-189
Space, metadata. *See* Structured
    metadata space
SQL (database software), 238-241
Standard Generalized Markup
    Language (SGML)
    Document Type Definition (DTD),
        102,196,208-209
    metadata cataloging and, 101-104,
        149,176,207-213,250-251
    Text Encoding Initiative (TEI), 102
Stokes, R., 88-89
Strategic impact of the Internet on
    education, 279-287
Structured metadata space

acronym definitions, 277
definition management, 269-272
document architecture and,
    243-261
filtering models of, 273-274
implementation of, 274-276
importance of, 276-277
introduction to, 263-264
metadata space, description of,
    265-269
problems associated with, 264-265
relationship with semantic
    structures, 272-273
research about, 276-277
Sutton, S., 116
Swedish cataloging system (SAB), 48
Synthesis Coalition, National
    Engineering Education
    Delivery System (NEEDS),
    191-202

TEI. *See* SGML
Tesauro Colombiano Educación
    (controlled vocabulary),
    47-48
Text Encoding Initiative (TEI). *See*
    SGML
Thesaurus of ERIC Descriptors
    (controlled vocabulary),
    25,47-48
Thesaurus tools. *See* Controlled
    vocabularies
Titterington, L.C., 61-62
Toronto Public Library, 67-77
Torres, A., 3,9,217-225
Tyler, T., 85

Undergraduate engineering resources,
    cataloging of, 191-202
UNESCO IBE Education Thesaurus
    (controlled vocabulary),
    47-48
UNESCO Thesaurus (controlled
    vocabulary), 47-48

United Nations, UNESCO, 3,47-48
United States
    Department of Education, Office of
        Educational Research and
        Improvement (OERI),
        53-65,244
    National Library of Education,
        109-126
    Navy, Office of Naval Research, 245
*Universal Decimal Classification
    (UDC)* (cataloging tool and
    standard), 46-47,151-152
Universities and colleges
    Brown University, 244
    Carnegie Mellon University, 128
    Deakin University, 203-216
    Iowa State University, 191-202
    Ohio State University, 55-65
    University of Michigan, 128
    University of New South Wales
        (UNSW), 207-208
    University of Toronto, 79-92
University of Michigan Digital
    Library, 128
University of New South Wales
    (UNSW), 207-208
University of Toronto, 79-92
UNSW. *See* University of New South
    Wales (UNSW)
USMARC documentation (cataloging
    tool and standard), 23-26.
    See also MAchine-Readable
    Cataloging (MARC)
Utah Education Network (UEN),
    122-124
UtahLink (online service), 122-124

Van Deusen, J.D., 25
VanderPol, D., 15,18
Verhoeven, B., 145-171
Vervaet, E., 145-171
Virtual libraries. *See* Digital libraries
Virtual Reference Library Project, 8,
    67-77
Vocabularies, controlled. *See*
    Controlled vocabularies

Ward, D., 15,18
Warkentyne, K., 145-171
Watson, T.D., 9,263-277
Watters, C., 83
Wehmeyer, L.M., 22-23
Weibel, S., 68-69
Wentland Forte, M., 145-171
Wiley, D., 9,263-277
Williams, M., 83
Wolff, C., 3,9,217-225
WoPEc. *See* Working Papers in
    Economics (WoPEc)

Working Papers in Economics
    (WoPEc), 229-230,238-241
World Bank Thesaurus (controlled
    vocabulary), 47-48

XML. *See* Extensible Markup
    Language (XML)

Z39.50 protocol, 34,81

AN EXCELLENT RESOURCE BOOK!

Find the best Web sites for academic research with the up-to-date information provided in this guidebook to the Internet!

ACADEMIC RESEARCH on the INTERNET
Options for Scholars & Libraries

NEW!

Over 400 Pages!

Edited by
Helen Laurence, MLS, EdD
System Librarian, Florida Atlantic University, Boca Raton, Florida

William Miller, PhD, MLS
Director of Libraries, Florida Atlantic University, Boca Raton, Florida

"Presents the reader with the best research-oriented Web sites in the field. A state-of-the-art review of academic use of the Internet as well as a guide to the best Internet sites and services."
—David A Tyckoson, MLS, Head of Reference, California State University, Fresno

Experts in specific subject areas provide up-to-the-minute assessments of the usefulness of the Internet for research in their respective fields. Each article includes a selected 'webliography' of key resources.

(A monograph published simultaneously as the Journal of Library Administration, Vol. 30, Nos. 1/2 and 3/4)
$79.95 hard. ISBN: 0-7890-1176-X.
(Outside US/Canada/Mexico: $96.00)
$49.95 soft. ISBN: 0-7890-1177-8.
(Outside US/Canada/Mexico: $60.00)
Available Fall 2000.
Approx. 414 pp. with Index.

Contents
- Introduction
- Getting What You Pay For?
- Anthropology and Sociology on and About the Internet
- Art on the 'Net: Enhanced Research for Art and Architecture
- Biology Sites on the World Wide Web
- Choosing Wisely from an Expanding Spectrum of Options
- Internet Resources for Educational Research
- Engineering Information Resources on the Web
- Sound, Image, Action
- Legal Information on the Internet
- English and American Literature Internet Resources
- Medical Reference Tools
- The Web of Life
- Internet Resources for Politics, Political Science, and Political Scientists
- Internet Reference Service
- The Philosopher's Web
- Index
- Reference Notes Included

AMEX, DINERS CLUB, DISCOVER, EUROCARD, JCB, MASTERCARD & VISA WELCOME!

CALL OUR TOLL-FREE NUMBER: 1-800-429-6784
US & Canada only / 8am–5pm ET; Monday–Friday
Outside US/Canada: + 607-722-5857

FAX YOUR ORDER TO US: 1-800-895-0582
Outside US/Canada: + 607-771-0012

E-MAIL YOUR ORDER TO US:
getinfo@haworthpressinc.com

VISIT OUR WEB SITE AT:
http://www.HaworthPress.com

FACULTY: ORDER YOUR NO-RISK EXAM COPY TODAY! Send us your examination copy order on your stationery; indicate course title, enrollment, and course start date. We will ship and bill on a 60–day examination basis, and cancel your invoice if you decide to adopt! We will always bill at the lowest available price, such as our special "5+ text price." Please remember to order softcover where available. (We cannot provide examination copies of books not published by The Haworth Press, Inc., or its imprints.) (Outside US/Canada, a proforma invoice will be sent upon receipt of your request and must be paid in advance of shipping. A full refund will be issued with proof of adoption.)

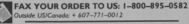

The Haworth Information Press
An imprint of The Haworth Press, Inc.
10 Alice Street, Binghamton, New York 13904–1580 USA

BIC00

TO ORDER: CALL: 1-800-429-6784 / FAX: 1-800-895-0582 (Outside US/Canada: + 607-771-0012) / **E-MAIL: getinfo@haworthpressinc.com**

☐ YES, please send me **Academic Research on the Internet**

— in hard at $79.95 ISBN: 0-7890-1176-X (Outside US/Canada/Mexico: $96.00)
— in soft at $49.95 ISBN: 0-7890-1177-8. (Outside US/Canada/Mexico: $60.00)

- Individual orders outside US, Canada, and Mexico must be prepaid by check or credit card.
- Discounts are not available on 5+ text prices and not available in conjunction with any other discount. • Discount not applicable on books priced under $15.00.
- 5+ text prices are not available for jobbers and wholesalers.
- Postage & handling: in US: $4.00 for first book; $1.50 for each additional book. Outside US: $5.00 for first book; $2.00 for each additional book.
- NY, MN, and OH residents: please add appropriate sales tax after postage & handling.
- Canadian residents: please add 7% GST after postage & handling. Canadian residents of Newfoundland, Nova Scotia, and New Brunswick, add 8% for province tax. • Payment in UNESCO coupons welcome.
- Please allow 3–4 weeks for delivery after publication.
- Prices and discounts subject to change without notice.

☐ **BILL ME LATER**($5 service charge will be added).

(Not available for individuals outside US/Canada/Mexico. Service charge is waved for/jobbers/wholesalers/booksellers.)

☐ Check here if billing address is different from shipping address and attach purchase order and billing address information.

Signature_____

☐ **PAYMENT ENCLOSED $**_____

(Payment must be in US or Canadian dollars by check or money order drawn on a US or Canadian bank.)

☐ **PLEASE BILL MY CREDIT CARD:**

☐ AmEx ☐ Diners Club ☐ Discover ☐ Eurocard ☐ JCB ☐ Master Card ☐ Visa

Account Number_____

Expiration Date_____

Signature_____

May we open a confidential credit card account for you for possible future purchases? ( ) Yes ( ) No

THE HAWORTH PRESS, INC., 10 Alice Street, Binghamton, NY 13904-1580 USA

FAX

Please complete the information below or tape your business card in this area.

NAME_____

INSTITUTION_____

ADDRESS_____

CITY_____

STATE_____ ZIP_____

COUNTRY_____

COUNTY (NY residents only)_____

E-MAIL_____

May we use your e-mail address for confirmations and other types of information? ( ) Yes ( ) No. We appreciate receiving your e-mail address and fax number. Haworth would like to e-mail or fax special discount offers to you, as a preferred customer. We will never share, rent, or exchange your e-mail address or fax number. We regard such actions as an invasion of your privacy.

☐ YES, please send me **Academic Research on the Internet** (ISBN: 0-7890-1177-8) to consider on a 60-day **no risk** examination basis. I understand that I will receive an invoice payable within 60 days, or that **if I decide to adopt the book, my invoice will be cancelled.** I understand that I will be billed at the lowest price. (60-day offer available only to teaching faculty in US, Canada, and Mexico.)

Signature_____

Course Title(s)_____

Current Text(s)_____

Enrollment_____

Semester_____ Decision Date_____

Office Tel_____ Hours_____

(10) (46) 09/00 BIC00

FAX